THE BIBLE IN THE CHURCH.

THE BIBLE IN THE CHURCH

A POPULAR ACCOUNT
OF THE COLLECTION AND RECEPTION
OF THE HOLY SCRIPTURES
IN THE CHRISTIAN CHURCHES.

BY

BROOKE FOSS WESTCOTT, D.D., D.C.L.
LORD BISHOP OF DURHAM.

Our Teacher said:
SHOW YOURSELVES TRIED BANKERS.

Wipf and Stock Publishers
199 W 8th Ave, Suite 3
Eugene, OR 97401

The Bible in the Church
A Popular Account of the Collection and Reception
of the Holy Scriptures in the Christian Churches
By Westcott, B.F.
ISBN: 1-59244-868-2
Publication date 9/16/2004
Previously published by Macmillan, 1901

TO THE

REV. CHARLES BRODRICK SCOTT,

HEAD-MASTER OF WESTMINSTER,

THIS ESSAY

IS AFFECTIONATELY INSCRIBED,

IN MEMORY OF

COLLEGE DAYS.

[1863]

NOTICE.

I HAVE made a few corrections and additions in this Edition, but the book remains substantially as it was originally written, and expresses fairly, as I believe, the facts and judgments which later investigations have confirmed. If at first it seemed strange to some that I spoke on several points with less confidence than was common twenty years ago, it is my happiness now to find nothing to retract or modify in the general view which I then gave of the history of the Christian Bible. The history is indeed a living lesson to us. Nowhere else can we trace more clearly the silent and unexpected ways in which the Spirit sent in Christ's Name works through the Society which is Christ's Body.

B. F. W.

CAMBRIDGE,
March 6, 1885.

PREFACE.

THE present book is an attempt to answer a request which has been made to me from time to time, to place in a simple form, for the use of general readers, the substance of my *History of the Canon of the New Testament*. It seemed to me that I could not do this by a mere abstract; and at the same time I felt that a History of the whole Bible, and not of the New Testament only, would be required, if those unfamiliar with the subject were to be enabled to learn in what manner and with what consent the collection of Holy Scriptures was first made and then enlarged and finally closed by the Church. The history of the Old Testament in the Christian Churches is intimately connected with the history of the New Testament. The two histories may be separated, but each illustrates the other in a remarkable degree, and when combined they show with the greatest clearness the principles by which the Church was guided in the ratification of the books of the Bible, and the power which she claimed to exercise in the work.

The task which I have undertaken is essentially historical. I wish to insist on this with marked distinctness, lest I should seem to have forgotten at any time that the Bible is more than a collection of Scriptures. The Bible may be treated historically or theologically. Neither treatment is complete in itself; but the treatments are separable; and, here, as elsewhere, the historical foundation rightly precedes and underlies the theological interpretation. The Bible has suffered, and is in danger of suffering more, from the inversion of this order. The truest and most faithful historical criticism alone can bring out into full light that doctrine of a Divine Providence separating (as it were) and preserving special books for the perpetual instruction of the Church, which is the true correlative and complement of every sound and reverent theory of Inspiration.

Within the limits thus marked out I have endeavoured to make this little book complete in itself. Every technical term is, I believe, explained when it first occurs; and the addition of slight historical characteristics of men or ages will enable the reader to appreciate fairly the relative importance of the evidence which they contribute. It would have been foreign to my object to have given the original texts which are quoted. The references will enable the scholar to verify them; and I have spared no pains to represent accurately in translation both their spirit and their words. But

PREFACE. ix

while the essay is intended to be simple and popular in its method, I have for this very reason aimed at the strictest accuracy. Indeed it is obvious that accuracy is nowhere so much needed as where (for the most part) it will not be tested. It has, therefore, been my desire to set down nothing which is not certainly justified by satisfactory evidence. In every case I have studied rather to understate than to overstate the positive conclusions which are to be drawn from the testimonies adduced; and wherever a conjecture has been introduced, for the purpose of connecting or explaining the statements of different fathers, this fact is expressly noticed. In numerous instances I have been enabled to correct what has been previously written upon the subject, by the investigation of fuller evidence or better texts. From the nature of the case the corrections are generally made silently, but it may be always assumed that where anything is stated otherwise than is generally done, the variation is deliberately adopted and on grounds which appear to me to be conclusive.

It may seem to be somewhat presumptuous to offer these explanations of the character and purpose of a very unpretending little book; but they seem to be due to the subject of which it treats. No one who has patiently laboured on the history of the Bible can fail to be deeply grieved by the hasty and peremptory tone with which it is commonly discussed. And it is hard to say whether

Holy Scripture is more injured by those who assail or by those who defend it. If the Bible were only a collection of ancient writings its readers would have a right to claim that those who deal with it should be conversant with the laws of literary criticism, and the methods of historical inquiry. And if it is, as we devoutly believe, the very source and measure of our religious faith, it seems impossible to insist too earnestly on the supreme importance of patience, candour and truthfulness in investigating every problem which it involves. The first steps towards the solution of a difficulty are the recognition of its existence and the determination of its extent. And, unless all past experience is worthless, the difficulties of the Bible are the most fruitful guides to its divine depths. It was said long since that 'God was pleased to leave difficulties upon the surface of Scripture, that men might be forced to look below the surface.'

Indeed the moral of the History of the Bible is full of the noblest lessons for all times, and not least for our own. If I am not wholly wrong in interpreting the sure facts which I have recorded, they teach us that the formation of the collection of Holy Scriptures was—to use a term which ought never to be supposed even to veil the action of a Present God—according to natural laws: that slowly and with an ever-deepening conviction the Churches received, after trial, and in some cases after doubt and contradiction, the books which we now receive: that the religious consciousness which was quickened by the words of prophets and apostles in turn ratified their writings. They teach us that the judgment which was in this manner the expression of the fulness of Christian life, was not confined in early times by rigid or uniform laws, but realized in ecclesiastical usage: that the Bible was not something distinct from, and independent of, the Christian body, but the vital law of its action: that the Church offered a living commentary on the Book, and the Book an unchanging test of the Church. They teach us that the extreme limits of the collection were not marked out sharply, but that rather the outline was at times dim and wavering, yet not so as to be incapable of satisfactory adjustment. They teach us that a corrupted Bible is a sign of a corrupted Church, a Bible mutilated or imperfect, a sign of a Church not yet raised to the complete perception of Truth. It is possible that we might have wished much of this or all this otherwise: we might have thought that a Bible of which every part should bear a visible and unquestioned authentication of its divine origin, separated by a solemn act from the first from the sum and fate of all other literature, would have best answered our conceptions of what the written records of revelation should be. But it is not thus that God works among us. In the Church and in the Bible alike He works through men. As we follow the progress of their formation, each step seems to be truly human; and when we contemplate the whole, we joyfully recognize that every part is also divine.

It would be ungrateful not to acknowledge the help which I have found in Hody's great work *De Bibliorum Textibus Originalibus*, especially with regard to mediæval writers. This contains in a very condensed form the most honest and accurate History of the Canon with which I am acquainted up to the time (1705) at which it was written. The *Scholastical History* of Bishop Cosin is essentially polemical and not historical, and must be read with the greatest caution. The best work on the Romanist side (as far as I can judge) is an Essay published anonymously (by J. Keil, I believe) in answer to E. Wernsdorff's treatise on the Maccabees (*Auctoritas utriusque libri Maccab. adserta* ......Viennæ, 1749). No book of Credner's can be without value; and I have been indebted to his posthumous *Geschichte d. Neutest. Kanon* (Berlin, 1860) for some suggestive remarks on the influence of Eusebius upon the Constantinopolitan Bible; but the work in its present form is certainly not such as Credner himself would have published, and the carelessness and inaccuracy of his editor have done grievous wrong to the memory of a most truthful and acute scholar.

It is with a feeling of no unworthy fear that I now commend my Essay to the Christian reader.

PREFACE.

The subject is one on which it is impossible to write without misgiving. If I have said anything which can be rightly construed as derogatory from the divine majesty of Holy Scripture, I am the first to wish it unsaid. If I have said anything inaccurately (and with all care it can scarcely be otherwise), I sincerely trust that I may be corrected. If I have said anything which may lead one student of the Bible to just and faithful views of its Divine authority, I thank God humbly for this fruit of painful and anxious work. *In His hand are both we and our words.*

B. F. W.

HARROW,
Christmas Eve, 1863.

NOTICE TO THE SECOND EDITION.

THIS Edition is a simple reprint of the First Edition with the exception of a few verbal corrections and a more accurate account of the MS. of the Syriac Bible in the Cambridge University Library. For the latter I am indebted to Mr R. L. Bensly, M.A. of Caius College, who has kindly collated the description in the Catalogue, which I followed before, with the manuscript itself, and furnished me with many important and interesting corrections.

B. F. W.

HARROW,
January 26, 1866.

CONTENTS.

INTRODUCTION.

	PAGE
THE Bible characterized by its connexion with a long history	1—6
A record of various revelations.	
Gradually extended.	
Successively acknowledged	1—4
Successive names	4—6
Difficulties arising from this fact	6—11
Traits from contrasted forms of life.	
Apparent conflict of successive dispensations.	6, 7
Fragmentariness of records	9
Periods of transition	10
Corresponding advantages	11—16
Unity not uniformity	11
A complete training	12—14
A witness in itself	14
Object: *not* to discuss *veracity: authority: inspiration* of the sacred Books; but *in what manner, when,* and with what *consent* or *variety of opinion* they were accepted as a written Rule of doctrine	16
Limits: the Apostolic age.	
The age of the Reformation	17

CHAPTER I.

The Bible of the Apostolic Age.

	PAGE
The *Dispersion* of the Jews in relation to the spread of the Bible	19—23
The Septuagint generally intelligible	23
i. The evidence of *Jewish* writers as to the contents of the Old Testament	24—38
1. JOSEPHUS (Palestine)	25—30
2. PHILO (Alexandria)	30—35
3. The TALMUD (Babylon)	35—38
ii. The evidence from the Apostolic writers as to the contents of the Old Testament	38—49
Collective titles for the Bible	39—41
Express quotations in	
1. The *Synoptic Gospels, Acts, Catholic Epistles*	41
2. The *Pauline Epistles*	42
3. The *Writings of St John*	ib.
No special quotation from the *Apocrypha*	44
Silent quotations	45
Express quotations of uncertain origin	46—49
Summary	49

CHAPTER II.

The Growth of the New Testament.

The Apostolic work	52—57
The oral teaching of the Apostles historical	57
An oral *Gospel* formed	57, 58
,, ,, committed to writing.	59
The origin of the Epistles	60

CONTENTS. xvii

	PAGE
Antagonism of *Jew* and *Gentile*	61—65
The writings of *St John*	65

CHAPTER III.

The Apostolic Fathers.

The close of the Apostolic age	67
Judaizing,	
Mystical,	
Pauline schools	69—72
The range of the *Apostolic Fathers*	73
i. Their relation to the Apostolic teaching.	
1. CLEMENT OF ROME	74—76
2. IGNATIUS	76—79
3. POLYCARP	79, 80
4. BARNABAS	80, 81
ii. Their relation to the *Gospels*	81—83
iii. Their quotations	
From the Old Testament and *Apocrypha*	84
From the New Testament	85
They do not recognize a New Testament, but prepare the way for it	86—89

CHAPTER IV.

The Age of the Apologists.

Characteristics of the age	90—94
PAPIAS	95—97
JUSTIN MARTYR	97—105

xviii   *CONTENTS.*

	PAGE
Memoirs of the Apostles	100—105
The *Clementine Homilies*	105, 106
Extent of references to the books of the New Testament up to this time	106
The Hebrew Canon of the Old Testament admitted to be a complete Bible	106, 7
HEGESIPPUS	107
HERMAS	108
Assaults on the Old Testament	108, 109
The Bible of MARCION	109—11
Note. Meaning of the word *Canon.*	
The *Muratorian Canon*	112—116

CHAPTER V.

The First Christian Bible.

Progress of Christianity in the Second Century	117
Retrospect of the history of the New Testament	118—120

1. *Asia Minor.*
   - IRENÆUS .... 121—123
   - MELITO 124

2. *Alexandria.*
   - Use of *Apocrypha* 125
   - CLEMENT OF ALEXANDRIA 125, 127

3. *North Africa.*
   - TERTULLIAN 127, 128
   - The *Old Latin* Version of the Bible .... 128—131

4. *Syria.*
   - THEOPHILUS. SERAPION 131
   - The *Old Syrian* Version (*Peshito*) 132, 133

	PAGE
Testimony to the disputed books of the New Testament (*Antilegomena*)	133, 134
ORIGEN	134—137
Asiatic and Syrian writers	138
Heretical and heathen writers	139, 140

CHAPTER VI.

The Bible Proscribed and Restored.

The characteristics of third century	141—143
Persecution of *Diocletian*	143—145
i. The Canon of the *Donatists*	145, 146
ii. The Canon of EUSEBIUS	146—158
Canon of the NEW TESTAMENT	148—153
Canon of the OLD TESTAMENT	153
Constantine's Bible	155—158
iii. The Canon of ATHANASIUS	158—162

CHAPTER VII.

The Age of Jerome and Augustine.

The growth of the Roman Church	163, 164
1. The Bibles of the East	165—176
i. *Asia Minor and Palestine*	166—171
GREGORY OF NAZIANZUS. AMPHILOCHIUS	166, 167
CYRIL OF JERUSALEM	168
Council of Laodicea	169—171
ii. *Alexandria*	171—173
DIDYMUS. EUTHALIUS. CYRIL	171
EPIPHANIUS	172, 173

CONTENTS.

		PAGE
iii.	*Syria.*	
	CHRYSOSTOM	174, 175
	The *Apostolical Constitutions*	175, 176
	Note. The *Apostolical Canons.*	

2. The Bibles of the West .... 177—190
    PHILASTRIUS 177
    RUFFINUS............ 178—180
    HILARIUS OF POITIERS 180
    JEROME............ 180—183
        Canon of the OLD TESTAMENT ...... 181—183
        Canon of the NEW TESTAMENT 183, 184
    AUGUSTINE .... 184—190
        Council of Carthage 188, 189

CHAPTER VIII.

The Bible of the Middle Ages in the West.

The character and work of the Western Churches   191, 192

§ 1. *The Church of North Africa.*
    PRIMASIUS. JUNILIUS 193, 194

§ 2. *The Church of Italy.*
    Papal Decretals .... 194—196
    Codex Amiatinus 196
    CASSIODORUS............ 197
    Later writers 198
    Council of Florence............ 199

§ 3. *The Church of Spain*............ 199—201
    Connexion with North Africa 201

§ 4. *The Transalpine Churches.*
    CHARLEMAGNE. ALCUIN 202, 203
    HUGO DE S. CARO, &c. 203
    PETER OF CLUGNY, &c. 204, 205
    NICOLAUS DE LYRA............ 206

CONTENTS. xxi

§ 5. *The Churches of Britain.*

The ancient [Irish] Church.
NOTKER of St Gall............................ 207
The Saxon Church.
ALFRIC.. 208
Epistle to the Laodicenes...................... 209
JOHN OF SALISBURY, &c. 210
The *Wycliffite Bible*........................... 211—213
Popular usage. R. GROSSETESTE........ 214, 215

CHAPTER IX.

The Bible of the Middle Ages in the East.

Decay of the Eastern Churches 216

§ 1. *The Greek Church* .... 217—229
  The *Quini-Sextine Council* 217, 218
  LEONTIUS OF BYZANTIUM 219, 220
  COSMAS INDICOPLEUSTES 220, 221
  JOHANNES DAMASCENUS.................
               222
  The *Canonists* 223, 224
  The *Sixty Books* 224
  The *Stichometry* of NICEPHORUS 225, 226
  Confusion of the lists...................... 226, 227
  Later history of the Canon............... 227, 229

§ 2. *The Nestorian Churches* 229, 234
  The *School of Nisibis* 230
  EBED JESU .... 231—234
Note. Syrian MS. of the Bible.

§ 3. *The (Monophysite) Coptic Church* 234, 235
§ 4. *The (Monophysite) Abyssinian Church*... 236—239
§ 5. *The (Monophysite) Armenian Church* ... 239, 240

CONTENTS.

	PAGE
§ 6. The *(Monophysite) Jacobite* Church......	240
The *Karkaphensian* Version	241
The *Hexaplaric* Version	ib.
Later Syrian writers	242
The Bible in the East never definitely fixed..	242—244

CHAPTER X.

The Bible in the Sixteenth Century.

The general religious character of the age	245—248
§ 1. *The Romish Church*	249—259
Earlier Scholars: XIMENES	249
ERASMUS	249—253
CAIETAN	253
CATHARINUS	255
The *Council of Trent*.....................	ib.
SIXTUS SENENSIS	258
§ 2. *The Saxon School of Reformers*	259—269
LUTHER on the *Apocrypha* of Old Testament...................................	260—262
,, ,, *Antilegomena* of New Testament	262—265
KARLSTADT	266—269
§ 3. *The Swiss School of Reformers*............	269—278
ZWINGLI	269
ŒCOLAMPADIUS	270
CALVIN	270—273
BEZA...	273
Public *Confessions*	275—278
§ 4. *The Arminian School.*	
GROTIUS	279, 280
§ 5. *The English Church.*	
Translations of the Bible.	
TYNDALE. COVERDALE. MATTHEW. CRANMER. *Bishops'. Authorized*......	281—287

	PAGE
Articles	288
Conclusion	293

APPENDIX A.

On the History of the Canon of the Old Testament before the Christian era .... 297—301

APPENDIX B.

On the Contents of the most ancient MSS. of the Christian Bible .... 302—311

§ 1. Codex Alexandrinus	303
§ 2. Codex Vaticanus	305
§ 3. Codex Sinaiticus	307
§ 4. The list of Sacred Books in the Codex Claromontanus................................	308
INDEX	313

INTRODUCTION.

There are diversities of workings, but the same God who worketh all things in all.—1 Cor. xii. 6.

IT is one of the chief characteristics of the Christian religion, that it is based upon a history. Its great doctrines are the simple interpretation or necessary results of facts. The Gospel, according to the instinctive judgment of ages, is emphatically a narrative of passages from the Life of Christ. This history, again, is not itself isolated, but bound up with a previous history which reaches to the primitive covenant of God and man. If the Coming of Messiah was in one sense sudden and unexpected, in another it was duly heralded and announced by other voices than that of the Baptist as near at hand. If His Doctrine was strange, yet it was strange only to those who had acquiesced in the superficial meaning of the Divine promises. To those who looked deeper the Life of our Blessed Lord was the consummation of long periods of struggle and repose, of Divine instruction and Divine silence, which can still be traced in clear outlines up to the first separation of a chosen people; and so, on the other hand, His teaching contained the fulfilment of all that had entered into the soul of

Christianity historical, and connected with a long history.

lawgiver, or psalmist, or prophet. Whatsoever was written aforetime served for the foundation of the Christian Revelation; and its own lessons were recorded not in one way only, but in many, that it might embrace all ages and all minds. It was preceded by a preparation most full and varied: it was portrayed in a record which reflects the most opposite sides of its doctrine. Thus it is that the whole Bible is rightly claimed as the pledge and type of the comprehensiveness and unity of the Christian Faith, a Book *manifold* by the variety of times and circumstances in which its several parts had their rise, *one* by the inspiring presence of the same spiritual Life.

For as Christianity is historical, so too almost every part of the Bible is historical. Not only is a large portion of both Testaments professedly a narrative of events, but even the special characteristics of psalms, prophecies and epistles reflect most distinctly the external circumstances in which they were composed. Other sacred books are, for the most part, purely ritual or speculative, avowedly the product of a brief period, or wholly separated from the region of fact; but the Bible is, in its origin, a slow growth of time, intimately connected with a long development of national life, bearing on its surface the impress of successive revelations, extended from time to time by the addition of new elements, accepted in its present form not by one act once for all, but gradually, and, as far as can be traced by the help of existing records, according to natural laws of criticism, exerted within definite limits.

The slow process by which the contents of the sacred volume were determined will be brought out as we proceed: the differences by which the several books themselves are marked are legibly inscribed upon them. There is no need of any detailed investigation to show that the constituent parts of the Bible, when looked at separately, have a distinct and peculiar meaning, and that long periods must (in the natural order of things) have intervened between particular books, and that others, more nearly contemporaneous in origin, are scarcely less broadly distinguished by the personal characteristics of their authors. Such lines of demarcation appear to exist between the Law and the Prophets, between the books of Kings and Chronicles, between the earlier and later Prophets, or, to take examples of a different kind, between the epistles of St James, St Paul and St John, and between the first three Gospels and the fourth. No one, indeed, would be inclined to question seriously the existence of these diversities of teaching, or even to deny that he finds special parts of the Bible best adapted to his own wants or to the wants of some particular phase of society; yet practically all err more or less, in regarding everything as spoken directly and in its original form to themselves. If the grosser faults which were defended in ruder times by the letter of Holy Scripture are now repressed by the moral influences of life, yet we are too apt to forget that in every age God spoke to men such as they *then* were and by men; and that consequently all true interpretation of the record must turn upon the relation of the act to the persons engaged in it, of the word to the speaker and the hearer, of the judgment to the spirit of which it witnessed. The unity of the Bible is not uniformity, and its variety is not discrepance; but

4 THE BIBLE

<small>INTRO-
DUCTION.</small>

rather, to borrow an image from Scripture, the whole is like a "living creature," made up of living creatures. The parts have a distinct life as well as the sum; the members are individually complete as well as the entire body. Each progressive phase in the development of the revelation has been preserved as well as the matured form; and thus at different points we can trace the rise and operation of different elements, which, though they contribute largely to the final result, might have been wholly unobserved if that result alone had remained.

<small>The Names of
the Bible in
Jewish and</small>

The very names of the Bible bear a striking witness to the instinctive sense which men have had from time to time of its manifoldness and its unity. Its proper Hebrew title is simply the enumeration of its triple division, 'The Law, the Prophets, and the [Holy] Writings;' and this title is recognized in the New Testament both in its full form, 'The Law, the Prophets, and the Psalms' (Luke xxiv. 44), and briefly 'The Law and the Prophets' (Matt. xi. 13; Acts xxviii. 23). More generally, however, the Old Testament is quoted simply as 'The Writings,' 'The Scriptures' (Matt. xxi. 42; Mark xiv. 49; Luke xxiv. 32; John v. 39; Acts xviii. 24; Rom. xv. 4; &c.), while the corresponding singular term,—'the Scripture'—is commonly used for a special passage and not as at present both for the part and for the whole (Luke iv. 21; John xx. 9; James ii. 8; &c.). At the beginning of the Christian era the Jews had in fact no singular name for their sacred books; nor was this strange, since at that time they could not have felt their entire completeness. Yet it is worthy of notice that the term 'The Law' was extended popularly to both the other divisions of the Bible, to the Psalms (John x. 34; xii. 34; xv. 25), and to the prophets (1 Cor. xiv. 21), for this was necessarily regarded as including in itself the whole growth of Judaism.

The establishment of Christianity gave at once a distinct unity to the former dispensation, and thus St Paul could speak of the Jewish Scriptures by the name which they have always retained since, as the 'Old Testament' or 'Covenant' (2 Cor. iii. 14), adapting and extending the earlier phrase for the Law 'the Book of the Covenant' (2 Kings xxiii. 2). At the close of the second century the terms 'Old' and 'New Testament' were already in common use, though a vain endeavour was made by scholars, both then and afterwards, to substitute for *Testament* the word *Instrument* (or Record). In such cases the popular habit prevails; and it is a matter of rejoicing that that title has been retained which represents the sacred books in connexion with their ultimate Giver rather than that which only regards them as official or authoritative documents.

The first simple collective title of the whole Bible appears to be that which is found in Jerome, in the IVth century, 'The Divine Library' (*Bibliotheca Divina*), which afterwards passed into common use among Latin writers, and thence into our own Anglo-Saxon language. About the same time Greek writers came to use the term 'The Books' (*Biblia*, pl.) for the Bible. In process of time this name, with many others of Greek origin, passed into the vocabulary of the Western Church; and in the XIIIth century, by a happy solecism, the neuter plural came to be regarded as a feminine singular, and 'The Books' became by common consent 'The Book' (*Biblia*, sing.) in

6   *THE BIBLE*

INTRODUCTION.

which form the word has passed into the languages of modern Europe.

Special value of several names.

'The Scriptures,' 'The Books,' 'The Library,' 'The Book,' each phrase is pregnant with meaning, and it were to be wished that no one had passed out of use, or been deprived of the fresh vigour of its original sense. Of all, perhaps, the Library, the term which seems to have been irrevocably lost, is the most expressive and includes the idea of 'the Book' and 'the Books' with the most felicitous simplicity. But the word which is denied to popular use still lives for the student, and as long as we regard the Bible as the divine Library, the treasury of divine records, of things old and new—the works of many authors, the products of many ages—we shall be protected from numerous dangers which are supposed to arise from a candid study of its history and contents, and prepared to feel to the full the infinite grandeur of the one message of love fashioned in a thousand shapes.

i. Difficulties which spring from the composition of the Bible.
1. Traits from contrasted forms of life.

For while the Bible is one it is manifold; and it is well if the apprehension of an inward rather than an outward unity leaves the mind free to observe the distinctness of the parts of which it is made up. The records which it contains extend over a period of twelve hundred years, on any theory, and probably over a much longer period. Whatever authoritative revision the books of the Old Testament may have undergone, the original substance at least remains unchanged, and presents pictures drawn from the most widely contrasted forms of life. If we compare with these the scenes reflected in the apostolic writings, the full width of the range of the Bible will be clearly felt. How great, for example, is the

IN THE CHURCH.

chasm between the freshness of patriarchal life and
that Roman prison from which St Paul wrote for
the confirmation of the churches: between the
discipline in the wilderness and the growth of
the Christian Church: between Leviticus and the
Pastoral Epistles; or even between the periods of
the judges, the kingdom and the hierarchy. The
intervals are undoubtedly filled up more or less
by periods of preparation and transition, but yet
there are crises of change; and the grandeur of
the scale on which the history is drawn encourages the student to note them. It would be
strange if it were not so. The rise and fall of the
empires of the ancient world are but as episodes
in the vast human drama which is contained in
the Bible. The Bible contains the history of man,
and not of a nation only. And in the course of
this living portraiture of human nature men in
every position bear and receive the Divine message, each according to the circumstances of his
character, his country, his age, furnished with
various gifts, actors at once and speakers on the
Divine stage, yet so acting and so speaking that
their personal characteristics form an essential
element of the part committed to them.

*INTRO-
DUCTION*

One of the chief difficulties which arise from
this manifold complexity of the Bible lies in the
practical interpretation of its contents, and though
this question is not now immediately before us,
it cannot be passed by wholly without notice;
for it belongs to the very constitution of the
Book. It is obvious that the records of the Divine teaching, addressed to societies thus widely
separated, by men who, while messengers of God
and prophets, were no less fellowmen of those
whom they addressed, must vary much as to the

*Consequent
difficulty of
Interpretation.*

form under which they present the truth. Their permanent lessons cannot be gained by one uniform and dead law of literal interpretation. There will be need, even as a first step towards entering into these several lessons, of a distinct conception of the meaning of the words when they were uttered, of the character of the act when it was wrought. No part of the Bible, it is true, will ever be antiquated, because all that is old there yet retains the spirit with which it was at first quickened, but still much in it belongs to modes of thought and life with which we are wholly unfamiliar. Our habitual use of language belonging to the past under new conditions, increases the difficulty of understanding its real import. A vigorous and constant effort is needed in order that we may remember that the associations which we attach to the words of Holy Scripture are no part of their original meaning.

2. Apparent conflict of successive dispensations.

The difficulty which has been thus briefly noticed is placed in its clearest light when we regard the different *series* of revelations (so to speak) which the Bible contains. These various phases of the progressive revelation answer in a great degree to the periods of social progress already marked out, but they present them under bolder and more comprehensive forms. If, for instance, we compare the revelations which God was pleased to make during the patriarchal period with those which accompanied the giving of the Law, we feel at once that they were not only addressed to men in different positions, but are also themselves different in scope and character. The difference is yet greater if we compare the letter of the Law with the writings of the prophets, and the prophets with the Apostles.

IN THE CHURCH.

Instinctively we make some adaptation and accommodation of the contrasted parts. We clear away difficulties by putting out of sight parts of the data from which they arise. But no solution of the many problems which arise from a comparison of Judaism and Christianity, and of various sides of Judaism and Christianity in their mutual relations to one another will ever be satisfactory, or even tend to place the harmony of Scripture in its true aspect, which is not based upon that principle of proportion which has been already indicated. The teaching of Scripture, as addressed to men, must be relative. To discover the relation of a dispensation or a message to those for whom it was primarily designed, is the first condition of ascertaining what is its bearing upon us and upon the general scheme of Divine Providence.

INTRODUCTION.

There is yet another feature inherent in the very formation of the Bible, which cannot be omitted in any estimate of its characteristics. It is fragmentary. With the partial exception of the Pentateuch, it does not anywhere present the semblance of completeness. Where we can trace the history of the component writings with the greatest precision, it does not appear that they were designed to form part of a written code of doctrine or discipline. Humanly speaking, they arose out of passing circumstances and were designed to meet occasional wants. That annals and prophecies and letters, thus (apparently) casual in their origin, should combine into a whole marvellously complete and symmetrical in its spiritual teaching is, indeed, a clear intimation of the presence of a controlling power both in their composition and in their preservation. But the

3. The Bible fragmentary.

10 THE BIBLE

INTRO-
DUCTION.

grand outline which they mark out is not everywhere complete. The several books necessarily present many gaps in their record which we cannot now fill up. The Divine stream sinks for a time, though it shortly reappears with undiminished strength. As soon as the whole history is examined critically, it is evident that much must remain obscure and perplexing. Yet the same criticism which brings difficulties to light fixes a practical limit to them. It is enough if we can see where our ignorance is a fair answer to objections, without interpolating imaginary combinations of events into the narrative of the Bible and perilling its truth on our own ingenuity.

4. The books mainly belong to critical epochs.

This fragmentariness of the Scriptures, when viewed in their outward and purely historic aspect, is made yet more marked by the general characteristics of the epochs in which they were composed. In the main they belong to periods of conflict and transition. They are the records of the Divine teaching by which the religious progress of the people of God was advanced from one stage of development to another. They are not (with rare exceptions) the products of times of silent growth and thought, but prophetic voices which prepared a nation for new phases of life. The Exodus, the first conquest of Canaan, the establishment of the Kingdom, the Fall of the divided kingdoms, the Captivity and the Return, leave a distinct impress on the groups of books which severally belong to them; and it is not without a strange significance that the Divine record closes when Israel was first brought into contact with Greece. At present comparatively little progress has been made in the study of the Old Testament in the light of its special history.

A narrow and unworthy view of the spiritual authority of its constituent parts still commonly leaves out of account the peculiar characteristics of each era and form of thought, as it refused to recognize for a long time the diversities of character and feeling in the sacred writers. In the New Testament more fruitful labour has been spent in this most difficult field of study, since the diversities of apostolic teaching, however pregnant with instructive difficulties, are confined within a narrow compass. But whether the fact yet be fully or partially acknowledged, it seems most certain that the Bible represents a progress by antagonism, a conflict and a reconciliation of partial views of one truth, a whole which is complete because it includes each separate element in a distinct and proportionate form. INTRODUCTION.

For while we admit most fully the momentous difficulties which are involved in the true appreciation and interpretation of Holy Scripture, yet it is evident that these difficulties are amply compensated by corresponding advantages. If the popular aspect of the Bible,—as one book, written in one dialect, fashioned in one mould, impressed with one moral and intellectual type, intelligible by one rule, no less than inspired by one Spirit—puts out of sight many perplexing questions, it neglects equally many of the most precious lessons which the Scriptures reveal to all ages. It is only by acknowledging the variety and distinctness of the parts of which the Bible is composed that we can gain any adequate sense of its real unity, of its inherent completeness, of its internal witness to its proper Divine authority. ii. Corresponding advantages.

The noblest external characteristic of the 1. Unity of the Bible, not uniformity.

INTRODUCTION.

Bible is its unity as distinguished from mere uniformity. Uniformity is the natural consequence of a limited design: unity is the outward expression of one great principle embodied in many ways. The one comes from without, the other from within: the one is the sign of constraint, the other of freedom: the one answers, in its highest shape, to organization, the other to growth. Take away the frank recognition of the human element in the Bible, widening with the increase of experience, which is of the very essence of the entire Divine word, and the necessary conditions on which its unity rests are at once removed. Deny the antithetic teaching of the Law and the Prophets, of St Paul and St James, and there remains nothing to lead to that fuller truth in which apparent contradictions are resolved. One Evangelist, or the first three Evangelists without St John, would have offered comparatively few difficulties, but any one can feel that the combination is the ground of a fuller harmony than could have been constructed from any uniform narratives.

2. The completeness of the moral training which it contains.

But the diversity of the Scriptures makes itself chiefly conspicuous in the completeness of the moral training which they convey. It is, as we have seen, one of their distinguishing marks that they belong to separate periods, to contrasted phases of life, to various forms of culture, to distinct habits of thought, and the peculiarities which they reflect are ever repeating themselves in history. No temptation is more subtle or more potent than that which bids us judge every-

Largeness of sympathy.

thing by one standard. Practically we are inclined to measure others by ourselves, other ages by our own, other forms of civilization by that under which we live, as the true and final measure of all. Against this error, which is sufficient almost to cloud the whole world, the Bible contains the surest safeguard. In that we see side by side how God finds a dwelling-place among nations and families in every stage of social advancement, and recognizes faithful worshippers even where they are hidden from the eyes of prophets. The absorbing cares of daily life, the imperious claims of those immediately around us, tend to narrow our sympathies, but the Bible shows to us, in an abiding record, every condition and every power of man blessed by the Divine Spirit. It lifts us out of the circle of daily influences and introduces us to prophets and kings and deep thinkers and preachers of righteousness, each working in their own spheres variously and yet by one power and for one end. It may be objected that devout students of the Bible have often proved to be the sternest fanatics. But the answer is easy. They were fanatics because they were students not of the whole Bible but of some one fragment of it to which all else was sacrificed. The teaching of one part only, if taken without any regard to its relative position in connexion with other times and other books, may lead to narrowness of thought, but the whole recognizes and ennobles every excellence of man.

Nor is it only that the various character of different parts of the Bible, if fairly regarded, widens our sympathy: it enlarges our conceptions alike of the destiny of the human race and of the working of Providence. There are times when men are inclined to regard religion merely as an individual matter, as a kind of righteous egoism, and then it is that we may dwell with especial

Breadth of view.

trust on those sublimer views of our social and national connexions which are opened in the broad outlines of the history of Israel and sanctioned afresh in the imagery used in the New Testament to portray the nature of the Church. All history as unfolded there is but a preparation for the establishment of 'the kingdom of God.' The single citizen is never disregarded, as was likely to be the case in some of the noblest systems of the ancient world, but he is never contemplated without reference to a divine commonwealth. And, again, when each part of the Bible is examined in relation to the rest, we cannot but be struck by what may be called the patience of God, the slow fulfilment of His counsels. The fabric of His Church, like the earth on which we live, advances almost imperceptibly from age to age, on what we might be tempted to call the ruins of the past. The laws of its progress, marvellous and inexplicable when contemplated in their special working, are yet seen on a wider view to be most natural, if by nature we mean (and a Christian can hardly mean anything else) man's apprehension of the expression of the one, harmonious, will of God. In this sense each separate book of Holy Scripture reveals some one portion of the growing work, and the perception of progress is gained by the comparison of successive records. Painfully, slowly, with many drawbacks and terrible chastisements, the people of Israel were trained to fulfil their task ; and their chequered history at once warns and encourages those who compare the tardy spread and scanty influence of the Gospel with the largeness of its claims and promises.

It seems to follow from what has been said, that the Bible contains in itself the fullest witness to its Divine authority. If it appears that a large collection of fragmentary records, written, with few exceptions, without any designed connexion, at most distant times and under the most varied circumstances, yet combine to form a definite whole, broadly separated from other books; if it further appear that these different parts when interpreted historically reveal a gradual progress of social spiritual life uniform at least in its general direction; if without any intentional purpose they offer not only remarkable coincidences in minute details of facts, for that is a mere question of accurate narration, but also subtle harmonies of complementary doctrine; if in proportion as they are felt to be separate they are felt also to be instinct with a common spirit; then it will be readily acknowledged that however they came into being first, however they were united afterwards into the sacred volume, they are yet legibly stamped with the Divine seal as 'inspired by God' in a sense in which no other writings are.

Thus the old analogy of Nature and the Bible is again forced upon us. The harmonious relation of facts, the subordination of details to great ends, the convergence of the separate phenomena towards one centre, the general laws of order and progress which rule the whole are equally characteristic of both. In both too there are residuary difficulties, some of which may perhaps be removed by wider knowledge, while others are probably inherent in the necessarily finite view which we must take both of the scope and method of the Divine plans.

The difficulties of the physical and moral worlds—all that is involved in the ideas of pain and sin—we bear almost unconsciously; and yet there are no difficulties in the written record of

INTRODUCTION.

Bible and Nature.

Final difficulties in both.

16　　　　　　　　*THE BIBLE*

INTRO-
DUCTION.

Origen,
Philoc. 2.

Object of the
Essay.

God's Word deeper or more perplexing than these. Nay the difficulties of Scripture spring, as we have seen, from the very conditions which determine its human and abiding value ; and to quote once again the pregnant words of the first great critic of Holy Scripture, 'he who has once received the Scriptures as derived from the Creator of the world, must expect to find in them also all the difficulties which meet those who investigate the system of Creation.' But that this may hold true in the highest sense, it is necessary that both Nature and the Bible should be investigated in the same manner. Each part must be interrogated faithfully and patiently. We must approach both as learners. There was a time when physical speculators indulged in the not very innocent occupation of forming imaginary worlds which should be free from the imperfections which they found in ours. Truer science has swept away their presumptuous dreams, and we may hope for the time when the student of Holy Scripture will look for what it contains, and not measure its contents by preconceived notions of the manner and form in which its lessons must have been given.

It has been the object of the preceding remarks to point out the necessity of the full recognition of the distinctness of the various parts of which the Bible is composed, both for the right understanding of their special lessons for us and for a comprehensive view of the progress of the Divine preparation for the Gospel. It is now possible to turn to the special subject of our inquiry, the history of the recognition of these detached records as a complete written rule of Christian doctrine. In tracing this history it is no part of our object to discuss the origin, the veracity, or the inspiration of the sacred books, but simply in what manner, when, and with what consent or variety of opinion they were accepted as containing an authoritative rule of faith. The problem is purely historical; yet in such a case history is the truest guide to right opinion. The limits of the inquiry are naturally fixed at the Apostolic age and the Reformation. The history of the Old Testament before the Apostolic age is most meagre and unsatisfactory;[1] and the era of the Reformation exhibited the last great array of authoritative judgments on the contents of the Bible, which have been variously elaborated and enforced in the last three centuries.

INTRO-
DUCTION.

The period thus marked out falls into several natural divisions. The first includes the Apostolic age (A.D. 30—80), in which we trace first the recognition and limits of an Old Testament as determined both directly by Jewish writers and incidentally by the Apostles and our Lord Himself (Chap. I.); and next the general circumstances which attended the composition of the New Testament Scriptures (Chap. II.). The second division (A.D. 80—120) is characterized by the organization of the Catholic Church, in which the distinguishing elements of the different books of the New Testament were embodied in the one Faith (Chap. III.). The third is the age of the Apologists (A.D. 120—170), in which Christianity appears in conflict with heathen and Jewish antagonists, and the writings of the New Testament begin to be used habitually in the same manner as those of the Old Testament (Chap. IV.). The fourth (A.D. 170—303) presents to us the first definite New Testament, varying slightly in its

Division of periods.

[1] See *Appendix* A.

contents, but in the main universally recognized throughout Christendom (Chap. v.). Then follows the eventful era in which the Bible (New Testament) was first proscribed and then restored (A.D. 303—397), (Chap. VI.). From this time the contents of the New Testament were practically fixed, but a division arose in the Western Church on the extent of the Old Testament, part including and part excluding the Apocrypha (Chap. VII.). The real history of the Canon, as far as it has any original value, closes here, but it will be interesting to follow the course of ancient opinion in the Western (Chap. VIII.) and Eastern Churches (Chap. IX.) till modern times, noticing in some detail the conflicting opinions which were maintained in the age of the Reformation (Chap. x), to which all recent theories may be referred.

CHAPTER I.

THE BIBLE OF THE APOSTOLIC AGE.

*What advantage then hath the Jew?...Much every way:
first of all that they were intrusted with the oracles
of God.*—Rom. iii. 1, 2.

AT the commencement of the Christian era the Jewish nation was already widely scattered throughout the old world. The fears or the policy of the successive conquerors of the East had settled colonies of Jews in Mesopotamia, Egypt, and Syria; and the influence of commerce increased and consolidated the power of these communities. Thus the 'Dispersion,' as it was called, gathered strength and consistency during upwards of five centuries and under the most varied circumstances. Many of the lessons of the captivity were permanently embodied in wide-spread societies, and Judaism was placed in close and lengthened contact with the teaching of Persia, Egypt, and Greece. It necessarily followed that from the time of the Exile this Dispersion became a most important element in shaping the character and fulfilling the destiny of the whole nation; and more than any one outward cause, prepared the way both materially and intellectually for the propagation of a universal faith.

CHAP. I.

A.D. 30—80.

The Dispersion of the Jews at the beginning of the Christian era.

It would be impossible here to enter with any detail into the history of the Dispersion. There is much that is obscure in the accounts of the

The origin and division of the Dispersion.

earliest colonies; but the contemporary writings of Philo and Josephus bear clear witness to the extent and character of the foreign Jewish settlements in the first age; and the books of the New Testament contain no less distinct proof of the influence which they exercised upon the spread of Christianity. At this time the Dispersion was divided into three great sections, the Babylonian, the Syrian, and the Egyptian. The Roman colony, which dated from the time of Pompey (B.C. 63), seems to have been confined within narrower limits and to have held closely to Palestinian traditions. The Babylonian 'Dispersion' was the oldest and claimed precedence before the others. It extended through Media, Persia and Parthia; and in later times Babylon became one of the most distinguished centres of Jewish learning. The Jewish colonies in Egypt owed their origin mainly to the wisdom of Alexander the Great and the earlier Ptolemies. From Alexandria the Jews advanced along the north coast of Africa, and a considerable Jewish population was settled at Cyrene and Berenice (Tripoli). The Syrian Dispersion was yet wider in its extent. Seleucus Nicator removed large bodies of Jews to his western provinces, and they spread rapidly through Armenia, Asia Minor, and Greece. But however widely removed from the 'Holy City,' however much despised by the stricter adherents of the Law, the Jews of the Dispersion still maintained a loyal connexion with the one Temple of their nation. All paid the customary tribute, and testified, though in various degrees, their dependence on the religious authorities at Jerusalem.

Apart from the religious effect of this Dispersion upon the Jews themselves—the necessary

THE BIBLE OF THE APOSTOLIC AGE.

relaxation of ceremonial observances, the steady spiritualization of worship, when prayer and exhortation were substituted for sacrifice, the recognition of a sacred bond of union between societies most widely separated by place and circumstances, the gradual substitution, in short, of the idea of a *faith* for that of a *kingdom*—its external effect was of the greatest moment. Everywhere the Jews formed a nucleus of pure monotheists. Their pagan neighbours became acquainted practically with the worship of one God; and the 'devout Greek' obtained a recognized connexion with Israel, without accepting the complete burden of the Law. The Apostles everywhere availed themselves of the opening thus created in the cities which they visited. Even when the Jews rejected the message which was first addressed to them, the imperfect proselytes who had gathered around them were eager to receive a Gospel of which they could feel the full value. Without some such preparation, the spread of Christianity in the first age would be historically inconceivable. The mode in which the preparation was effected offers one of the most remarkable examples of Divine Providence which we are allowed to contemplate.

CHAP. I.
A.D. 30—80.
Dispersion as a preparation for Christianity.

But dismissing all detailed discussion of the effects of the Dispersion upon the progress and development of Christianity, whether by furtherance or by antagonism, we must yet notice one special point with which we are directly concerned. As far as can be ascertained the Jews, however widely scattered, carried their sacred books everywhere with them. '*Moses*,' St James says '*from generations of old hath in every city them that preach him, being read in the synagogues every*

The consequent circulation of the Old Testament.

Acts xv. 21.

sabbath.' No testimony could express more strongly the extent of Judaism, or the universal use of the ancient Scriptures in the Apostolic age; for, as we learn from other passages, the special mention of Moses does not exclude the public recitation of the Psalms and the Prophets. Not to speak now of the intimate acquaintance with almost every part of the Old Testament which is assumed by our Lord to exist in all his hearers, and afterwards by the Apostles within the limits of Judæa, we find a like acquaintance apparent everywhere wherever we can catch a glimpse of the religious life of the Jews. The Ethiopian chamberlain no less than the Jews of Berœa and Rome '*searched the Scriptures.*' At Antioch, at Thessalonica, at Corinth, at Ephesus, at Rome, St Paul took for granted that his Jewish hearers were familiar with Scripture, and ready to abide by the conclusions which could be drawn from it. Philo, as will be seen, shows that the same was the case in Egypt. From Babylonia alone all contemporary evidence fails us; but the testimony of a later age proves that there is no reason to suspect that there was any variation here from the general feeling of the Jews.

We find then at the beginning of the Apostolic age ' the twelve tribes scattered abroad' throughout the civilized world—and it is instructive to notice that the Dispersion itself obliterated the ancient division of the nation and restored its spiritual unity:—we find them everywhere in possession of sacred books, described generally as '*the Law and the Prophets;*' we find that these books, or parts of them, were habitually read, and that their contents were recognized as authoritative. The Jews had then at that time a '*Bible*' of some

THE BIBLE OF THE APOSTOLIC AGE.

kind, sanctioned by ancient usage, and it remains to inquire whether there is sufficient evidence to determine its contents. For this purpose it will be most convenient to examine first the evidence of Jewish writers (i), and then the evidence which can be drawn from the New Testament (ii).

But before doing this it may be well to notice a difficulty which may occur to some who have not realized the condition of the Roman world at the Christian era. What provision, it may be asked, was made by the translation of the Hebrew Scriptures for their circulation through so many distant provinces? The answer is most simple. The Greek Version—the Septuagint—which was made gradually at Alexandria, at various dates, from about the middle of the third century B.C. sufficed (to speak generally) for all. It is, indeed, possible that parts of the Old Testament were already translated into Syriac and Latin, but the direct evidence for this opinion is slight; and there is little reason to doubt that Greek was understood in the cities of the far East, and it was certainly well known throughout the chief towns of Africa, Syria, Asia Minor, Italy, and Gaul. During the early period of the Empire a single rule embraced the known world, and a single language opened the way to all hearts. But that language was the proper language neither of the Conqueror nor of the Teacher. Jerusalem gave the Divine message wrought out in a world-long history, during which she had gathered in struggles and sufferings all the wisdom of the East: Greece gave the language which had gained from the labours of poets, philosophers, and orators, a power and plasticity never since equalled: Rome gave the

CHAP. I.

A.D. 30—80.

The Old Testament generally intelligible in the Greek Translation (the LXX.)

24 *THE BIBLE IN THE CHURCH.*

CHAP. I.
A.D. 30—80.

i. The evidence of Jewish writers as to the contents of the Old Testament.

facilities of imperial organization and the dignified protection of sovereign law, unknown before that marvellous epoch, which in every aspect was indeed 'the fulness of time.'

i. These great facts, the broad unity of the Roman Empire and the Dispersion of the Jews, coextensive with its limits, and yet bound together round one centre, form the foundation of all understanding of the Apostolic age. At a later time the destruction of Jerusalem put an end to the external connexion of the Jewish societies, and the Christian Churches made no attempt, till long afterwards, to embody the Catholic Faith in one outward organization. But during the lifetime of St Paul every condition was realized for proclaiming the Gospel to the whole world, and reaping the full fruits of the earlier preparation for its message. There was variety in the form and relations of Judaism combined with substantial unity. This unity, it will appear, was preserved by the use of the same Scriptures as well as by the observance (more or less complete) of the ritual which was based upon them. It is with the first point alone that we are now concerned. And when we inquire what contemporary Jewish evidence there is as to the contents of the Sacred Volume in the first century, two writers at once offer themselves, Josephus in Palestine, and Philo at Alexandria, representing the two chief sections of the Jewish Church; for though the Alexandrine Dispersion was inferior to that of Babylon in antiquity and to that of Syria in extent, it was superior to both in intellectual vigour. The testimony of Babylon we must draw from a later source; that of Syria from the casual notices in the Apostolic writings.

THE BIBLE OF THE APOSTOLIC AGE. 25

1. FLAVIUS JOSEPHUS (that is, Joseph, born A.D. 37, died *after* A.D. 97), in whose Romanized name we do not at first recognize the name of the Patriarch, was eminently fitted by birth, character and education to be the historian of his nation. He was of priestly descent and connected on his mother's side with the noble family of the Maccabees. At an early age he studied with diligence the tenets of the various Jewish sects, and at a later time gained an extensive acquaintance with Greek literature, especially such as bore on the history of the East. It is unnecessary to follow the course of his life during the war of independence. After a distinguished but unavailing resistance he surrendered himself to Vespasian, whose future elevation he is said to have foretold, though he did not immediately gain his confidence. At length, on the accession of Vespasian to the imperial throne, Josephus was released from confinement; and during the reign of the Flavian emperors Vespasian, Titus and Domitian (whose family name he assumed), he was treated with great distinction. His works—The History of the Jewish War, The Antiquities of the Jews, his Autobiography, and the Books against Apion, on the Antiquity of the Jews— were composed at Rome, and the first, at least, was admitted into the Palatine Library. His Treatise on the Antiquity of the Jews (or against Apion, as it is commonly called) was composed some time after A.D. 93, and was intended to maintain the belief in the early origin and records of the Jewish nation against the objections drawn from the silence of the Greeks. With this object Josephus points out the late introduction of writing to the western nations, and the absence of

CHAP. I.

A.D. 30—80.

1. JOSEPHUS.

A.D. 67.

A.D. 69.

26   *THE BIBLE IN THE CHURCH.*

CHAP. I.

A.D. 30—80.

His special testimony.

c. Ap. i, 7. 9

early authentic registers of public events among them. In skill of composition, the East, he says, yields to Greece, but not in the accurate history of antiquity, and still less in the special history of different nations. In illustration of this statement he quotes first the primitive annals of the Egyptians, Babylonians and Phœnicians; and then goes on at once to speak of the Jewish records in greater detail, as the fact of their antiquity was not equally familiar to his readers. The whole passage, though long, is of the highest interest; dismissing all inquiry into the records of Egypt, Babylon and Greece, as it is universally admitted that they date from the earliest time, "I shall endeavour," he says, "to show briefly that our forefathers exhibited the same care as the nations already mentioned in the record of events, for I do not stop to maintain that it was even greater, as they enjoined this duty on the high priests and prophets, and [further, I shall show] how this custom has been preserved up to our time with great exactness, and, to venture on a bold assertion, how it will still be preserved. For not only did we commit this charge in the first instance to the best men and those who were devoted to the service of God, but we also took care to preserve the priestly race constantly pure and unmixed...
...(even) in Egypt and Babylon, and in any other place in the whole world, where any of the priestly race are scattered......Our accuracy in this respect is most conclusively proved by the fact that the descent of our priests is preserved in our records by name from father to son two thousand years back......Naturally, therefore, or rather necessarily [this accuracy is found in our Archives] inasmuch as the making the record did not rest upon

the simple will of any, and there is no discrepancy in the facts recorded; but the prophets only [composed our annals] who narrate the most remote and ancient events through the inspiration of God, and compiled exactly the history of the occurrences of their own time. For we have not tens of thousands of books discordant and conflicting, but only *twenty-two*, containing the record of all time, which have been justly believed to be Divine. And of these *five* are the books of Moses, which embrace the laws and the tradition of the creation of man reaching up to his (Moses') death. This period is little short of three thousand years. Next, the prophets who succeeded, compiled the history of the period from Moses to the reign of Artaxerxes the successor of Xerxes, king of Persia, in *thirteen* books, [relating severally] what was done in their times. The remaining *four* books embrace hymns to God, and practical directions for men. From the time of Artaxerxes to our own time each event has been recorded; but the records have not been deemed worthy of the same credit as those of earlier date, because the exact succession of the prophets was not continued. But what faith we have placed in our own writings is seen by our conduct; for though so long a time has now passed, no one has dared either to add anything to them, or to take anything from them, or to alter anything. But all Jews are instinctively led from the moment of their birth to regard them as decrees of God, and to abide by them, and, if need be, gladly to die for them. So ere now many of our captive countrymen have been often seen to endure tortures and all kinds of deaths in theatres, that they might utter no word against the laws and the records which are united with these. And what Greek would endure such a test in like case? Nay, rather, no Greek will endure even an ordinary loss to save the whole literature of his nation from destruction."

Conclusions from his statements.

When every allowance is made for the rhetorical character of the passage, and the evident desire of Josephus to adapt his statements to the feelings of heathen readers, several important conclusions may be certainly deduced from it.

(1) The Sacred Writings were distinctly limited in number; and this number (it appears) was admitted by universal consent.

(2) The reign of Artaxerxes (*c.* 450 B. C.) was regarded as the extreme limit of the Divine history (*i. e.* according to Josephus, the Book of Esther).

(3) The books were esteemed Divine, and this without any distinction between the three classes into which they were divided (Law, Prophets, Psalms, or, to use the technical term, Hagiographa, *i.e.* Holy Writings).

His arrangement of the Books of the Old Testament.

At present we are concerned only with the first of these conclusions, the number of the Sacred Books. This number itself, the number of the letters in the Hebrew alphabet, indicates an artificial arrangement, and in later times was adapted to various mystical speculations. But Josephus divides the books in an unusual manner, and as he gives no special enumeration of them, some doubt has arisen as to the way in which he reckoned up his thirteen books of the prophets, and four books of the Hagiographa. The usual enumeration gives eight books of the Prophets (*Joshua, Judges* and *Ruth*, 1, 2 *Samuel*, 1, 2 *Kings, Isaiah, Jeremiah, Ezekiel* and *Lamenta-*

tions, and 12 *minor Prophets*), and reckons the remaining nine as Hagiographa. Sometimes *Ruth* and *Lamentations* are reckoned separately, and added to the Hagiographa, in which case the total number of books is *twenty-four* instead of *twenty-two*. Josephus follows a different arrangement; and if we observe the peculiar definitions which he gives of the two classes, it will appear that he necessarily includes *all* the historical books among the writings of the prophets, so that the books of *Chronicles, Ezra, Nehemiah* and *Esther*, as well as *Daniel* and *Job*, are included in the second class; while *Psalms, Canticles, Proverbs* and *Ecclesiastes* alone satisfy the description which he gives of the third class.

Thus the list of the books of the Old Testament given by Josephus exactly coincides with our own; and there is nothing in his language to countenance the suspicion that he is expressing the opinion of one sect or country. The popular belief that the Sadducees, like the Samaritans, received only the Pentateuch, rests on no adequate evidence. It is possible that they (like the Alexandrine Jews) drew a less sharp line of division between the books of the Old Testament and other books; but if they had rejected all the sacred writings except the books of Moses, Josephus could hardly have omitted such an important trait in the description which he elsewhere gives of the opinions of the sect, as he expressly notices their rejection of tradition.

The casual quotations in Josephus give the same result. With the exception of *Proverbs, Ecclesiastes* and *Canticles*, which furnished no materials for his history, and *Job*, which, even if historical, lay without his scope, he quotes all the remaining books included in his list, either as divinely inspired or as authoritative sources of truth. On the other hand, while he uses the *first book of Maccabees* as the basis of his history of the period of which it treats, he definitely excludes it from the list of sacred books by the chronological limit within which he confines them. With the remaining books of the Apocrypha he shows no acquaintance[1]; though *Judith* and 2 *Maccabees* must have been noticed by him, if he had known them and held them to be trustworthy.

2. Our next witness PHILO is somewhat earlier in date than Josephus, but his evidence is less precise. He was born at Alexandria, probably about the year B.C. 20, and, like Josephus, was of priestly descent. The one important fact in his life, of which we have certain information, was an embassy to Rome, which he undertook A.D. 40, with four others of his countrymen, in the hope of obtaining from the emperor Caius (Caligula) some mitigation of the decree by which he had enjoined even on the Jews the adoration of his image. The embassy failed in its object, but the death of the emperor in the following year averted the worst dangers which it was intended to remove. At the time of this mission, Philo was already advanced in years, and he appears to have devoted all his earlier life to study. It would, indeed, be difficult to imagine any Jew, still faithful to the Law, who could have entered with a larger sympathy into the speculations of Greek philosophy before the spread of Christianity. Christianity has necessarily changed our appreciation of Judaism, but Philo was emphatically a Jew before Judaism was widely declared

[1] Except 2 Esdras, which is not included in the Roman Canon.

THE BIBLE OF THE APOSTOLIC AGE. 31

to culminate in a universal religion. Many, without doubt, had preceded him in the endeavour to reconcile the precepts of the Law with the teaching of philosophy, but he combined into a system what was before fragmentary, and at the outset announced his great thesis, that "the true servant of the Law is necessarily the true citizen of the world."

CHAP. I.
A.D. 30—80.

It would carry us too far from our immediate purpose to indicate the method by which Philo extracted the spiritual lessons which he supposed to be hidden under the veil of patriarchal history. All the Law appeared to him to be full of profound allegories and subtle harmonies; and he recognized with equal readiness the truths which had been laid open by Greek (and Eastern) philosophers, so that it was a common saying, "Either Philo teaches Plato (Platonizes), or Plato teaches Philo." The reverence which he shewed for the letter of the Law, as the sure groundwork of its spiritual significance, is remarkable on many grounds. The ecclesiastical constitution of the Alexandrine Jews was comparatively lax. The Old Testament existed among them only in a Greek translation, and that made at different times, by different persons, without any unity of plan or execution, and apparently without any final and authoritative revision or sanction. At the same time other books which, though of high religious interest, were not acknowledged as of Divine authority in Palestine, were translated into Greek, (for instance 1 *Maccabees*, *Ecclesiasticus*, &c.), and circulated together with the translations of the Hebrew Scriptures. Some books of similar character were also written at Alexandria itself, and by their intrinsic worth challenged wide

His general relation to the Old Testament.

32   *THE BIBLE IN THE CHURCH.*

CHAP. I. respect (as *Wisdom*). All these circumstances must
——— have tended to obscure the notion of a definite
A.D. 80—80. Bible, or at least to have modified its contents,
either by confining it to the Law, or by including
within its range (as we shall see was actually the
case at a later time) all the writings which were
sanctioned in any way by public or ecclesiastical use.

His special In spite of these disturbing influences by which
testimony he was surrounded, Philo appears to have held
to the contents of the the same opinion as Josephus on the number of
Old Testament. the sacred books. The Pentateuch, indeed, as
was natural, occupied the first place in his regard.
The later books, according to his principles of interpretation, were but partial elucidations of its
teaching, and their writers "companions of Moses"
or "members of his sacred band." Of the Law he
says, that "after a lapse of more than two thousand years [the Jews] had not changed a single
word of what had been written by [Moses], but
Fr. p. 628. would sooner endure to die a thousand times than
Euseb. *Pr.*
Ev. viii. 6. consent to violate his laws and customs;" and all
his works are based upon a verbal criticism of
the Septuagint text, which he accepts as the faithful reflex of the Divine original. But while the
Law is thus prominent in his writings, some books
from each of the other divisions of the Old Testament are quoted, though far less frequently than
the Pentateuch, as Divine or authoritative. Thus of
the 'former prophets,' *Joshua, Judges,* 1 *Samuel,*
1 *Kings* are quoted as 'the sacred word,' 'the
Divine oracle,' or mystically interpreted; of the
'later prophets,' *Isaiah* and *Jeremiah* of 'the
greater,' *Hosea* and *Zechariah* of 'the less,' are
said in various places to have spoken by Divine
inspiration; of the 'historical Hagiographa,'

1 *Chronicles* and (probably) *Ezra* are quoted; of the 'poetical Hagiographa,' *Psalms, Proverbs* and *Job*. On the other hand, though it is impossible that Philo should have been unacquainted with some (at least) of the Apocryphal writings (as *Ecclesiasticus*), yet he never makes a quotation from them[1].

CHAP. I.
A.D. 30—80

It further appears from a remarkable passage in Philo's description of the life of the Therapeutæ—the true forefathers of the Christian monks— that the threefold division of the Palestinian Bible was not unknown in Egypt. "In each house of these ascetics there is," he says, "a temple which is called...a monastery (a solitary cell), in which they perform the rites of a holy life, introducing therein nothing...which is needed for the necessities of the body, but *laws*, and oracles delivered by *prophets*, and *hymns* and the other [books] by which knowledge and piety are mutually increased and perfected." The last words are somewhat ambiguous, still from the connexion in which they stand it is not unreasonable to suppose that already some addition was made to the contents of the three divisions of the sacred books which were recognized in Palestine; and perhaps these new writings formed a distinct class and were not incorporated in the several parts of the Bible with which they were specially connected.

His division of the sacred books.

De Vit. Cont. § 3.

It is possible then that we may trace in Philo the conflict between the traditional view of the Jews on the Old Testament, and the looser opinions which, as has been already remarked, were almost forced upon him by the circumstances

Summary of Philo's testimony.

---

[1] The passage in *De Praem.* § 19, which is commonly said to have been taken from some unknown apocryphal book, is an obvious adaptation of Ex. xxiii. 26 (LXX.).

3

of his position, as well as by the general character of his speculations. Like other Jews, he held the Pentateuch to be the spring of all later teaching, the complete record of the Divine law. But he held this view with peculiar distinctness: nor could it be otherwise. The Pentateuch was raised into preeminence at Alexandria not only by its intrinsic character, but practically scarcely less by the fact that for some time it was the only book accessible to a Greek-speaking population. The books of Moses formed then the first Bible. Round them the other books which were received in Palestine were gradually collected, but in such a way that the sense of their unity as parts of one whole was obscured or even destroyed; and at the same time other writings came into popular use, and may have been joined in the same volume with the older books. Yet Philo, in the midst of this confusion, retained a hold upon the definite belief of the Palestinian Jews. Though he drew his chief illustrations from the Pentateuch, which formed the subject of his work, yet he also explained a few passages from the later historical books in a mystical sense, showing that he did not regard them as differing in kind from the books of Moses. His system led him to regard every one who shares in the Divine reason as being in some sense a prophet, yet even for him "the prophets" were a definite body, through whom "the Father of the Universe gave oracles." But it is easy to see even in Philo a tendency to break down the boundaries of the Old Testament, by an undue exaltation of the Pentateuch in comparison with the other books. This tendency, which was restrained in his case by a familiarity with the opinions of his countrymen in Palestine, was ne-

THE BIBLE OF THE APOSTOLIC AGE. 35

cessarily far more powerful among less educated Alexandrines; and it is not unlikely that the Greek Bible popularly received among them was already enlarged beyond the limits of the original Hebrew Bible. Yet this enlargement, whether it was already commenced or took place at a later time, was a result of habit and not of judgment. It was not determined by any conflict or agreement, but by the circumstances under which the books themselves were first introduced and afterwards studied.

CHAP. I.
A.D. 30—80.

3. It is necessary to come to a much lower date to obtain the judgment of the Babylonian Jews. This first appears in a written form about the close of the 5th century in the TALMUD, the great summary of the unwritten law, which had been preserved in very many cases by exact tradition from the time of the Return from Captivity, or even from a yet earlier age. The account given of the formation of the Old Testament appears to be in substance of the most venerable antiquity, and probably contains the most ancient opinion of the Jews upon the subject which has been preserved. In estimating its historical value it is well to bear in mind the tenacity with which Orientals retain a definite traditional record, and yet more, the special repugnance of the Eastern Jews to committing their opinions to writing, till the successive persecutions and destruction of their schools made this the only method of saving them from complete oblivion. The passage in question is contained in the Babylonian Gemara[1], in the

3. The TALMUD.

Baba Bathra, f. 14 b.

---

[1] The Talmud consists of two parts: the text, *Mishnah* (a *repetition*, i.e. a second law), which was committed to writing in the third century, and a commentary, *Gemara*. There are two Gemaras, that of

3—2

section which treats of the division of property. It runs as follows: 'But who wrote [the books of the Bible]? *Moses* wrote his own book, the section about Balaam and Job. *Joshua* wrote his own book and [the last] eight verses of the Pentateuch. *Samuel* wrote his own book, the books of Judges and Ruth. *David* wrote the book of Psalms [of which some were composed] by the ten venerable elders, Adam the first man, Melchizedek, Abraham, Moses, Haman, Jeduthun, Asaph, and the three sons of Korah. *Jeremiah* wrote his own book, the books of Kings and Lamentations. *Hezekiah* and his friends [wrote the books included in] the memorial book JAMSHAK, *i.e.* Isaiah, Proverbs (*Meshalim*), Canticles (*Shir hashirim*), and Ecclesiastes (*Koheleth*). The *men of the Great Synagogue*, [the books included in] the memorial word KANDAG, *i.e.* Ezekiel, the twelve (minor prophets), Daniel, and Esther. *Ezra* wrote his own book and continued the genealogies of the books of Chronicles down to his own times.... But who completed them (the books of Chronicles)? *Nehemiah* the son of Hachaliah.'

The context of the passage.

This remarkable passage stands in close connexion with two others which bear upon the same subject. One of these treats of the binding together of the sacred books, the other of their order. From the former it appears that a question had been raised whether the *Law* should be alone, the *Prophets* alone, and the *Hagiographa* alone, but it was decided that he who bound all toge-

Jerusalem and that of Babylon: the former is somewhat earlier in date and covers a larger range, but the latter is much more full. Of the 63 treatises of the *Mishnah*, 36 have a *Gemara* in the Babylonian and 49 in the Jerusalem Talmud.

THE BIBLE OF THE APOSTOLIC AGE. 37

ther did rightly. The second passage gives a list of books according to the three divisions, *Law, Prophets, Hagiographa*, reckoning *Ruth* and *Lamentations* as separate books among the Hagiographa. But these traditions are far inferior both in interest and (as it appears) in antiquity to that which has been quoted. For it is important to notice that this contains no trace of the triple division of the books, which is found in the context, and on the contrary places together books from the Hagiographa and the Prophets. It is also another most striking feature in the tradition that while several of the books are said to have been '*written*,' that is, reduced to their present form by others than their proper authors, yet it does not appear that anything was supposed to be detracted from their Divine authority by this revision.

CHAP. I.
A.D. 30—80.

Its importance.

The functions of the men of 'the great assembly[1],' as described in this earliest notice of their labours, are confined within very reasonable and trustworthy limits. In later times this tradition— for it is impossible not to believe that it is substantially præ-Christian— was fabulously embellished. Thus in the Second Book of *Esdras*, which cannot be much later than the close of the first century, Ezra is represented as writing again by immediate inspiration the sum of the divine revelation, and delivering to the people twenty-four books in place of those which had been lost[2]. The same story is repeated by many early Christian Fathers, for example, by Irenæus, Clement of

Later traditions.

2 Esdr. xiv. 20—40.

[1] See *Appendix* A.
[2] The true reading in 2 Esdr. xiv. 44 is "*ninety and four.*" When the "*seventy*" books reserved for "the wise among the people" (v. 46) are removed, this number gives the contents of the original collection.

38 *THE BIBLE IN THE CHURCH.*

CHAP. 1.
A.D. 30—80.

Alexandria, and Tertullian. As a singular pendant to the popular story of the origin of the Septuagint the legend is not without historical interest; but at present it is chiefly remarkable as a striking testimony to the recognized number of the public sacred books of the Old Testament; and an indication of the manner in which the later apocryphal writings were connected in theory with the original collection.

Summary.

Thus far we have seen the substantial unity of the opinion of the Jewish churches in Palestine, Egypt and Babylonia upon the contents of the Old Testament. All agree in confirming the authority of those twenty-two or twenty-four books only which we receive; but this agreement is combined with characteristic differences[1]. In Palestine the books appear in a definite and symmetrical arrangement completely marked off from all the other literature of the people. In Alexandria the line of separation is practically on the point of being obliterated or even broken. In Babylonia the tradition of the origin of the books is connected with the enumeration of them. We next pass to the examination of the evidence which can be gathered from the apostolic writings, which, though casual and disconnected, is of the highest interest and importance.

ii. The evidence of the Apostolic writers as to the contents of the Old Testament.

ii. One of the most important characteristics of the apostolic writings in their historical aspect, in which alone we now regard them, is their variety.

[1] The uniformity of the contents of the Hebrew Bible at later times will be seen in the catalogues of Melito, Origen and Jerome, which are based on Jewish authorities.

The limitation of the Samaritan Bible to the Pentateuch was the necessary consequence of historical and political conditions (*App.* A).

THE BIBLE OF THE APOSTOLIC AGE. 39

Even on the most cursory view it is obvious that they fall into distinct groups which represent typical forms of thought and feeling. These groups, as will be seen afterwards, are distinguished by broad lines of difference. Thus their independence multiplies the force of their testimony; and so far as they combine in presenting the same general result as to the contents of the Old Testament, the result depends not on one witness but on the concurrent evidence of several. Speaking roughly we may divide the books of the New Testament into three such groups. The first group includes the first three (synoptic) Gospels, the *Acts*, the *Apocalypse*, and the *Epistles of St James, St Peter*, and *St Jude:* the second group, the Epistles of St Paul with the *Epistle to the Hebrews:* the third group, the writings of St John.

CHAP. I.

A.D. 30—80.
Variety of Apostolical writings.

Before proceeding further we may notice the indications which these different groups contain of the existence of a definite collection of sacred writings generally known and recognized. The plainest of these lies in the name by which the books of the Old Testament are most commonly called '*the Scriptures*,' '*the Writings*.' This title, which is as definite in its apostolic use as with us, is found in each group (Matt. xxii. 29; Acts xvii. 11; 1 Cor. xv. 3; John v. 39), and the records to which it is applied are assumed to contain the sum of the divine revelation (Matt. xxvi. 54; 1 Cor. xv. 3, 4), and to be the source of authoritative argument (Luke xxiv. 27; Acts xviii. 28). This general title is further explained by the fuller phrase *the Law and the Prophets* (or *Moses and the Prophets*, Luke xvi. 29, 31), which is also used in each group to describe the whole of the Old Testament (Matt. vii. 12; Rom. iii. 21; John i. 46);

Collective titles for Holy Scripture.

the title of *the Law* itself is extended by a remarkable usage, which has been already noticed, to the *Psalms* (John x. 34; xv. 25), and Prophets (1 Cor. xiv. 21), and the Old Testament generally (John xii. 34). In one passage the triple division of the books is clearly recognized, where it is said that 'all things must be fulfilled which were written in *the Law of Moses* and in [*the*] *Prophets* and in *Psalms*....' (Luke xxiv. 44); though the certain omission of the article in the last clause and its suspiciousness in the second, point to the conclusion that the reference is rather to different parts of the sacred writings and not to the Bible as a whole under its complex title.

Importance of this usage.

The existence of these collective titles, the universal assumption of their intelligibility, the absence of all trace of doubt as to their application in the districts over which the evidence extends, the unhesitating appeal to the writings described by them, the absolute equality of the different parts which are recognized in the whole collection, have an important bearing both positively and negatively upon the special testimonies to separate books. They extend the testimony from one book to a group of books, and they exclude the inference that a possible use of other books places them on the same footing with those which belonged to the recognized collection.

The Hebrew collection of sacred books preserved by the study of the original text.

The definiteness of this collection of sacred books was secured in Palestine by a special guarantee. Whatever may have been the general currency of Greek in social intercourse, however widely or even universally the Septuagint may have been used in public and private religious exercises, yet it is certain that an influential school

THE BIBLE OF THE APOSTOLIC AGE. 41

of public teachers still maintained the study of CHAP. I.
the Hebrew text. Thus there was no danger in
Palestine, as in Egypt, that the original limits of A.D. 30—80.
the Old Testament should be obscured. Popular
usage, even if it went astray, was corrected by the
presence of the original records; and there is not
the slightest evidence to show that the Hebrew
Bible ever included any more books than are now
contained in it.

The range of the express quotations from the 1. Express
Old Testament in the first group of the Apostolic quotations in
writings extends (in each division) to the Law,
the Prophets and the Hagiographa, without any
difference in the mode of citation. In the synop- The first
tic Gospels the quotation is made sometimes by three *Go-*
the Lord Himself, sometimes by the Evangelist, *spels.*
sometimes by the Jews, in a way which shows beyond all doubt the equality of authority which was
attributed to all the sacred books, the unanimity,
with which this authority was admitted, and the
extent of the collection of Scriptures within narrow limits. Thus our Lord quotes passages from
Genesis, Exodus, Numbers, Deuteronomy, 1 *Samuel, Psalms, Isaiah, Daniel, Hosea, Jonah*
and *Malachi,* with the most distinct recognition
of their binding moral force; and it is worthy of
notice that St Mark, who introduces no quotation in his own person except in the preface to
his Gospel (xv. 28 is an interpolation), yet agrees
with the other Evangelists in preserving those
which occur in the Lord's discourses. The list of
books quoted in the first three Gospels is increased by St Matthew and St Luke, by the addition of *Leviticus, Jeremiah, Micah,* and *Zechariah.* The quotations in the Acts spread over The *Acts.*
the same field, including passages from *Genesis,*

42 *THE BIBLE IN THE CHURCH.*

CHAP. I.
A.D. 30—80.
The *Catholic Epistles*.

Exodus, Deuteronomy, Psalms, Isaiah, Joel, Amos, and *Habakkuk.* In the Catholic Epistles (with the exception of the Epistles of St John) quotations occur from *Genesis, Isaiah* and *Proverbs.* The wide extent of these references when compared with the brief compass of the books in which they occur is a remarkable proof of the familiar acquaintance of the Jews with the Old Testament; and the fact that in each subordinate group of books passages are found from all the three classes into which the writings of the Old Testament were subdivided, seems to show that no practical difference existed in the use of them.

2. Express quotations in the *Epistles of St Paul.*

In the Epistles of St Paul, or rather in that great group of his epistles which is composed of 1, 2 *Corinthians, Galatians* and *Romans,* the range of quotations is a little more extensive, including *Genesis, Exodus, Leviticus, Deuteronomy,* 2 *Samuel,* 1 *Kings, Job, Psalms, Isaiah, Jeremiah, Hosea, Habakkuk,* and *Malachi;* but in his remaining epistles there are only three or at most four express quotations. In the Epistle to the Hebrews the quotations are proportionately still more numerous, and it is a characteristic difference that they are in every case introduced by a word which implies the living voice of the speaker—'*he saith,*' '*he spake,*' '*he beareth witness*'—and not merely the testimony of the record—'*it hath been written.*' The quotations in this Epistle are made from *Genesis, Exodus, Deuteronomy,* 2 *Samuel, Psalms, Proverbs, Isaiah, Jeremiah,* and *Haggai.*

The *Epistle to the Hebrews.*

3. Express quotations in *St John.*

In the Gospel of St John passages are quoted from *Exodus, Psalms, Isaiah,* and *Zechariah.* In his epistles and the Apocalypse no express quotations occur, though the latter is in a great

THE BIBLE OF THE APOSTOLIC AGE. 43

measure constructed out of the language of the Old Testament.

For it must be remembered that the express quotations in the Apostolic writings include only a very small portion of the passages borrowed from the Old Testament. It is scarcely possible to read many consecutive verses in any part of the New Testament without meeting with words or phrases which are obviously reminiscences of the Septuagint; and the ease and naturalness with which these are introduced prove more distinctly than anything else could do, how completely this great Greek version was inwrought into the minds of the devout Jews of the Apostolic age. But setting aside silent quotations and coincidences, every book in the Hebrew Bible is distinctly quoted in the New Testament with the exception of *Joshua*[1], *Judges*, *Chronicles*, *Canticles*, *Ecclesiastes*, *Ezra*, *Nehemiah*, *Esther*, *Obadiah*, *Zephaniah*, and *Nahum* ; and, with the limitations already noticed, there is no perceptible difference between the different groups of the Apostolic books as to the range or character of the quotations which they contain.

The general evenness of the biblical quotations throughout the New Testament may be conveniently exhibited by a brief summary of the direct quotations in the several groups of books. Some differences may arise in the enumeration of them, but the number of distinct references, not reckoning repetitions in the same group, is approximately as follows:

CHAP. I.
A.D. 30—80.
Such quotations only a small part of biblical reminiscences.

General summary of quotations.

[1] The words in Heb. xiii. 5 correspond more nearly with Deut. xxxi. 6 than with Josh. i. 5. They probably represent a traditional form of the saying. See note *l.c.*

44 THE BIBLE IN THE CHURCH.

CHAP. I.

A.D. 30—80.

		Law.	Prophets.	Hagiographa.
i.	Synoptic Gospels	15	21	6
	Acts	7	9	7
	Catholic Epistles	4	1	2
ii.	The Epistles of St Paul	25	28	13
	Epistle to the Hebrews	11	4	11
iii.	The writings of St John (Gospel)	2	6	6

Of special books *Isaiah* and the *Psalms* furnish by far the largest number of references, as might naturally be expected from their extent and character; and the absence of quotations from the books which have been mentioned is to be explained by the peculiar and limited nature of their contents.

No special quotation from the *Apocrypha*.

On the other hand there is not one direct quotation in the whole of the New Testament from any of the books included in the Apocrypha, though the book of *Wisdom* has very numerous points of contact with Christian doctrine. This fact is universally admitted, and is of the greatest interest, for even if it appear that some of the Apostolic writers were acquainted with one or other of the books of the Apocrypha, yet their knowledge and use of the books prove nothing as to their reception among the Canonical Scriptures,

Acts xvii. 28, 29.
Tit. i. 12.

unless the same claim be conceded to Aratus or Epimenides. So far as the clear evidence extends, the books of the Hebrew Bible are quoted as writings *sui generis*, and as forming part of a definite and known collection, the limits of which are fixed by independent witnesses in such a way as to harmonize exactly with the casual quotations of the Apostolic writers. But it is nevertheless evident that it would be impossible to determine the contents of the Old Testament

THE BIBLE OF THE APOSTOLIC AGE. 45

by the express quotations in the New, without the complementary evidence of direct testimony. Quotations and general references are necessarily valid only as far as they actually extend. They have in themselves no negative force. And it is only when taken in combination with explicit catalogues of the sacred books that they show in the clearest manner how the formal belief was actually ratified in practice.

This corroborative power belongs properly and in its full weight only to express quotations; if, however, account be taken of coincidences of thought or expression, the extent of the evidence is very greatly enlarged. In this case the whole number of quotations in the New Testament from the Old cannot be less than seven hundred, and is probably still greater. Yet most of these references are taken from the same books as furnish the direct quotations, though it appears certain that passages of *Joshua*, 1 *Chronicles*, and probably also of *Esther*, were present to the minds of the apostolic writers. On the same grounds it seems likely that St Paul and (perhaps) St James were acquainted with the book of *Wisdom;* and the author of the Epistle to the Hebrews alludes to the facts related in 2 *Maccabees*, though he may not have derived his knowledge of them from that book. The alleged references to *Ecclesiasticus* are extremely doubtful; and there are certainly none to *Judith*, *Tobit*, or any other of the Apocrypha[1].

CHAP. I.

A.D. 30—80.

Extent of silent, verbal, and historical coincidences.

Old Testament.

John iv. 5.
‖ Jos. xxiv. 32.
James ii. 25.

Apocrypha.
Acts vii. 47 ‖
1 Chron. xvii. 12.
Mark vi. 22,23
‖ Esth. v. 3.
Hebr. xi. 37.

---

[1] It may be well to add that this statement is made after a careful examination of the passages alleged in the late thorough discussion of the question in Germany. The most striking parallels which have been adduced are: Wisd. v. 18—21 ‖ Eph. vi. 13—17.

46   *THE BIBLE IN THE CHURCH.*

CHAP. I.

A.D. 30—80.

Express quotations of doubtful origin.

Luke xi. 49—51.

But there are four or five apparently distinct references to "passages of Scripture" in the New Testament of which the original sources cannot be certainly traced, and it has been frequently supposed that these must have been derived from lost Apocryphal books[1]. The passages occur in Luke xi. 49, 51; James iv. 5; 1 Cor. ii. 9; Eph. v. 14; John vii. 38. Each of these requires a short notice. The passage in St Luke is introduced by the phrase '*Therefore also said the Wisdom of God*,' and the substance of the words which follow is assigned to the Lord Himself in Matt. xxiii. 34. Thus both the mode of reference, which is without a parallel, and the character of the quotation are unfavourable to the belief that it was directly borrowed from any writing. The general tenor of the passage is contained in 2 Chron. xxiv. 19; and it is not improbable that those words had been remoulded at an early time, and preserved, like other traditional sayings, till they were

---

Wisd. xv. 7 || Rom. ix. 21. Wisd. ii. 12 || James v. 6. Wisd. vii. 27 || Hebr. i. 3. Ecclus. v. 11 || James i. 19. Ecclus. vii. 10 || James i. 6. Tobit iv. 16 || Matt. vii. 12. Wisd. ii. 16—18 || Matt. xxvii. 43—54. Any one who will examine the character of the coincidences in these passages, and their relation to the language of the Old Testament, will readily feel how slender the evidence is on which the apostles are affirmed to have been acquainted with the writings in question. The last parallel is, in many respects, the most remarkable, and one which appears to be most certainly casual.

[1] As the words *Apocrypha*, *Apocryphal* are ambiguous, it may be well to notice that I have limited the terms *Apocrypha* or *books of the Apocrypha* to the ecclesiastical books added to our Bibles. *Apocryphal books* or *writings*, on the other hand, are those which are admitted to be unauthentic. This distinction will be always observed in the following pages.

THE BIBLE OF THE APOSTOLIC AGE. 47

finally ratified by the Lord[1]. The passage in St James is much more difficult. *Or do ye think that the Scripture saith in vain, Doth the Spirit that dwelleth in us* (or rather *which He caused to dwell in us*) *lust to envy?* As the words stand it has been thought most natural that the words *Doth the Spirit......envy?* are a quotation, and according to the true reading, a quotation from a *Christian* writing. The chief alternative is to suppose that the verse consists of two distinct questions, and that the first has reference only to the general scope of the teaching of Scripture. But such a use of '*saith*' is apparently without a parallel; and, on the other hand, there is not the slightest trace of words like the assumed quotation in any other place. The supposition that the reference is to a Christian writing gains some confirmation from Eph. v. 14. *Wherefore he* (or *one*) *saith, Awake thou that sleepest and arise from the dead, and Christ shall give thee light.* For here it seems almost certain that the words quoted are part of a Christian hymn, an opinion supported by Severian early in the fifth century, though some Fathers referred the quotation to an apocryphal book of Elias[2]. Another quotation of St Paul, 1 Cor. ii. 9, *As it is written, Eye hath not seen,*

CHAP. I.
A.D. 30—80.
James iv. 5.

Eph. v. 14.

1 Cor. ii. 9.

---

[1] The reference in Matt. ii. 23 which was spoken by *the prophets* is not wholly dissimilar; for in this it appears that the general scope of several prophetic passages was summed in a phrase which does not occur in any one of them. Compare John i. 46 with Is. liii. 3, Ps. xxii. 6.

[2] The phrase in 1 Tim. v. 18, *The labourer is worthy of his hire*, is apparently only a popular proverb, and not a reference to Luke x. 7. Compare John iv. 37, 2 Pet. ii. 22 (the second proverb).

48 *THE BIBLE IN THE CHURCH.*

CHAP. I.
A.D. 30—80.

nor ear heard, neither have entered into the heart of man, the things which God hath prepared for them that love Him, was also referred at a very early time (at the beginning of the third century by Origen, or perhaps at the middle of the second by Hegesippus) to an Apocalypse of Elias. From the direct testimony of several competent witnesses there can be no doubt but that the passage did occur in an apocryphal writing in this form; but it seems equally certain that the groundwork of the passage is Is. lxiv. 4, and in this (as in some other places) St Paul seems to have availed himself of a traditional rendering, which may have been widely current. There is, at least, no evidence to show that the Apocalypse of Elias was earlier than his Epistle[1]. The words

John vii. 38.

in St John vii. 38, *He that believeth on Me, as the Scripture hath said* (or *said*), *out of his belly shall flow rivers of living water*, appear to be (like Luke xi. 49—51) a free adaptation of Old Testament imagery (Is. xliv. 3; Zech. xiii. 1), but with this difference, that the adaptation was one suggested by the immediate circumstances of the discourse, and moulded by our Lord to suit the figure which He had used immediately before (*drink, out of his belly*).

Quotation of St Jude from Enoch.

There yet remains the remarkable quotation of *St Jude* from *Enoch* (Jude 14, 15): *Enoch also, the seventh from Adam, prophesied of these saying, Behold the Lord cometh......against*

[1] Traces of Jewish tradition are found 2 Tim. iii. 8 (Jannes and Jambres); Jude 9 (Michael and Satan); Hebr. ix. 19 (the book), &c.; and the phrases in Matt. vii. 2 (*with what measure...*); Matt. vii. 5 (*cast the mote...*); Matt. xii. 25 (*every kingdom divided...*), &c., appear to have been proverbial.

THE BIBLE OF THE APOSTOLIC AGE. 49

Him. The words thus quoted exist substantially in the Apocryphal book of Enoch, which is still preserved in an Æthiopic translation. From the form in which the quotation occurs, it is impossible to determine whether St Jude derived it from tradition or from this so-called Apocalypse. Yet as the book of *Enoch* was widely circulated at a very early time, it seems almost certain that the quotation was made directly from it; and it is needless to inquire from what ulterior source the words were originally taken. It is enough that St Jude simply adopts the language of his time in speaking of words with which his readers were probably familiar. They may have been handed down orally from primitive times—many will be inclined to think that it must have been so from St Jude's use of them—but of this there is not the slightest external evidence.

CHAP. I.
A.D. 30—80.

From what has been said it will be evident how little ground there is for believing that our Lord or the Apostles sanctioned the authoritative use of the Apocrypha or Apocryphal books. The books with which they offer certain coincidences were never admitted into the Hebrew Bible, nor, as far as is known, ever made a claim to admission to the Christian Bible till late times when, with the partial exception of *Enoch*, they were universally rejected. Yet, on the other hand, the passages last quoted from *St Jude*, *St James*, and *Ephesians* tend to show that the formulæ of the citation of Scripture were not always used with exclusive strictness; and the wide freedom of citation which was admitted is seen in the other references.

The general conclusions which follow from the review of all the earliest evidence as to the con-

General result.

4

tents of the Jewish Bible may be briefly stated. (1) The books which are definitely enumerated as part of the collection of Holy Scripture are exactly the same as those books of the Old Testament which are now received; and there is no trace of any explicit difference of opinion on the subject, or of any attempt to extend the collection by the addition of later writings. (2) The casual testimony of the New Testament harmonizes completely with the direct evidence obtained from other sources, both as to the existence of a recognized body of 'Scriptures,' and as to the books contained in it. (3) In Palestine all the books included in the collection—'The Law and the Prophets'—are placed on the same footing as authoritative sources of divine truth, without any distinction of character; and no conclusion can be drawn from the use of the books in the New Testament as to the peculiar preeminence of any part of them. But, on the other hand, (4) In Egypt, and probably wherever the influence of Palestine was not predominant, the Law was placed in such a position of supreme and complete authority, that the distinction between the remaining books of Scripture and the ordinary religious literature of the people was in danger of being disregarded.

Such was the Bible at the time when it was destined to receive its final complement. In the next Chapter we shall trace the circumstances under which a New Testament gradually and without conscious purpose grew up by the Will of Providence under the shadow of the Old. The mode of this growth, which can be followed with tolerable exactness, will explain better than anything else the corresponding process in the for-

THE BIBLE OF THE APOSTOLIC AGE.

mation of the Jewish Bible. Indeed, in the absence of adequate original evidence, it is only in this way that we can understand how the Old Testament was formed historically; nor is it an essential difference between the two cases, that the productive energy of the divine teachers was extended in the one case over many centuries while it was limited in the other to a single generation[1].

[1] A sketch of the history of the formation of the Hebrew Bible, as distinct from the history of the origin of the separate books, is given in *Appendix* A.

CHAPTER II.

THE GROWTH OF THE NEW TESTAMENT.

> *Not unto themselves, but unto us they did minister the things which are now reported unto you by them that have preached the Gospel unto you with the Holy Ghost sent down from heaven.*— 1 Pet i. 12.

CHAP. II.

A.D. 30—80.

The critical study of the Apostolic age a source of hope.

IF it is always difficult to realize the beginning of any great movement, to picture the external appearance which it must have presented to those among whom it arose, to appreciate without reference to later experience the judgments which must have been passed upon it, to follow out the partial or conflicting developments which it must have received, before it gained its final shape, this difficulty becomes almost overwhelming in studying the rise of Christianity. Not only are the conditions of the problem in this case complicated beyond all example, but the subject is necessarily veiled under a halo of religious awe. It seems to be irreverent to attempt to analyse the first forms of that life which animates all Christendom, to separate what has been united by the instinct of centuries, to contemplate as history wrought out upon earth, in the midst of misunderstanding and conflict and error, that which is now seen most readily in its heavenly power;

THE GROWTH OF THE NEW TESTAMENT. 53

yet Christianity not only admits a purely critical inquiry into the outward circumstances under which it arose and spread, but even invites it. It was the consolation of St Paul that Christ's *strength is made perfect in weakness.* And if on a closer scrutiny traces of human infirmity can be discovered in that earliest age of the Church, in which the presence of a Divine power is most certainly visible, the result will be not a lessening of the majesty of the past, but a bringing of hope and confidence to the study of other periods, where the darkness of present misconceptions still hides the working of Providence. The temper which isolates the first age does injustice to its abiding power, and takes away a large measure of that instructiveness which we may believe it was designed to preserve for all time. The more free and more truly reverent study of its records finds that they have a vital connexion with our life. The apostles though *full of the Holy Ghost and of power,* could yet proclaim that they were *men of like passions* with their Gentile hearers; and conversely as we picture to ourselves their working, we may believe that in spite of divisions and disappointments, the promise of Christ has not yet failed, according to which He *is with His Church always, even to the end of the world.* [CHAP. II. A.D. 30—80. 2 Cor. xii. 9. Acts xiv. 15. Matt. xxviii. 20.]

In order to appreciate the Apostolic age in its essential character, it is necessary to dismiss not only the ideas which are drawn from a collected New Testament, but those also, in a great measure, which spring from the several groups of writings of which it is composed. The first work of the Apostles, and that out of which all their other functions grew, was to deliver in living [The work of the Apostles *to preach,* not to *write.*]

words a personal testimony to the cardinal facts of the Gospel—the Ministry, the Death, and the Resurrection of our Lord. It was only in the course of time, and under the influence of external circumstances, that they committed their testimony, or any part of it, to writing. Their peculiar duty was to preach. That they did in fact perform a mission for all ages in perpetuating the tidings which they delivered, was due not to any conscious design which they formed nor to any definite command which they had received, but to that mysterious power which is for men the outward expression of the action of God, Who uses the results of our free agency for the fulfilment of His designs.

Their training makes the New Testament a moral miracle.

Everything in the national and spiritual position of the Apostles was unfavourable to the formation of a written record of Christian history or doctrine. The training of the Palestinian Jews was exclusively oral. The Old Testament was an inexhaustible field for study, which admitted no rival and seemed to require no supplement. Even those teachers who, like Gamaliel, were acquainted with Greek literature, remained faithful to the ancient tradition, which forbade them to commit anything to writing. And this discipline under which St Paul was schooled, must have been less incompatible with literary effort than the rude life of Galilee. As soon as the Apostles are seen in their historical relations, the supernatural energy with which they were inspired is revealed beyond all cavil. That the New Testament should have been written by Jews—and St Luke is the only Gentile, if, indeed, he was a Gentile, among the apostolic writers—is a moral miracle of overwhelming dignity, if only account be taken of the

THE GROWTH OF THE NEW TESTAMENT. 55

traditions and prejudices among which they, like all their countrymen, were born and reared.

CHAP. II.

A.D. 30–80.

The general disinclination of Jews for literary work must have been greatly increased in the case of the Apostles by the spiritual position which they occupied. For them *the kingdom of God* was already *at hand* in the fulness of its completed triumph. The close of the old dispensation appeared to coincide with the final consummation of the new. The slow development of countless ages was brought together in their perspective in the one awful scene of the revelation of the Lord. The time seemed to be imminent when they *which were alive and remained should be caught up to meet Him*. The future to which they looked forward was one in which there would be no need for written monuments of the first coming of Christ, for it was to be enlightened by the abiding glory of the Saviour.

The Apostles looked forward to no long historic future.

1 Thess. iv. 17.

Rev. xxi. 23.

But while the Apostles, like the prophets in former times, failed to see the full meaning of their own work, the same circumstances which hid from them the history of following generations enabled them to pierce through all that is seen and temporal to the spiritual and eternal. 'Men wrote history, as it had never been written, whose present seemed to have no natural sequel ; and unfolded doctrine with far-seeing wisdom, while they looked eagerly for that divine presence in which all partial knowledge should be done away.' They erred not in their spiritual apprehension of things, but as to the temporal dress in which they arrayed them. The 'Lord came' and His 'kingdom' was established, yet not so as to dispense with the long labour of men in realizing its blessings. Thus it is that the writings of the Apostles

Their insight into the Eternal, one sign of their inspiration.

56 　THE BIBLE IN THE CHURCH.

CHAP. II.
———
A.D. 30—80.

and Evangelists are instinct with inexhaustible lessons. If we look at them on their historical side it is this peculiarity of their origin which is the condition of their divine authority. They reach forward to the end of the dispensation in which we are living. Like Christianity itself they belong to no one age. Their authors wrote in the immediate contemplation of that glorious triumph of Christ in which it culminates. 'Heaven lay about them,' and as that light faded from the world, a Christian literature succeeded to a New Testament.

The teaching of the Apostles *oral* not *written*.

Acts i. 21, 22.
Gal. i. 12, 16.

Acts vi. 4.

1 Cor. i. 17.

Acts iv. 20.

1 John i. 1.

Rom. x. 14.

The need of a written record felt later.

The records which have been preserved of the working of the Apostles fully confirm the view which has been given of their office. They first witnessed by oral teaching to the facts of the Life of Christ, and then proclaimed the truths which flowed from them. The qualification for the Apostolate was to have known Christ personally; and St Paul himself claimed this direct and personal knowledge. The common work of the twelve was *prayer and the ministry of the word;* and St Paul writes that *Christ sent him…to preach the Gospel.* The message with which they were charged was to be enforced by the living voice: *they could not but speak the things which they had seen and heard.* The Gospel was what the witnesses of Christ had *seen…and looked upon and…handled of the word of life.* The question which expressed best the spirit in which they went forth was *how shall* men *hear without a preacher?* As yet it was impossible that they could feel that the brightness of the image of Christ could fade away from the minds of men, or the memory of His words be effaced. The repeated experience of many ages has even yet hardly suf-

THE GROWTH OF THE NEW TESTAMENT. 57

ficed to show that a permanent record of His words and deeds, open to all, must coexist with the living body of the Church, if that is to continue in pure and healthy vigour. In the first glow of Christian love it might seem that such a power needed nothing from without to sustain and temper it. That which is still a life can rarely be apprehended as a history or a doctrine.

CHAP. II.
A.D. 30—80.

But while the work of the Apostles lay chiefly in preaching, this was substantially historical. The narrative of the Acts contains several examples of the way in which the Gospel message was delivered. Two may be taken to represent the general character of all. St Peter before Cornelius, and St Paul in the synagogue at Antioch, base their teaching on the facts of the Saviour's life. Both briefly sketch the outlines of His ministry from the Baptism of John to the Resurrection; and the discourse of St Peter, which was the immediate preparation for Baptism, is, as it were, a brief commentary on the events which are included in the Apostles' Creed. Everywhere one fact—the Resurrection—was the starting-point of the Apostolic teaching. By all alike and in every place this was set forth as the spring of all faith. In Palestine, in Asia Minor, in Greece, in Italy, before popular assemblies, in the council and in the synagogue, the same witness was delivered. The Gospel claimed to be an announcement of facts, and in the first generation it triumphed in virtue of its claim.

Their oral teaching in substance historical.

Acts x. 37—43.
Acts xiii. 23—31.

One of the first effects of this oral historical teaching of the Apostles must have been the separation of a cycle of facts which formed the centre of their message. Out of the infinite mul-

The formation of an *oral Gospel*.

58   THE BIBLE IN THE CHURCH.

CHAP. II. titude of those *things which Jesus did* and suf-
A.D. 30—80. fered, a few only could be preserved for the in-
John xxi. 25. struction of the Church: *how few*, perhaps we
can hardly realize, without reckoning up what a
small number of days contribute all the incidents
of the Gospels, and how little remains even in the
record of those to bear witness to the labours
Mark vi. 31. which left *no leisure so much as to eat*. Thus the
selection of representative facts from the history
of the Lord was one of the first steps towards the
establishment and instruction of a Christian society. Apart from all considerations of immediate
Divine guidance, it is obvious that the experience
which the Apostles gained in their preaching
would define the general character of the facts
suited to the fulfilment of their work, and the
limits within which they ought to be confined.
Thus gradually an oral Gospel would be constructed, varying slightly in its contents from
time to time, but fashioned according to the
same general model. By constant repetition,
especially in the instruction for Baptism, the form
of each constituent narrative would gain a certain
consistency; and at the same time the prominence
given to particular acts and discourses of the Lord,
would tend to destroy the recollection of those
other incidents in His Life, which were not allowed by Divine Providence to be included in the
Evangelic cycle.

Traces of a   There are several traces in the Epistles of the
historic tra-
dition in the existence of this Evangelic tradition, which con-
Epistles.   stitutes the first stage in the composition of our
1 Cor. xi. 23: Gospels. Thus St Paul speaks of '*delivering*' to
xv. 3.   others what he had himself '*received*' as to the
details of the Last Supper, the Passion and the
Resurrection. St Luke, again, speaks of the ac-

THE GROWTH OF THE NEW TESTAMENT. 59

count of the Lord's Life which *they delivered* CHAP. II.
which from the beginning were eyewitnesses and A.D. 30—80.
ministers of the word. And in close connexion Luke i. 2.
with these distinct traces of a historical tradition,
must be taken those other passages which speak
more generally of the *deposit* committed to the
Evangelist, or of the revealed *mystery of godli-* 1 Tim. vi. 20.
ness, which is described in words that seem to 2 Tim. i. 12.
reflect the outlines of a primitive Creed. 14; iv. 5.
1 Tim. iii. 16.

While the Gospel thus gradually assumed a *The oral* definite shape in the oral teaching of the Apostles, *Gospel committed to* many, as it seems from St Luke's words, endea- *writing.* voured to commit it to writing; and some, perhaps, formed collections of the words of the Lord, others of His acts, others of the events of the Passion. In doing this they gave a new form to that which was the common inheritance of Christians (Luke i. 2...as they delivered them *unto us*); but there is nothing to show that they attempted either to enlarge or to modify the contents of the oral Gospel. They designed to do what was afterwards done under Apostolic sanction. As long as the twelve were still at Jerusalem, they were in themselves abiding witnesses to the facts which they announced; and, if we may believe the accordant traditions of the early Church, it was not till they were scattered and their work of preaching well nigh finished, that the first authoritative record of the Gospel was composed. Thus St Mark is said to have written down the substance of St Peter's public preaching. "St Luke," in like manner, "committed to a book the Gospel which Paul used to proclaim;" and, though this rests upon a later authority, St Matthew, when he was about to go to a fresh field of labour, left his Gospel to supply the place of his oral teaching in

60 *THE BIBLE IN THE CHURCH.*

CHAP. II.
A.D. 30—80.

Palestine. The Gospel of St John belongs to a yet later period, and is wholly separated from the cycle of oral narratives. It is essentially a personal witness of the one beloved disciple, and not a reflection of the common public witness of the twelve. And, unlike the others, this Gospel was composed in its present form with a definite purpose, and without any direct reference to what was already known: *these* (signs) *are written that ye may believe that Jesus is the Christ, the Son of God; and that believing ye may have life in His name.*

John xx. 30, 31.
Comp. Luke i. 1—4.

The origin of Epistles.

The extension of the work of the Apostles gave rise to another form of composition, which probably contributed the first written elements of the Christian Scriptures. The founders of scattered Churches had need to counsel or reprove or instruct those whom they had admitted to the faith. Such was the origin of most of the Epistles of St Paul. Others again felt drawn by peculiar ties towards large societies of men on whom they wished to enforce special aspects of truth, as St Paul in writing to the *Romans*, St John in the *Apocalypse*, and the author of the *Epistle to the Hebrews*; and with a more general scope St James, St Peter and St Jude. As the Churches grew, some directions were needed for their management, and thus the *Pastoral Epistles* were written. At a still later time St John, looking back over a whole generation of believers, could address to his 'children' the earliest type of a Christian pastoral (1 *John*). And besides all these, there must have been need of much individual communication between Christians, of which specimens yet remain in 2, 3 *John*, and the *Epistle to Philemon*.

THE GROWTH OF THE NEW TESTAMENT.

All this took place in the natural way of history. The Apostles when they speak claim to speak with Divine authority, but they nowhere profess to give in writing a system of Christian doctrine. Gospels and Epistles, with the exception, perhaps, of the writings of St John, were called out by special circumstances. There is no trace of any designed connexion between the separate books, except in the case of the *Gospel of St Luke* and the *Acts*, still less of any outward unity or completeness in the entire collection. On the contrary, it is not unlikely that some epistles of St Paul have been lost; and though in point of fact the books which remain do combine to form a perfect whole, yet this completeness is due, not to any conscious co-operation of their authors, but to the Will of Him by whose power they wrote and wrought.

CHAP. II.
A.D. 30—80.
No combined design in the composition of the different books.

Indeed it appears from what has been already said that the Old Testament was the Bible of the Apostolic Church. In embracing Christianity, the Jewish convert found the key to the mysterious words of the Prophets. What was obscure before was now flooded with a new light. It was seen that *all the prophets from Samuel and those that follow after, as many as have spoken,* foretold the fortunes of Christ and His Church. The old Scriptures were felt to be *able to make men wise unto salvation through faith which is in Christ Jesus.* There was no sense of incompleteness in their record, no desire for any permanent supplement to their contents, no purpose of composing any new Law to interpret the old. For the Gentiles, on the other hand, the simple facts of the Apostolic message were sufficient. The tidings of the Resurrection was for them a

The Old Testament still felt to be a complete Bible by the Jew.

Acts iii. 21, 24.

2 Tim. iii. 15.

The Gentile felt no want of a Bible.

62 THE BIBLE IN THE CHURCH.

CHAP. II.
A.D. 30—80.

complete Gospel. Yet silently and in distant places the New Testament was written, so that when the want of it was first felt, the Jew might read there in unfading characters the fulfilment of the earlier dispensation, and the Gentile be led to trace back through the ancient Scriptures how by the discipline of ages that Church was prepared, into the fulness of which he was admitted.

Antagonism of Jew and Gentile in the Apostolic age.

This fundamental contrast of feeling between Jew and Gentile, which exercised a considerable influence on the collection of the Christian Scriptures, was manifested in a yet more striking difference of teaching. Difference soon degenerated into antagonism, and the Apostolic writings reveal the speedy development of the great forms of heresy, which in various shapes have ever continued to disturb the Church. Even within the Church the fulness of truth was only slowly realized; and the earliest heresy was simply the perverse and obstinate retention of that which had once been the common belief, after that a wider view had been sanctioned by Divine authority. Thus in its primitive form the Apostolic Church was simply a congregation of Jews, who added to the observance of the Law a belief in Jesus as

Acts iii. 21.

the Messiah, with the immediate hope of a *restitution of all things*. In this stage there was no idea of the abrogation of the Law before the Second Coming of Christ. The Hellenist Stephen

Acts vi. 13, 14.

first proclaimed the *change of the customs which Moses delivered*, and the storm which followed on his teaching sufficiently shows the novelty of its form. Afterwards, when a mightier Stephen was already prepared in the person of 'Saul the persecutor,' the full privileges of the Church were

Acts x. xi.

extended to 'devout' Gentiles, of whom Cornelius

was the type, yet not without misgivings and op- CHAP. II.
position from those that *were of the circumcision*.
The same opposition was repeated with greater A.D. 30—80.
violence, when, through the preaching of St Paul,
God *had opened the door of faith unto the Gen-* Acts xiv. 27.
tiles. Cornelius rendered at least a partial homage to the Law, and a Divine sign testified to his
acceptance, but the work of St Paul was based on
the broad principle of the openness of the Gospel Acts xv.
to all alike. Again the law of progress was affirmed, and freedom was assured to the heathen converts. Yet another step remained. The Jews
hitherto had held to their Law by common consent. Jerusalem was still the seat of the twelve:
the Temple was their habitual place of worship:
the national Festivals were still hallowed by their
observance. St Paul conformed in practice to
the customs of his countrymen, but after a little
experience in his Divine work, he declared that
the keeping of the Ceremonial Law was a matter
of indifference even to Jewish converts. This was
the last struggle, and the *Epistle to the Galatians*
bears witness to the fierceness with which it was
contested. Perhaps it may be said that the issue
would have been doubtful but for the fall of Jerusalem and the abolition of the Temple service,
which ratified by an awful judgment the perfect
liberty of the Christian Church.

Till this consummation, however, two great par- This antagoties of Christians were necessarily opposed to one nism reflected
another within the Church, those who observed the Testament,
Law and those who neglected it. The opposition of both in the
the leaders was in reality an alliance based upon the Gal. ii. 7.
recognition of complementary work; but among
their followers the observance of the Law degenerated into Judaism, and the rejection of it into

a denial of its Divine institution and significance. The Judaizers were inclined to dwell exclusively on the teaching of the Lord as the Fulfiller of the Old Testament, the disciples of St Paul to rest absolutely in the apprehension of the facts of the Lord's life. Thus each party had to witness to a true principle against the exaggeration of its correlative, and the New Testament contains memorials of their contrasted teaching. On the one hand, the *Epistle of St James*, who was recognized as a martyr even by many among the Jews, speaks with the voice of the ancient Prophets, denouncing common vices and enforcing active virtues. The work of Christ almost disappears from it, and every part of it is quickened with the spirit of the Law. In the *Epistles of St Paul*, on the other hand, all action is regarded as springing out of the freedom of Faith; and in the *Epistle to the Hebrews* the same principle is extended to the interpretation of the Law and History of Israel. Between the two come the *Epistles of St Peter*, combining something of the character of both, as the great Apostle himself was chosen to found the Jewish and Gentile Churches. Corresponding differences can be traced in the first three Gospels, which are all moulded on a common outline. *St Matthew*, with his prophetic references, and symmetrical discourses, and shadowings of regal dignity, has ever been felt to draw, as it were, a Judaic picture of Christ's life. *St Luke* again, the companion of St Paul, by parables, and scattered traits of patient love and mercy, has given that image of our Lord which seems to harmonize most exactly with the teaching of the Apostle of the Gentiles. And it cannot be merely fanciful to connect the vivid portraiture with which *St Mark*

THE GROWTH OF THE NEW TESTAMENT. 65

presents the acts of Christ with the spirit of *St* CHAP. II.
Peter. Such differences occur naturally in sepa- ⎯⎯⎯⎯
rate records of any great events, for they lie deep A.D. 30—80.
in the mental characteristics of men; but that
which makes their presence in the Gospels full of
instruction is, that each form finds its representation in a particular treatment of common materials, and that the Gospels are connected in this
way with distinctive types of Apostolic doctrine
and critical phases of Apostolic history.

The destruction of Jerusalem, which decided The writings
for ever the earliest controversy in the Church, of St John
brought another question to a head. If the Gospel
had vindicated its essential freedom from Judaism,
what points of connexion could it show with the
wider aspirations of humanity? The answer to
this inquiry came from one of the first Apostles,
who in this sense had fulfilled the spiritual meaning of His Lord's words, and 'tarried till He came.' John xxi. 22.
St John, without the appearance of any conscious
purpose, beyond that most general one which he
describes, shows how the spiritual teaching of St John xx. 31.
Paul had its foundation in the words of the Lord;
how from the first a preparation had been made for
the gradual establishment of a universal Church;
how, finally, throughout all time the Word, Who John i. 3—11.
at last *became flesh*, had been present in the
world which He had created as *the light of men*.

The writings of St John complete the cycle of The historic
the Apostolic Scriptures, and contain the fullest variety of the
revelation which has been given of those highest New Testa-
forms of Truth in which the differences of the ment a sign
early Church are resolved. Yet it is evident that of its divine
the understanding of St John depends in a great authority.
measure upon the recognition of previous differences. And at the same time each part of the

5

New Testament gains immeasurably in solemn meaning when it is regarded in its true light as the monument of an epoch in the growth of the Church. In this aspect the wide range over which the Apostolic writings extend as to their authors, their subjects, their dates, gives a historic grandeur to their sum, of which all sense is lost when the circumstances of their origin are disregarded. He only who watches how each writing was called forth by some passing need, how it was welcomed and preserved by some section of the Church, how it was related to other manifestations of the one infinite Truth,—who marks the sovereign authority which is everywhere assigned to the Scriptures of the Old Testament, and the assumed completeness of their teaching which underlies the use which is made of them,—who recognizes the complete absence of design in the relations of the several books, the utter unconsciousness of a common purpose in their writers, the directness with which they seem to be addressed to present wants, can truly feel the marvel of their unity, which is the outward pledge of their divine power, or fully understand how the New Testament is the historical symbol of the Catholic Church. How it became so will form the subject of the next Chapter.

CHAPTER III.

THE APOSTOLIC FATHERS.

> ...*All the body being supplied and knit together through the joints and bands, increaseth with the increase of God.*—Col. ii. 19.

AT the close of the apostolic age the external prospects of the Christian Church were perhaps as much overcast by danger and discouragement as at any later time. The writings of St Paul are full of anxious forebodings for the future. Even in one of his earliest epistles *the falling away* was put forward as one of the necessary conditions of the manifestation of Christ to which he was eagerly looking forward. At a subsequent time he noticed the fulfilment of his sad prophecy at Miletus, when he told Timothy *that all they which are in Asia* were *turned away from* him. The same dark traits appear in the picture which St John draws of the seven churches in the Apocalypse. Of these some had left their first love, and were in danger of speedy and fatal judgment. So-called *Apostles* were active among them which were indeed *liars;* and others there were *of the synagogue of Satan which* said *they were Jews, and were not;* and others which held *the doctrine of the Nicolaitanes.* Thus the words of

CHAP. III.

A.D. 80—120.
The dark aspect of the close of the Apostolic Age.

2 Thess. ii. 3

Acts xx. 29.
2 Tim. i. 15.

Apoc. ii. 2.
Apoc. iii. 9.
Apoc. ii. 15.

CHAP. III.
A.D. 80—120.

Speculation then quickened into marvellous fertility.

the Lord received their accomplishment, in which He spake of the false prophets who should arise before His coming to judgment on Jerusalem, and of the power which they should exercise upon those who had followed Him.

Nothing, indeed, is more remarkable in the history of Christianity than the rapidity with which it passed through the most varied developments. In a single generation the germs of the new life were embodied in every variety of form; and from the same vivifying source men quickened for themselves shapes of partial truth or prevailing error. The intellectual advance which was made in the apprehension of the work of Christianity—to regard the subject in no other light—during the course of the apostolic preaching was as marvellous as it is commonly unnoticed. If the discourse of St Peter on the day of Pentecost be compared with the first epistle of St John, it is hard perhaps to realize that the whole interval between them is filled up by the ministry of a single life. And no other fact has been so fruitful in specious error as the disregard of this extreme fertility of thought among those to whom the message of the Gospel was first given. It has seemed to many that a longer period than one generation is needed for the growth of the various opinions which are noticed in the New Testament: and the suspicion would have been just if the world had not been then waiting for that which kindled all the hopes, pure or wild, which it cherished. The tidings of the Advent fell upon the ears of men already prepared to interpret it according to their aspirations; and in the record which has been preserved of its reception an outline is drawn for all time of the varied

working of the Gospel upon the human mind, CHAP. III.
which was given, according to the prophecy of A.D. 80—120.
Simeon, *that the thoughts of many hearts may* Luke ii. 35.
be revealed.

It would be impossible to follow out in any The great divisions of opinion.
detail the divisions which thus arose, yet some
brief sketch of them is necessary, both to show
how the exaggerations of heresy witness to the
manifold teaching of the Catholic Church, and
also to place in a yet clearer light the fulness of
the New Testament, as preserving the essential
truths which lie at the base of each typical development of Christianity. Several great lines of
difference in the first apprehension of the Gospel
have been already noticed. These ended in the
formation of distinct parties. The oldest, and for The extreme Jewish party: Ebionites. Acts xxi. 20.
some time the most powerful section in the apos-
tolic Church, was that of *Jews zealous for the*
Law, who still retained their earliest form of
Christian belief, though the divine leading guided
them to larger views, and thus fell gradually more
and more into the position of adversaries to the
true faith. Their distinguishing characteristic was
Legalism, and as they began by regarding the
Lord as a Teacher, so they naturally lost in the
course of time those higher views of His Person
and Work which were unfolded by St Paul and
St John. Under the name of *Cerinthians* and
Ebionites they continued to exist as separate societies long after the close of the apostolic age;
but their real power ceased with the destruction
of the Temple, and they remained isolated and
purposeless, like fragments of an earlier system
left standing in a new world.

Others, starting at first from the same point, The orthodox Jewish party: *Nazarenes.*
clung with a lasting devotion to the ancient Law,

though they did not insist on its observance: such was the Church at Jerusalem, which retained for several generations the succession of Bishops of the circumcision. These occupied an important position in a period of transition. They remained as living witnesses to the divine and permanent significance of the Old Testament, and still continued to fulfil their mission when the fall of Jerusalem had finally put an end to the literal observance of the Mosaic ritual. Their work was only transitory, but it was of the greatest moment for the complete development of the Church. For while St Paul himself had maintained in essence the principle which they embodied, the example of Marcion, two generations afterwards, shows that those who professed to follow his teaching felt themselves at liberty to cast aside all allegiance to the past. Against this error the Nazarenes, as these Jewish believers were called, protested. And even when the Catholic Church had definitely accepted the truth to which they bore witness, some of them retained their ancient customs, and combined a faith generally orthodox with the partial observance of the Jewish ritual.

The mystical school: Gnostics.

The characteristic of Judaism in Palestine was in one shape or other Legalism, a complete devotion to the letter of the Old Testament, to the form and order of Divine revelation: in Egypt and in parts of Asia Minor it was Mysticism, an attempt to penetrate, as it were, to the very soul of things, and to realize by thought the final truths of which all outward institutions are the veils and symbols. Both tendencies correspond with natural instincts of man, and claim satisfaction from Christianity. The first, as we have seen, which was by many exaggerated into a heresy, contri-

THE APOSTOLIC FATHERS. 71

buted an important element to the constitution of the Church, and preserved through all the crises of change a faith unbroken in the coherence of the old and new dispensations. The second came into play somewhat later, but exercised even a more lasting influence upon the fortunes of the Church. The search after knowledge (*Gnosis*) occupied for nearly two centuries many of the subtlest minds among those who professed to follow Christianity. Heathenism, which probably first excited this form of speculation among the Jews, continued to mould its later phases. At one time it was connected with physical questionings, at another with strange sorceries, at another with intellectual dreams of creation, but it always centred in the effort to determine the relation of nature to man and to God, to pierce below phenomena to the mysteries of *being* and *becoming*. The Gnostic passed by insensible gradations into the heathen, just as the Judaizer passed into the Jew. Meanwhile the Church welcomed such elements of a true Gnosticism as were given in the doctrine of the Creative, Illuminative Word, as shadowed out by St John, and in the typical interpretations of the Law sanctioned by St Paul and the Epistle to the Hebrews. So much lay within the scope of the Church. What was more than this was no necessary part of her teaching.

CHAP. III.
A.D. 80—120.

At first sight it may seem strange that the logical development of Christian truth which was drawn out by St Paul was not made the foundation of any sect in the Apostolic age. Some indeed called themselves by his name during his life-time, but the first great body who professed to follow his peculiar teaching (the *Marcionites*) was not founded till seventy years after his death;

The extreme Pauline party: Marcionites.

and then his characteristic doctrines, as they represented them, were greatly modified by the admixture of foreign tenets. Yet, perhaps, it will appear that in the first age St Paul was more likely to act on individuals than on large congregations. In such a period of society the mass of men had need of a system more external or more contemplative; and thus it happened that till the full awakening of new races in the xvth and xvith centuries his power was nearly dormant in the Church at large.

The truths contained in the partial teaching of sects combined in Catholic Christianity. The Apostolic Fathers.

But though at one time the principle of order and legal observance, at another the principle of mysticism, at another the principle of logical exposition, has been most powerful in the Christian Church, yet from the first all were embraced within it, all are ratified by the New Testament. Some time elapsed before the separate societies, or the separate books, were formally united; but the catholicity which was realized in combined action, and the complete Bible which was gradually built up by the guidance of the Holy Spirit, are implicitly recognized in the earliest Christian records of the sub-apostolic age. These scanty remains, which consist only of a few epistles, a vision, and some scattered fragments, occupy a most important position in the history of Christianity. Like the Apocrypha of the Old Testament they form a connecting link between the literature of inspiration and the literature (so to speak) of art or reason. They belong to an age which was conservative and not creative. Their authors write rather with authority than with argument. They composed not essays or apologies, but letters. They were impelled to write not by any literary impulse, but by the deep sense

THE APOSTOLIC FATHERS. 73

of their fellowship with believers as members of CHAP. III.
the one great family of Christ. They were not
yet far enough from the first age to appreciate A.D. 8^—120.
consciously its full majesty, and yet their instinct,
if nothing else, taught them to repose absolutely
in its lessons. Thus they bear a twofold witness
to the Bible, to its contents and to its use. And
specially they show that the representative forms
of doctrine which are recognized in the New Testament—or, in other words, the characteristics of
the different groups of books of which it is made
up—were simultaneously present in the Church
from the first; and that, even if the Apostolic
books were not absolutely gathered into a collection, parallel to the Old Testament, in the generation which followed the death of their authors,
they were still thus early looked upon as invested
with a special authority. They prove that the
teaching of every part of the Bible was active in
shaping the opinions of Christians, and that the
principles on which the New Testament was formed
were already acknowledged and in operation.

Three figures stand out with marked pre-emi- The range of
nence in the sub-apostolic age, CLEMENT of Rome, the *Apostolic*
IGNATIUS of Antioch, and POLYCARP of Smyrna. *Fathers*.
BARNABAS and HERMAS (who really belongs to a
later period) are little more than names known
by the writings to which they are attached. The
work of PAPIAS falls within the verge of the next
generation. It may be a mere coincidence, yet it is
worthy of notice, that these three represent three
provinces of the Church, and stand in connexion
with the received centres of the Apostolic labours
of St Peter, St Paul and St John. The exact
historic position of Ignatius and Polycarp can be
determined with greater certainty, but Clement

74 *THE BIBLE IN THE CHURCH.*

CHAP. III.
A.D. 80—120.
1. CLEMENT of Rome.

has been invested by tradition with a shadowy dignity which is without parallel in the annals of the Ante-Nicene Church. It seems tolerably certain that he was a disciple of St Peter and that he presided over the Roman Church, yet in what order of succession must remain doubtful. At a very early time he was taken as a chief character in a Christian romance, and thus his real personal history was lost in the part which he was made to play as the representative of the spirit of order and organization among his contemporaries. But though his character has been painted by imagination, yet it is evident that the traits which the picture presents were not arbitrarily chosen. There can be little doubt that he occupied a position corresponding to that of St Peter in the first age. He was the acknowledged mediator between the Judaizing and Gentile believers and the first legislator of the Christian society.

His alleged writings.

The writings which bear the name of CLEMENT are numerous and extensive, including the earliest law-books of the Church (the *Apostolical Canons* and *Constitutions*), and the earliest romance (the *Clementine Homilies* and *Recognitions*), which under the form of a personal history contains strange depths of thought and wisdom; and if often wild and unsound, yet reveals the existence of a singular power of speculation in the primitive Church. Two Greek epistles attributed to him are included in the list of the books of the Bible in the Alexandrian MS. The latter of these, lately recovered in a complete text, is a homily and spurious. The former is undoubtedly genuine.

His *Epistle to the Corinthians*.

This *Epistle to the Corinthians*, written in the name of the Church of Rome, both by its style, its doctrine and its theory of Church government, confirms the view which has been given of the relation of Clement to the Apostles. It was probably written at the close of the first century (*c*. A.D. 95), and it shows in each respect a definite advance, a fusion of elements formerly contrasted, which harmonizes completely with the idea of a considerable interval of silent growth between it and the Apostolic writings. Two or three examples must suffice. In speaking of justification, Clement uses the same examples as were used by St James and St Paul, and combines the complementary truths which they drew from them. 'Through faith and hospitality a son was given to Abraham in old age, and by obedience he offered him a sacrifice to God.' 'Through faith and hospitality Rahab was saved.' 'We are not justified,' he says, 'by ourselves...nor by works which we have wrought in holiness of heart, but by our faith, by which Almighty God justified all from the beginning of the world:' and then he adds shortly afterwards, in the spirit of St James, 'Let us then work from our whole heart the work of righteousness.'

Again, it is impossible not to feel the mind of St John in such passages as these. 'The blood of Christ gained for the whole world the offer of the grace of repentance.' 'Through Him we look steadfastly on the heights of heaven: through Him we view as in a glass His spotless and most excellent visage: through Him the eyes of our heart are opened: through Him our dull and darkened understanding—like a flower in a sunless cavern (such is the image)—is quickened with new vigour on turning to His marvellous light.'

Once more: the language of the *Epistle to the*

Hebrews is so constantly repeated by Clement that an old tradition ascribed to him the authorship of it. In immediate connexion with the passage last quoted he proceeds: 'Through Him our Lord wished us to taste of immortal knowledge, *Who being the brightness* of His majesty is *so much* greater *than angels, as He hath obtained by inheritance a more excellent name.*'

Thus in the narrow compass of a single letter we find the clearest traces of the certain presence of each of the typical forms of Apostolic doctrine which are contained in the New Testament. There is no effort, no design: Clement simply shows that the Church in which he lived welcomed the teaching, not of one Apostle only, nor of one group of books, but of all; he shows that if the Catholic Church was not yet universal in range, it was from the first universal in its grasp of truth.

The Epistles of IGNATIUS carry us forward to a still later epoch in the history of the Church. They were written on his way to martyrdom, A.D. 107 (or, according to some, A.D. 116), and contain the parting charge of one who felt that he was called away from his flock at a momentous crisis, when the government of bishops was not yet firmly established in the place of that of Apostles, and heresies within and persecutions without endangered the unity of the weakened Church. The energy of his language is to be explained by the peculiarity of his position; and it is hard to say how a Christian bishop could have written otherwise who 'believed that episcopacy was the bond of unity, and unity the safety of the Church.'

The Epistles, as is well known, exist in three distinct forms, a longer Greek recension, a shorter

Greek recension, and a still shorter Syriac recension. The first is undoubtedly interpolated; and it seems scarcely less clear that the last is epitomized. The shorter Greek recension forms a complete and harmonious whole, bound closely together by unity of thought and language; and the light which has been thrown lately on the history of early heresies goes far to explain some difficulties which had been urged as fatal to its authenticity. But in fact if the letters are reduced within the narrowest limits which can be justified by historical criticism, the character of Ignatius stands out with vivid individuality. And the traits which it presents are in part at least not those which would have been feigned by a writer of a later age. Zeal against schism might be simulated at any time (though perhaps hardly with the speciality which it has in the Ignatian letters); but not so the denunciation of Judaism and of the errors of the Docetæ, who supposed that the Lord as manifested to men was a mere phantom. 'When Christ came to Peter and those with him,' so Ignatius writes to the Church at Smyrna, 'He said to them: "Take hold, handle Me and see, that I am not an incorporeal spirit." And straightway they touched Him and believed, being convinced by His Flesh and by His Spirit...If these things were done in appearance by our Lord, I too am bound in appearance. Yea, why have I delivered myself to death, to fire, to the sword, to wild beasts? But he that is near the sword is near God.'...In such words there seems to be a reality and vividness which attests their authenticity.

CHAP. III.

A.D. 80—120.

The characteristic feature of the letters of Ignatius is the prominence which is there given

Their characteristics
The idea of the Church.

to a definite ecclesiastical order. In them first 'the Catholic Church' is distinctly drawn, according to the image of St Paul, as the body of Christ. In this body the bishop is the visible representative of Christ, the spiritual Head. He is the centre of unity in each congregation as the Father Himself is "Bishop of all." Or briefly, as the idea is expressed in the most startling passage, the Bishop presides in the congregation 'as representative of God, and the presbyters as representatives of the Apostolic Council.' But while Ignatius defines and systematizes very much that is left open in the New Testament, yet the polity which he constructs is based upon a logical development of the cardinal passage of St Paul. And it is in this that the historical importance of his writings chiefly lies. They present the last stage of an order which is seen to be gradually evolved in the Pastoral Epistles and the Epistle of Clement. The principles were given by the Apostles. The combination and practical adaptation of them to the wants of the Christian society was left to their successors. And when the process of construction can be traced in various stages following one another harmoniously, as far as they can be seen in the scanty records of the early Church, up to the fundamental teaching of apostolic writings, it follows as a certain conclusion that these writings contain what was accepted by Christians as the rule of action from the first.

Though the Pauline type of thought is most predominant in the letters of Ignatius, owing to the character of the subjects with which he deals, there are abundant traces in them of the influence of St John. 'Faith,' he says, 'is the beginning, and love the end of life.' 'Faith is our guide upward, but love is the road that leads to God.' 'Jesus Christ the Son of God is the Eternal Word by whom God manifested Himself to men,' 'the Door by which we come to the Father.' The true meat of the Christian is 'the bread of God, the bread of heaven, the bread of life, which is the flesh of Jesus Christ,' and his drink is 'Christ's blood, which is love incorruptible.' Such phrases as these, and they do not stand alone, could not have been used unless it had been assumed that those for whom they were written were familiar with the teaching of the fourth Gospel[1].

CHAP. III.
———
A.D. 80—120.

ad Eph. xiv.
'the *ad Eph.* ix.
ad Magn. VIII.
ad Philad. IX.
ad Rom. VII.

The short Epistle of POLYCARP contains far more clear references to the writings of the New Testament than any other work of the age. It was written shortly after the martyrdom of Ignatius, and in part reflects the image of the same dangers against which Ignatius contended. In one passage Polycarp seems even to have caught the language of his predecessor, where he says that Christians 'are to be subject to the priests and deacons, as to God and Christ.' The phrase is important, as showing the urgency of the feeling by which it must have been dictated; and it is further characteristic of the position which Polycarp occupied that he is called in the contemporary account of his martyrdom (*c.* A.D. 167) 'bishop of the *Catholic* Church at Smyrna[2].' The title

3. POLYCARP.

c. A.D. 107 (or 116).

c. v.

---

[1] The account of the *Martyrdom of Ignatius* seems to be mainly authentic. It contains coincidences of language with *Romans, Corinthians* (1, 2), *Galatians,* and 1 *Timothy.* The parallelisms with the *Acts* (chapp. iii, iv) are yet more remarkable, as references to that book are comparatively rare in early times.

[2] It is in the letter of Ignatius to this church that the term first occurs.

had thus become a technical one in the course of half a century; and the description which is given of Polycarp praying 'for the churches throughout the world,' shows in what way he practically realized some of the lessons which it conveys. This last trait conveys a true impression of the martyr. His soul seems centred in the practical work of faith. He speaks generally with the tone of St Peter, as enforcing the idea of the Christian Law, so that the similarity of his epistle to the *first Epistle of St Peter* was noticed by Eusebius. But there is nothing exclusive in his teaching. His references to St Paul, and especially to the Pastoral Epistles, are clear and frequent. St John has left the slightest impress upon his writing, though one passage in his Letter is a close parallel to words in *St John's first Epistle*. The fact is not without interest, for it was with this Apostle that he was directly connected. He heard St John, and was himself heard by Irenæus. His testimony connects two ages. His life and work extend over the whole period of the consolidation of the Church. In his extreme old age he taught 'that which he had learned from the Apostles, and which continued to be the tradition of the Church.'

The letter of BARNABAS, which is found together with *The Shepherd* at the close of the New Testament in the Sinaitic MS. of the Bible, is very different in character from the letters which have been hitherto noticed. It was probably written at the beginning of the second century; and is addressed generally to Christians ('sons and daughters'), without any apparent historical occasion. In this latter respect, no less than in its whole scope, it occupies the same position among the writings of the Apostolic Fathers as the *Epistle to the Hebrews* among the writings of the New Testament. The resemblance between the two Epistles as to object, principles, and materials, is most striking; and the contrast of method and effect not less complete. In the *Epistle to the Hebrews* there is a reserve in dealing with typical interpretation, a confinement to broad and fruitful illustrations of its use, an instinctive sense of the proportion of one part of the dispensation of God to another, a recognition of the growth, so to speak, of the Divine plan as manifested among men; but in the Epistle of Barnabas it is far otherwise. The author insists on the value of the lessons which he teaches for all; he descends to the minutest details with reckless confidence; he misrepresents the very purpose of the Law as a discipline; 'he makes Judaism a mere riddle of which Christianity is the answer.' The other writings of the sub-Apostolic age illustrate the history of the New Testament, by showing in what way the teaching of its constituent parts contains the germ and rule of the varied thought of the generation which followed their composition. The Epistle of Barnabas does more. It exhibits in a crucial example (to use Bacon's expressive phrase) the unspeakable difference between the ordinary products of early Christian labour and piety and those writings of the first age which the experience of a later time has welcomed as containing the written rule of Christendom.

Thus far it has been shown that the Apostolic teaching, as preserved in the Epistles of the New Testament, was the basis of the teaching of the next generation. Every characteristic form of doctrine which is found in them reappears in the

The relation of the Apostolic Fathers to the Gospels.

scanty records of the following age, and that without the addition of any new principle. But nothing has been said yet of the relation of our Gospels to the writings of the Apostolic Fathers. The occurrence of a key-word, or marked phrase, from one of the Epistles, in a later writer, is sufficient to show that he was acquainted with the source in which it first occurs, or at least that the phrase must be referred to that definite origin. But it is not so in the case of the Gospels. Silent coincidences in facts and words with the Evangelic texts in themselves prove nothing as to the use of the Gospels by those in whose writings they occur. The Gospels were, as has been seen, based on an oral tradition, and that tradition still lived after it had been reduced to a permanent shape. Those who had heard the voice of Apostles necessarily cherished the memory of the spoken word more than the letter of the record. There is always something more direct and personal in the fruits of immediate intercourse than in the remote relationship of books. This sentiment was powerful, as we shall see, even in the next generation, and with those who had seen the Apostles it must have been paramount. It can then create no surprise if the testimony of the Apostolic Fathers is to the substance and not to the authenticity of the Gospels. With the single exception of Barnabas, no one of them quotes any words contained in our Gospels as 'written.' But though their testimony is thus circumscribed, it establishes an important fact. Even in the first generation after the Apostles the contents of the Gospel were fixed within their present limits. Some mysterious working of Providence suppressed the countless multitude of *things which Jesus did* of which the

THE APOSTOLIC FATHERS. 83

Apostles could have told. Two sayings of our CHAP. III.
Lord are preserved in the letters of Barnabas A.D. 80—120.
and Ignatius, which are not contained in the
Gospels, and may possibly be independent and
original[1]; but otherwise the great outlines of His
life and teaching which can be drawn from the
Apostolic Fathers, exactly coincide with those
preserved in the first three Gospels. The Incarnation, the Baptism, the Passion, the Resurrection, the Ascension—the historic substance of the
ancient creeds—form the sure and broad ground
of the hope of the early Christians. These facts
were from the first the 'glad tidings' which were
proclaimed without ceasing to the world. Yet
in this glorious circle a difference may be observed. Other events are noticed more rarely,
by one writer or another, but the Resurrection
(as in the New Testament) is the common theme
of all.

In the direct citation of Scripture the usage Their citations of Scripture anonymous.
of the Apostolic Fathers agrees generally with
that of the Apostles. They continued to look
upon the Old Testament as a full and lasting
record of the revelation of God. In one remarkable particular they carried this belief yet further
than it had been carried before. With them the
individuality of the several writers falls into the
background. They practically regarded the whole

[1] Another saying is commonly attributed to our
Lord on the authority of the Latin translation of the
Letter of Barnabas: *Let us resist all iniquity and hold
it in hatred.* The lately recovered Greek text in the
Codex Sinaiticus shows that the words which precede
it should be (by the change of three letters in the
Latin) 'as *becomes sons* of God,' and not, as it stands
at present, 'as *says the Son* of God.' This example
may serve to show with what facility a grave error
may arise and be propagated.

84 THE BIBLE IN THE CHURCH.

CHAP. III.
A.D. 80—120.

Book as one Divine utterance; and, with the exception of Barnabas, no one of them ever makes a distinct reference by name to any book of the Old Testament. *Clement* sometimes uses the common formula 'It is written;' and more frequently 'God saith,' or 'One saith;' sometimes he introduces the language of the LXX. into his text without any mark of quotation. The two quotations from the Old Testament in *Ignatius* are introduced simply by 'It is written.' In the Greek text of *Polycarp* there is no mark of quotation at all; and little confidence can be placed in the Latin Version in which formulæ of scriptural reference are applied to passages from the Old and New Testaments. *Barnabas*, on the other hand, makes several explicit references to passages from the Law, the Psalms and the Prophets, and it is in him first that a saying of the Lord is quoted as the words of Scripture[1].

The range of their quotations from the Old Testament.

The range of the quotations which they make from the Old Testament is nearly identical with that in the New Testament. The *Psalms* and *Isaiah* furnish to them also by far the largest number of passages. In addition to the books quoted by the Apostles, *Clement* makes use of the history of *Esther*; and *Barnabas* quotes a verse from *Zephaniah*. On the other hand, *Clement* uses the narrative of *Judith* in exactly the same manner as that of *Esther*; and *Barnabas*, as might have been expected from an Alexandrine writer, appears to have been familiar with *Wisdom* and *Ecclesiasticus*, and he quotes the *Second book of Esdras* (4 Ezra) as the work of a prophet. The

c. LV.
c. XII.

l. c.

cc. VI, XIX.
c. XII.

---

[1] The Greek text of the *Codex Sinaiticus* places the reading beyond doubt; c. 4, As it is written, *Many are called, but few are chosen.* (Matt. xx. 16.)

references of *Clement* to *Wisdom* and of *Polycarp* to *Tobit* are very doubtful.

Of the New Testament by far the greater number of the didactic books were certainly used by them. There are clear traces in their writings of the Epistles of St Paul to the *Romans, Corinthians* (1, 2), *Galatians, Ephesians, Philippians,* and to *Timothy* (1, 2); of the *Epistle to the Hebrews;* of the Epistles of *St James,* 1 *St Peter,* and 1 *St John.* The allusions to the Epistles of St Paul to the *Thessalonians, Colossians,* to *Titus* and *Philemon* are very uncertain; and there are, I believe, no coincidences of language with the Epistles of *St Jude,* 2, 3 *St John,* and 2 *St Peter;* or with the *Apocalypse.* The only certain reference to the historical books is that to *St Matthew,* which has been already quoted from *Barnabas.*

In addition to these passing adaptations of apostolic language, there are three definite notices of Epistles of St Paul on the several occasions when it was natural to expect them. 'Take up the Epistle of the blessed Paul, the Apostle,' is the charge of Clement to the Corinthians; '......in truth he spiritually charged you concerning himself and Cephas and Apollos.......' 'Those who are borne by martyrdom to God,' Ignatius writes to the Ephesians, 'pass through your city. Ye share the knowledge of mysteries with Paul, the sanctified, the martyred, worthy of all blessing... who in every part of his letter (*or* in every letter) makes mention of you in Christ Jesus.' 'The blessed and glorious Paul,' says Polycarp to the Philippians, 'wrote letters to you[1], into which if

[1] Thus it appears that the letters of St Paul were a common possession of the churches.

ye look diligently ye will be able to be built up to [the fulness of the faith given to you.']

The Apostolic Fathers have no definite idea of a New Testament.

It cannot, however, be denied that the idea of a New Testament consisting of definite books and equal in authority to the Old, was foreign to the sub-Apostolic age[1]. Such an idea is necessarily the growth of time. Distance is a necessary condition for the right estimate of objects of vast proportions. If it be true that a prophet is not received in his own country, it is equally true that he is not received in his own age. His full majesty is not seen till his whole work can be contemplated in the history of the times in which he lived. And if the person of the prophet cannot be duly appreciated by his contemporaries, still less can his writings. These at most are fragmentary and occasional, and only long experience can prove their Divine worth. Yet further, the New Testament is made up not of the writings of one prophet only, but of many, differing widely both in work and character. Thus the difficulties which beset the recognition of the practical completeness of the fragmentary records of one prophet's teaching are multiplied tenfold; and it would have been unnatural, opposed, that is, to all that we can learn of the dealings of God with man, that the New Testament should have been stamped from the first with that distinctive character of plenary authority with which it was invested in after times.

But they prepare the way for it by separating the

The immediate successors of the Apostles did not, then, we fully admit, perceive that the written

[1] Polycarp speaks (c. VII.) of those who 'pervert the oracles of the Lord to their own desires;' but these, as the context shows, were spoken and heard, and not written.

memoirs of the Lord, and the scattered writings of His first disciples, would form a sure and sufficient source or test of doctrine when the current tradition had grown indistinct or corrupt. Conscious of a life in the whole Christian body, and realizing the present power of its Head, as later ages cannot do, they did not feel that the Apostles were providentially charged to express once for all in their *writings* the substance of the New Covenant. Trained for the most part in mystic schools, they found a rich depth of meaning in the Scriptures of the Old Testament, which is hidden from more critical eyes, and fancied that these alone contained the sum of all Christianity. The position which they held did not command that comprehensive view of the nature and fortunes of the Church by which the true relation of its original records to its subsequent development is suggested and confirmed. But still they certainly had an indistinct sense that their own work was essentially different from that of their predecessors. They declined to perpetuate their title, though they may have retained their office. Already they began to separate the Apostles from the teachers of their own time, as possessed of an originative power. Without any exact perception of the completeness of the Christian Scriptures, they began to draw a line between them and their own writings. As if by some providential instinct, each one of those Fathers who stood nearest to the Apostolic writers plainly contrasted his writings with theirs, and placed himself upon a lower level. The fact is most significant; for it shows in what way the formation of a New Testament was an intuitive act of the Christian Body, derived from no reasoning, but realized in the course of

CHAP. III.
A.D. 80–120.

its natural growth, as one of the first results of its self-consciousness.

Clement, the earliest of the Fathers, lays aside the individual authority of the Apostle in writing to the Church of Corinth, and writes simply in the name of the Church of Rome. He even apologizes in some measure for the tone of authority which he uses, and at the same time refers them to the Epistle of the blessed Paul, who wrote to them 'spiritually,' and certainly with the fullest assertion of absolute power.

cc. VII, XLVII.

Polycarp, in like manner, who had listened to St John, freely confesses that 'neither he, nor any like him, is able to attain fully to the wisdom of the blessed and glorious Paul.'

ad Phil. III.

Ignatius, who, if we receive the testimony of the writings attributed to him, was little inclined to disparage the power of his office, twice disclaims the idea that he wished to 'impose his commands like Peter and Paul. They were Apostles,' he adds, 'while I am a condemned man'—condemned to death, that is, and no less spiritually guilty.

ad Rom. IV.

Barnabas, again, twice reminds his readers that he speaks 'as one of them,' not as a teacher with authority, but as a member of Christ's Church.

cc. I, IV

The Bible and the Church grew silently.

Thus silently and slowly, without any formal deliberations or open contests, the work of God went forward. The principles which the Apostles set forth separately were combined and systematized. The societies which they founded were more fully organized according to the outlines which they had drawn. The writings which they left were preserved and studied, and exercised more and more a formative authority. The para-

ble of the mustard-seed was fulfilled. The Church CHAP. III.
rose and spread, not by any sudden miracle, but
by the gradual assimilation of all around which   A.D. 80—120.
could contribute to its growth, in virtue of the
action of that Spirit which is its Life.

But though we have heard voices from An- The Church
tioch and Alexandria, from Smyrna and Rome[1], at Jerusalem as yet silent.
one Church is as yet silent. The Christians of
Jerusalem contribute nothing to the written portraiture of the age. The peculiarities of their
belief were borrowed from a system destined to
pass away. They embodied no permanent form
of Apostolic doctrine. The Jewish Church was
an accommodation, if we may use the word, and
not a substantive form of Christianity. Its teaching was inherently defective and transitory. How
far, nevertheless, it prevailed and influenced the
early Church, will be seen in the next Chapter.

[1] The *Proverbs* of XYSTUS (Sixtus), which have
been recently found in a Syriac translation, exhibit
the influence of St James and St John (Ewald, *Gött.
Gel. Anz.* 1859, p. 266); but the history of these
fragments is too doubtful to allow of their being used
as a production of the first Roman Bishop of the
name (A. D. 119—127).

The recently discovered *Doctrine of the Apostles*
contains two express quotations from the prophetic
books of Old Testament (cc. 14, 16, and incorporates
a phrase from Ecclesiasticus (iv. 31). It has also one
quotation from an unknown source (c. 1). It contains
clear traces of a written Gospel (cc. 8, 11, 15). The
Evangelic words quoted are mainly parallel with the
text of St Matthew, but they also contain passages
characteristic of St Luke. The Eucharistic prayers
offer many striking coincidences with the language and
thoughts of St John.

The Evangelic citations belong to the class of
'*Oracles*' in the narrower sense. No fact of the
Lord's Life is definitely referred to. The references
to St Paul's Epistles appear to be doubtful.

CHAPTER IV.

THE AGE OF THE APOLOGISTS.

...First the blade, then the ear, then the full corn in the ear.—St Mark iv. 28.

That is not first which is spiritual, but that which is natural; then that which is spiritual. — 1 Cor. xv. 46.

CHAP. IV.

A.D.120—170.

Contrast of the state of Christianity in the *sub-Apostolic age* and the *age of the Apologists*.

IT appears from the evidence which has been adduced, that before the end of the first quarter of the second century, the chief part of the apostolic letters which are included in the New Testament were familiarly known and generally used by Christians; that the great types of apostolic teaching which are represented in them were simultaneously active in shaping the popular views of doctrine; that the contents of the Evangelic tradition coincided very closely with the records preserved in our Gospels, though, from the nature of the case, the earliest Fathers refer more commonly to the words and sufferings and resurrection of Christ than to the acts of His ministry. But as yet there was no recognized New Testament, or rather the New Testament was still a collection of *facts*, and not a collection of *books*, of the spirit, and not of the letter. The substance of the apostolic doctrine was thus em-

THE AGE OF THE APOLOGISTS. 91

bodied in a period of comparative quiet: the CHAP. IV.
necessity of a written rule was enforced by times
of sharp and protracted conflict within and with- A.D. 120—170.
out. Till some years after the close of the first
century the Church grew up silently and almost
secretly. To the mass of superficial observers
the Christians had hitherto seemed merely a sect
of the Jews, and had enjoyed with them a con-
temptuous toleration, interrupted only by popular outbreaks, as at Rome in the time of Nero.
Individuals had attracted attention and suffered
for their faith in the provinces, but as yet such
cases were extremely rare. The famous letter A.D. 104.
of Pliny to Trajan marks the beginning of a new
era. The Christians had at length grown so
numerous that as a body they called for the special notice of the civil government; and the peculiarities of their belief became too well known to
allow them to be confounded with Jews. Meanwhile the false teaching, which had been fragmentary and unformed in the apostolic age, was
systematized and supported by the arguments of
philosophy. Thus during the next stage of its
history the Church had to maintain an open
struggle against official persecution, organized
heresies, and philosophic controversy. In little
more than half a century the battle was won,
though the times of suffering were not past; and
the close of the 'age of the Apologists' leaves us
in the presence of a vast Christian society, Catholic in range and doctrine, formidable in numbers, illustrious by the genius of its champions,
armed against error by the possession of a Bible
made up of the 'scriptures of the prophets, the
evangelists, and the apostles.'

The Christian literature of the sub-Apostolic Extent of

92 THE BIBLE IN THE CHURCH.

CHAP. IV.
A.D. 120—170.
Christian literature in the age of the Apologists.

age was all of the same form. A few letters bore witness to the mutual intercourse of Christians and to the presence of a common faith among them. The writings of the next age were varied in accordance with the changed position of the Church. Letters, chronicles, essays, apologies, visions, tales, and even poems, attested the activity and exhibited the claims of the new faith. But of these by far the greater part have perished. The Letter to Diognetus, some of the writings of Justin, the Clementine Homilies, and nearly all the Shepherd of Hermas, alone remain in their original Greek. In addition to these there is a complete Latin translation of the Shepherd, a Syriac translation of the Apology of Melito, and a series of precious quotations from lost books, due mainly to the industry of Eusebius. The Exposition of Papias, the treatises of Justin and Agrippa Castor against Heresies, the didactic and controversial works of Melito, the Chronicles of Hegesippus, have perished, and with them the most direct sources of information on the history of this period of the Church.

Its characteristics.

But the works which have been preserved possess a distinctly representative character. The Apologies of Melito and Justin, and the Letter to Diognetus, offer three very different types of treatment of the same subject; and the Shepherd and the Clementines, which have many points of resemblance, illustrate in a striking manner the different developments of a *legal* view of Christianity within and without the Church. Above all, the writings of Justin, which are by far the most extensive literary remains of the period, reflect the spirit of the age most clearly. No one could exhibit better than he does the character of the Greek apologist. For him philosophy was truth, reason a spiritual power, Christianity the fulness of both. The Apostolic Fathers portray the vigour of the Faith among believers; their successors point out how it satisfies the deepest wants of men. It remained for the Latin Apologists at a later period to establish its right to supplant as well as to fulfil what was partial and vague in earlier systems. The time was not ripe for this when Justin wrote. For as Christianity was shown to be the completion of Judaism before the Church was separated from the synagogue, so it was set forth as the Truth towards which the old philosophies converged, before it was declared to supersede them.

CHAP. IV
A.D. 120—170.

This was one great work of the period, to proclaim Christianity as the Divine answer to the manifold questionings of heathendom. Another was to separate Christianity finally from Jewish observances. Hitherto the Jewish Church of Syria had continued to exist in the north of Palestine, the cradle of the Faith, retaining one of the oldest names of believers—*Ebionim*, 'the poor'—stationary while all other churches moved onwards in obedience to the leading of God, clinging tenaciously to an imperfect creed, and a falsified hope, but yet still honoured in some degree as the mother Church of Christendom. After the founding of Ælia upon the site of Jerusalem and the establishment of a Gentile Church there, the 'Ebionim' sank into the rank of a sect. Some cherished still more fervently what they held to be the substance of their ancient observances, others transferred the spirit of their party to Rome and embodied it in a new shape. The sect speedily became a heresy, and though it lin-

The final separation of Judaism from Christianity.

A.D. 130.

gered on till the beginning of the fourth century, its power was gone before the close of the second. So fell the Church which by outward descent claimed to be the Church of the Twelve, the Church of the Brethren of the Lord. Nowhere perhaps has a false conservatism issued in a more tragic end.

Yet before it fell the Jewish Church did good service to the Christian cause. Papias, Justin and Hegesippus, sympathized more or less with one at least of its great principles—the superior prominence given to the prophetic office of the Lord over the Apostolic interpretation of His work, and it is to Judaizing sources that we must look for the first direct evidence for the authority of our written Gospels. As yet we have traced only the influence of the Apostolic doctrine and Epistles and of the oral Gospel. Papias and Justin, with the Clementine Homilies, will fill up the gap which remains. It is natural that they should do so. One essential difference between the Catholic and Judaizing parties in the Church was, as has been said, that the former rested their faith on the interpretation of the Lord's life and work by the Apostles, the latter on the Lord's explicit teaching. For the one the Apostolic tradition was of the highest moment, for the other the Evangelic tradition. The difference is one confined to no single age or country. There are always some who will look rather to what Christ *said* than to what He *was;* and in this aspect the history of the *Ebionim* is not without the deepest interest for our own times[1].

[1] Nothing perhaps strikes the student of Church history more than the spread of this essential Ebionism

THE AGE OF THE APOLOGISTS. 95

The earliest account of the Gospels is given by PAPIAS, who was bishop of Hierapolis in Phrygia at the beginning of the second century. He was a friend of Polycarp and of others who had known the apostles. His congregation appears to have been in close connexion with the Churches of Judæa; and the Epistle of St Paul to the neighbouring Church of Colossæ shows the characteristic dangers of the country—the home of the wildest heathen fanaticism—from which Papias himself does not seem to have wholly escaped. The work by which his name is known was 'An Exposition of Oracles of the Lord, based upon the teaching of the elders.' The exact translation of the title, which has been strangely misinterpreted, plainly shows that the object of Papias was not to write a Life of Christ—a Gospel—from current traditions, but rather to give an explanation of some of the Lord's sayings, illustrated by such reports of what the Apostles had said as he could collect. With this object he might well say that 'The information which he could draw from books was not so profitable as that which was preserved in a living tradition.' For there is nothing to indicate that the 'books' of which he speaks were (as many have assumed) our Gospels, and not commentaries like his own, of which many were current at a very early time among heretical sects.

CHAP. IV.
A.D.120—170.
The 'Exposition' of PAPIAS.

Ap. Euseb. H. E. III. 39.

The manner in which Papias speaks of two of our Gospels confirms the view which has been given of his own object. 'Matthew,' he said,

His testimony to the Gospels of St Matthew and St Mark. Euseb. l.c.

in the present day. How often is it said that the Sermon on the Mount is the sum of Christianity. Judaism in ritual and Judaism in doctrine are opposite poles of the same error.

'compiled the oracles[1] in Hebrew; but each one interpreted them as he was able.' 'This also,' he writes, 'the Elder [John] used to say: Mark having become Peter's interpreter wrote accurately all that he [Peter] mentioned, though he did not [record] in order that which was either said or done by Christ. For he neither heard the Lord nor followed Him; but subsequently, as I said, [attached himself to] Peter, who used to frame his teachings to meet the wants [of his hearers]; and not as making a connected narrative of the Lord's discourses. So Mark committed no error, as he wrote down some particulars as he [Peter] related[2] them; for he took heed to one thing—to omit nothing of what he heard, and to state nothing falsely in his record.'

How the Testimony applies to our present Gospels.

But it has been argued that these notices of Papias cannot refer to the Gospels at present received as St Matthew's and St Mark's. The 'oracles' which St Matthew is here said to have compiled were in the Aramaic dialect of Palestine, and the narrative of St Mark was not 'in order,' while the arrangement of his Gospel at present is at least as orderly as that of the Gospels of *St Matthew* and *St Luke*. To these objections the answer is really simple. There can be no doubt that Papias speaks of the original collection of 'the oracles' of the Lord made by St Matthew, of which our Greek Gospel is the representative and not the exact reproduction;

---

[1] It is important to observe the definite article in this case, which is omitted in the title of Papias' treatise.

[2] The original word is ambiguous. It may mean, 'as he (Mark) called them to mind.' So also the word above translated 'mentioned' may mean 'remembered,' in which sense Papias elsewhere uses it.

but at the same time he speaks of it in such a way as to show that in his time it already existed substantially in Greek. On the other hand, the account which he gives of the origin of St Mark's Gospel is exactly that which, as we have already seen, holds true of the first three Gospels. They were not intended to be chronological Lives of Christ, but were simply designed to preserve a summary of representative facts, given according to a moral and not a historic sequence in the oral teaching of the Apostles, to satisfy the requirements of those to whom they preached the Gospel ('some particulars, not in order, to meet the wants of his hearers').

CHAP. IV.
A.D. 120—170.

pp. 57, ff.

While Papias was busy in collecting the scattered traditions of the first age in this remote city, regretting, it may be, the growing freedom of Christian thought, and shaping wild dreams of a speedy millennium, JUSTIN MARTYR was now actually engaged in proclaiming to Jew and Gentile alike the New Philosophy which he had found. Justin has left us a slight sketch of his life, and his writings are in complete harmony with his early history. He was of Greek descent, but his family had been settled for some time at Flavia Neapolis, which was founded by Vespasian on the site of the ancient Sichem. His countrymen, he tells us, were still in his time (*c.* A.D. 100—120) addicted to the errors of Simon Magus; but he himself escaped this delusion, and sought for truth in the schools of Greek philosophy. He applied in succession to Stoics, Peripatetics and Pythagoreans, but without gaining that for which he longed. At last a better hope was beginning to dawn upon him in the teaching of a Platonist, when a new master appeared. As

JUSTIN MARTYR.

Euseb. H. E. l. c.

His early life.

he sought a place of calm retirement on the sea-shore, an aged man, meek and venerable, turned his thoughts in a fresh direction, from Plato to the prophets. 'Pray before all things,' were the last words of this strange teacher, 'that the gates of light be opened to you; for [the truths for which you seek] are not comprehensible by the eye or mind of man, unless God and His Christ give him understanding.'

'Immediately a fire was kindled in my soul,' Justin adds, 'and I was possessed with a love for the prophets and those men who are Christ's friends; and as I discussed his arguments with myself I found Christianity to be the only philosophy that is sure and suited to man's wants. Thus then and for this cause I am a philosopher.'

In the strength of his new faith he travelled far and wide to spread the truth which he had found; and the large list of his writings attests his intellectual zeal and activity. Of those which now bear his name two Apologies and the Dialogue with Trypho are genuine beyond doubt; and present a lively picture of the relations of Christianity, not indeed to the Christian Church, but to Judaism and heathenism. This distinction is of the greatest importance in dealing with the evidence which they furnish on the history of the Christian Scriptures. From a disregard of the original destination of Justin's essays the most false deductions have been drawn. It is obvious that the life of Christ and not the apostolic teaching would be the centre of his arguments both with Jew and Gentile. Prophecy and history were the open provinces in which he could freely work. He may have been, and pro-

THE AGE OF THE APOLOGISTS. 99

bably was, constitutionally inclined to dwell on CHAP. IV.
this external aspect of Christianity, as distin- A.D. 120—170.
guished from its logical development; but under
any circumstances his work necessarily led him
to rest in it, at least in those writings which have
come down to us. It was enough if he could
bring men to listen to the fuller instruction of
the Christian teacher. It was not his task to
anticipate the discipline or duties of the catechist.
To forget this limitation of his office was to forget
the very business of an Apologist. Thus we may
expect from him the outlines of the Gospel, but
not an exposition of Christian doctrine.

This expectation is largely fulfilled. It would His testimony
be possible to re-write from Justin's works a con- to the contents and
siderable part of the records of Christ's Life as
given by the first three Evangelists[1]. By putting
together various passages from these we can collect almost all the details of the history of the
Birth and Infancy of our Lord, of the mission of
John, of the Baptism, of the Passion, Resurrection and Ascension, which are given in the synoptic Gospels. The references which they contain
to the Miracles are naturally very few. On the
contrary, with the exception of the Parables,
quotations occur from most of the Lord's Discourses. At times the narratives of St Matthew
and St Luke are interwoven: here and there the
addition of some minute trait, or the higher colouring of the picture, marks the freedom with
which the rhetorician uses his materials; but
generally Justin's references present the closest

[1] The character of St John's Gospel—the Gospel
for Christians—evidently placed it out of the range of
Justin's arguments. In casual phrases he shows his
acquaintance with it.

7—2

100   *THE BIBLE IN THE CHURCH.*

CHAP. IV.
A.D. 120—170.

resemblance both in range and substance to the contents of our Gospels.

Style of the Gospels.

Nor is the general resemblance of the quotations which he makes from Christ's teaching to the style of the Evangelists less striking. However much he condenses, combines, transposes, the words which they have preserved, yet, with very few exceptions, he retains through all these changes the characteristics of the New Testament dialect without the admixture of any foreign element.

The source of his quotations. Memoirs of the Apostles.

We are not, indeed, wholly left to conjecture as to the source from which Justin derived his knowledge of the Gospel history. Hitherto all the references to the words of Christ (with one exception) have been anonymous. These were still for some time after the close of the first century utterances of a living voice unconnected with any written record. But Justin, while he habitually represents Christ as speaking, and not the Evangelist as relating His discourse, distinctly refers to 'Memoirs of the Apostles' in which he found written '*all things* concerning Jesus Christ.' The statement is significant. It shows that tradition had now no special store. Papias, in Justin's judgment, might illustrate the meaning of the Evangelic narratives, but he could not add anything essential to their completeness. The purpose of Justin did not call for any exact description of these 'Memoirs,' but he mentions incidentally several points of interest about them. In his first Apology he refers to them twice directly. When explaining the celebration of the Eucharist he adds: 'The Apostles in the Memoirs made by them, which are called Gospels[1], have

Apol. 1. 66.

[1] It is foreign to our purpose to enter into details

THE AGE OF THE APOLOGISTS.

handed down that it was thus enjoined on them.' ...And again, when describing the Christian service, he notices that 'the Memoirs of the Apostles or the writings of the Prophets are read as long as the time admits.'

In the Dialogue the references to the Memoirs are more numerous, fifteen in all; for Trypho himself was acquainted with the written 'Gospel.' Of these, two deserve special notice. In one Justin describes the authorship of the Memoirs somewhat more exactly than by a general reference to the Apostles. 'In the Memoirs,' he writes, 'which I say were composed by the Apostles and *those who followed them*, [it is written] that sweat, as drops [of blood], streamed down [from Jesus], as He was praying and saying "Let this cup, if it be possible, pass away from me."' The description, it will be seen, precedes the quotation of a passage found only in St Luke, the follower of an Apostle, and not an Apostle himself. In the other place he refers to 'the Memoirs of Peter' for a fact which is contained only in the Gospel of St Mark, whose Gospel, as we have already seen, was believed to be the record of St Peter's teaching[1]. A passage of Tertullian

CHAP. IV.
A.D. 120—170.
Apol. 1. 67.

The authorship of these *Memoirs*.

Dial. 103.

Dial. 106.

of criticism, yet it may serve as an illustration of the perverse ingenuity which has been brought to bear upon the question, to notice that one of the ablest and most trustworthy scholars who has discussed Justin's quotations says that, if he had had our four Gospels in his mind he must have said '*the four Gospels.*' What missionary now would speak so?

It may be noticed that the name *Memoirs* was evidently chosen by Justin himself (after the model of Xenophon's *Memoirs of Socrates*) to suit a literary taste.

[1] See p. 96. The original word for *Memoirs* is the substantive derived from the verb there used for '*related.*'

CHAP. IV.
A.D. 120—170.
Adv. Marc.
IV. 2.

seems to fix the sense of Justin's words beyond all doubt When discussing the authorship of the New Testament he says, 'In fine, John and Matthew, out of the number of the Apostles, implant faith in us; Luke and Mark, out of the number of their followers, renew it...'

The coincidence of express quotations of the Memoirs with our Gospels.

The remaining references made by Justin to the Apostolic Memoirs all contain facts or words which are found in our Gospels. Of the seven passages which give quotations from them, five agree verbally (excepting one slight variation) with the Evangelic text, as given by good early authorities; the sixth gives a reading supported by considerable patristic evidence; the seventh appears to give only a free adaptation of words of St Matthew and St Luke.

The general argument for the identity of the Memoirs with our Gospels.

Briefly then this is the sum of what Justin says of the Memoirs which he used. They were several and yet one: they were called Gospels: they contained a record of *all things* concerning Christ: they were known and admitted by Christians generally: they were read in their public services habitually with the books of the Old Testament: they were of Apostolic authority though not exclusively of Apostolic authorship. Further than this we gather that they recorded facts which are severally peculiar to each of the Synoptic Gospels, and that they contained nothing which these do not substantially contain. If we include in our consideration the whole mass of Justin's anonymous references to the Life and Teaching of Christ the general effect is the same. In the one case the coincidence is more complete, in the other it is more extensive. And when account is taken of the general notoriety and official use of the documents which he employs as authentic, it

THE AGE OF THE APOLOGISTS. 103

seems to be a necessary conclusion that they were no other than the Gospels which we receive, unless arguments can be brought forward on the opposite side more difficult to face than the idea of a revolution in the practice of the Christian Church,—a revolution which in the course of a single generation entirely changed the records of the life of Christ publicly used by Christians.

Objections to the identification.

Some have thought that such arguments can be found. It is urged that Justin nowhere mentions the Evangelists: that the text of his quotations in many instances differs materially from that of our Gospels: that he introduces apocryphal additions into his narrative. To answer completely these objections to the identification of the Memoirs with our Gospels requires a full analysis of all the passages in question, and likewise an examination of Justin's quotations from the LXX. At present it must suffice to give very briefly the results of such an inquiry.

These objections groundless or insufficient.

The first objection is based upon inattention to the usage of the Apologists. As a rule the later Apologists always quote the Gospels anonymously. Tertullian, for example, who in his other writings quotes the Gospels continually and mentions every Evangelist by name, nowhere cites the Gospels in his Apology, while he gives in it a general view of Christ's life and teaching. Of the books of the Old Testament, Justin quotes the prophets constantly by name—it was needful that he should do so—and the only book of the New Testament which he assigns to a special author is the *Apocalypse*, the one prophetic book in the collection, which was written, he says, by revelation, by 'a man named John, one of the Apostles of Christ....' *Dial.* 81.

104 THE BIBLE IN THE CHURCH.

CHAP. IV.
A.D. 120—170.

The inexactness of Justin's quotations from the Gospels is completely illustrated by his mode of dealing with the LXX. In texts which he professedly cites from this, he frequently combines distinct passages, adapts others to his immediate purpose, and yet more frequently errs by defect of memory, ascribing words to wrong authors, and differing widely from himself in a second and third citation of the same text. But it is further urged that some of Justin's peculiar readings in his Evangelic references occur more than once; while some are found also in the Clementines or in fragments of heretical Gospels. The latter cases are very rare, and outweighed by differences from the unauthoritative texts far more numerous and important. The former may be due in part to that facility with which a peculiar form of words becomes habitual, and in part to real variations of reading. It is not, indeed, an exaggeration to say that one known MS., the *Codex Bezæ*, contains more peculiar readings in the same space than an average sample of Justin's quotations.

The occurrence of Apocryphal details in Justin's references is no more than might have been expected from a writer at his time: there are even more in *Codex Bezæ*, to recur to the example which has been given above, a MS. which represents a very early and widely-current text of the Gospels. Yet in the most remarkable incident which he gives, the kindling of a fire in the Jordan, when Christ descended into the water, he evidently distinguishes the traditional detail from what was recorded by the Evangelists. 'When Jesus,' he says, 'came to the Jordan, where John was baptizing, when he descended to the water,

Dial. 88.

both a fire was kindled in the Jordan, and *the* CHAP. IV.
Apostles of Christ Himself recorded in writing ──────
that the Holy Spirit as a dove lighted upon A.D. 120—170.
Him.'

It follows from what has been said, that Our Gospels
there is no reason to believe that Justin made the written
use of any written record of the Lord's Life ex- Justin used.
cept our Gospels, and that it is to these only he
refers when he speaks directly of Memoirs of the
Apostles. At the same time, most of his references are manifestly not taken directly from
books. He is the representative of an age of
oral teaching. The texts both of the Old and
New Testament in his time were popularly
moulded afresh in many cases, and tradition,
though formally set aside, yet contributed some
few details to the sum of the evangelic records.
But this fact does not detract from the value of
his testimony. On the contrary, it shows with
what definite accuracy the received Gospels represented and controlled the traditional accounts
of Christ's Life, and thus carries back their substantial authority to a time earlier than that at
which they were in general or exclusive use.

What has been said of Justin's quotations The *Clemen-*
applies almost without modification to the quo- *tine Homilies.*
tations in the *Clementine Homilies,* the most c. A.D. 160.
remarkable product of philosophic Ebionism. In
these also there is great freedom of citation in
passages both from the Old Testament and from
the Gospels ; and at the same time they preserve
phrases characteristic of each of the four Gospels.
For in one respect they supplement the evidence
of Justin. The allusions to St John's Gospel in
his writings are confined to casual coincidences of

language. In the Homilies there is a very distinct quotation from the history of the restoration of the man born blind. St John's Gospel was also largely used by the Ophites, one of the earliest heretical sects; and its teaching is reflected clearly in the exquisite fragment which closes the Letter to Diognetus.

If we extend our inquiry from the Gospels to the remaining books of the New Testament, it appears that shortly after the middle of the second century every book which it contains is recognized as familiarly known, if not authoritative among Christians, except 1 *Thessalonians*, 2 *Peter*, 2, 3 *John*, and *Jude;* for the silent incorporation of the language of Scripture in another writing is a sure sign of the familiar use of it. And it must be remembered that the evidence thus gained is collected from writings which are not, if put together, much larger in bulk than the New Testament itself. Thus the references of the earliest Fathers to the New Testament are proportionately more complete and extensive than those of the Apostolic writers to the Old Testament.

The quotations from the Old Testament in Justin and the Clementine Homilies confirm exclusively the books of the Hebrew Bible. There is no quotation, I believe, in these books of the *Apocrypha* of the Old Testament, though *Wisdom*, at least, would have fallen in with much of Justin's reasoning. Indeed, to use the words of a contemporary writer, it was regarded as a 'work of Divine Providence that the books which were of critical importance to the Christian religion were preserved in the hands of Jews.' In

THE AGE OF THE APOLOGISTS. 107

another respect Justin offers a marked contrast to the Apostolic writers. In dealing with the Old Testament, he allows himself a license of mystical interpretation which is bound by no rules. It could hardly be otherwise. The prophets according to him 'proclaimed the same truths which Christ taught:' the Holy Spirit 'proclaimed beforehand through them *all things* concerning Jesus.' For him the Old Testament was a complete Bible, historically and doctrinally.

CHAP. IV.
A.D. 120—170.

Dial. 48, 119.
Apol. 61.

For it must be again repeated that even at this time there is no clear sense anywhere expressed of a New Testament corresponding to the Old Testament. The idea of such a collection of Christian Scriptures was doubtless present to many of the most far-seeing teachers of the age, and was in part practically carried out, for it is found firmly established in the next generation. But at present the collection was incomplete, and not fixed by an express rule. The time was not yet ripe for any universal decision on the subject. *Papias,* who 'quoted testimonies from the former Epistle of John and that of Peter,' appears to have made no allusion whatever to the *Gospel of St Luke,* the *Acts* or the *Pauline Epistles.* As a friend of Polycarp he could not have been unacquainted with them, but it is probable that his sympathies remained with 'the Twelve,' according to the narrow interpretation of their teaching, and that he declined to admit the writings which bore the stamp of the Apostle of the Gentiles as having a decisive authority for the Church. The *Ebionim,* again, even before they sank into a heretical sect, definitely declined to accept St Paul's teaching; and it is not unlikely that HEGESIPPUS formally shared their judgment, though

No New Testament recognized at present.

The Judaizers within the Church rejected St Paul.

HEGESIPPUS.
c. A.D. 140.

he found the 'right principles' of the faith at Corinth, where, as he relates, the Epistle of Clement was still read, in which the authority and doctrine of St Paul is distinctly affirmed. For the Judaizing party were already accepting practically the fulness of the Apostolic faith. Intercourse and experience had broken down the barriers of isolated congregations and cherished prejudices. In other words, Rome, the centre of the world, and not Jerusalem, was the centre of the Church; and the effect appears in the new limits imposed upon Judaizing thought. The Shepherd of *Hermas*, which is most legal in its spirit, and bears the same relation to the other writings of the first century after the Apostles that the Epistle of *St James* does to the remainder of the New Testament, yet recognizes clearly each typical form of Apostolic doctrine, and shadows forth under a remarkable image the outward building of the Catholic Church from many different elements.

Meanwhile the authority of the Old Testament was called in question. At the time when Justin was urging the letter of the prophets on Jew and Gentile, as conveying clear proof of the truth of Christianity, others were labouring to overthrow partially or entirely the divine claims of the old dispensation. Those who failed to apprehend the proportionate and progressive character of the revelations of God, culminating in Christianity, maintained either that the Mosaic revelation had been corrupted in successive transcriptions, or that it was not originally divine. The two opinions found able and energetic supporters; and modern controversies may find their prototypes in the history of the second century. Here it is sufficient to have indicated that the Church had to win, so to speak, the whole Bible: to maintain the Old Testament against the false literalism which stereotyped its precepts, and the false literalism which ignored its spirit: to construct the New Testament out of scattered books which consecrated for the use of all ages every essential form of Christian truth. The one work was wrought in conflict, the other comparatively in silence: the one was an effort of thought, of reason: the other an operation of instinct, of life. Both were achieved essentially at the same epoch; and the next Christian writers who meet us witness to their accomplishment. Both were combined with the firmest belief in the immediate teaching of the Spirit; or rather it was this belief in a living Word which gave to true Christians a lively trust in the written Word. To use the noble language of a writer who sums up the blessings and the faith of the age in which he lived, at this time 'the fear of the Law is chanted, and the grace of the Prophets is recognized, and the faith of the Gospels is established, and the tradition of the Apostles is guarded, and the grace of the Church has free and exulting course. And if thou dost not grieve His grace,' he adds, 'thou shalt further learn what the Word communicates [in intercourse with us], through whom He chooses, when He wills. For all that we were moved to declare by the will of the Word which bade us, with toil, from love of that which has been revealed to us, we impart to you.'

CHAP. IV.
A.D. 120—170.
The whole Bible gained by the Christian Church.

Ep. ad Diogn. c. 11.

One definite attempt, indeed, was made within this period to define a Christian Bible. Marcion, the son of a bishop of Sinope, claimed to vindicate Christianity from the corruptions which

The Bible of MARCION.

had grown round it. His object was to restore the Gospel of St Paul to its original simplicity, and to cast out all Jewish elements from the Christian faith. With this view he formed a collection of sacred books as the basis and test of his teaching. This was divided into two parts, the *Gospel* and the *Apostolicon*. The Gospel was an adaptation of St Luke—a conclusion in which critics of the most opposite schools now acquiesce: the Apostolicon consisted of ten epistles of St Paul, excluding the *Pastoral Epistles* and the *Epistle to the Hebrews*. There is no evidence to show on what grounds Marcion limited his collection of the Pauline letters. The writings which depended on the authority of the other Apostles, and the Acts which ratified their teaching, he necessarily rejected; but it does not follow that he regarded them as unauthentic because he rejected them as unauthoritative.

Such is the first clear notice of a Canon[1] of

---

[1] The word *Canon*, which springs from a root found in its simplest form in Hebrew, Greek, and Latin (*kaneh, cannê, canna*) for a *reed*, (Engl. *cane*), is connected with a large class of derivatives (*canal, channel, cannon*) in which the idea of 'straightness' prevails. *Canôn* itself, which is a classical Greek term, signifies properly *a straight rod*, especially *a carpenter's rule*. Thus the word came to be used for the *standard* in art and literature and morals. At the same time it was also used *passively* for that which was definitely measured (comp. 2 *Cor.* x. 13—16).

In the first three centuries the word is not used of the Scriptures, but of the traditional *Rule (Canon) of the Church, Rule of Truth, Rule of Faith,* the law by which the progress of the Church was regulated, and specially of the *Creed* in which that law was embodied. Afterwards by a natural transition the special decisions made on points of Christian discipline were called '*canons.*'

THE AGE OF THE APOLOGISTS. 111

Christian Scriptures, of a written rule, that is, of Apostolic doctrine. Yet it is most improbable that Marcion first carried the idea of such a collection into effect. He is more likely to have followed an example which he found, than himself to have given an example to the Church at large. His adversaries, in fact, always represent him as mutilating something which already existed, and not as imposing a new kind of test of truth. But if, as seems most probable, similar collections of Apostolic writings existed before his time in the orthodox churches, they probably were confined to separate districts, and differed, more or less, as to their contents[1].

The first application of the word to Scripture is in the derivatives *canonize* and *canonical*. The authoritative books of the Bible are spoken of as those which *are* or *have been canonized*, that is ratified by the rule of the Church. And the first meaning of *canonical* was also in all probability passive, 'admitted by rule,' and not (as at a later time) 'giving the rule.'

In the fourth century *Canon* itself was applied to the Bible. After a list of the sacred books has been given it is said 'this would be the most unerring Rule (Canon) of the Inspired Scriptures' (Amphilochius. See Ch. vii.), that is the *measure* for testing them, and thus approximately, an *index* or *catalogue*. From this sense *Canon* was naturally transferred to the collection of books included in the index.

The chief point of interest to be observed in these fluctuating meanings of the terms is that the *verb* and not the *substantive* is first applied to the Bible. That was first tried by a *rule* and ratified, which afterwards became itself the *rule*.

In the following pages the word Canon will be used in its proper sense for 'the measure of the contents' of the Bible.

[1] The indication of such a collection is found in a phrase of DIONYSIUS, of Corinth (c. A.D. 160—170), referring to the conduct of Marcion. It is not marvellous that 'some,' he says, 'have attempted to adul-

112   *THE BIBLE IN THE CHURCH.*

CHAP. IV.

A.D. 120—170.

The Muratorian Fragment.

The memorial of one such collection has been preserved by a most remarkable chance—if such a word can be rightly used—in the famous Muratorian *Fragment on the Canon*, which forms an appropriate conclusion to this part of our inquiry, and offers a striking contrast to the partial New Testament of Marcion. This precious relic was first published by Muratori (1740) from a MS. in the Ambrosian Library at Milan, which had originally belonged to the great Irish monastery of Bobbio. It was found in a volume of Latin fragments and translations which dates apparently from the VIIIth century. But the fragment itself was evidently copied from a MS. of much higher antiquity; for it was mutilated both at the beginning and end before it was transcribed. The writer claims to be a contemporary of Pius, who was bishop of Rome in the middle of the second century; so that its date may be fixed with tolerable certainty between A.D. 160—170. The text of the fragment is not only mutilated, but corrupt. The Latin in which it is preserved is evidently a rude translation from a Greek original; and this copy is unusually disfigured by the manifold errors which abound in Irish MSS. of the period when it was written. But notwithstanding these defects the general scope of the fragment is clear, and it expresses with fair distinctness the first known judgment

terate *the Dominical Scriptures*, when they have laid hands on those which are not such as they are' [quoted by Euseb. *H. E.* II. 25]. So a little later MELITO (*c.* A.D. 170—180) speaks of 'the Old Books,' 'the Books of the Old Testament,' phrases which clearly imply the existence of a New Testament, a written anti-type to the Old.

of 'the Catholic Church' on the sum of the Christian Scriptures.

The author is entirely unknown. He was probably an Italian, as may be concluded from his intimate knowledge of the Roman Church, but not a resident in Rome, for he speaks of the city by name. From the internal character of the passage it seems to have been taken from a controversial rather than from a historic work, and probably from some book against heresy. If this conjecture be correct, it confirms what has been said before of the necessary limitation of the early evidence for the use of the Apostolic writings, from the character of the works of the oldest Fathers which have been preserved. If any of the earliest treatises against heresy, as those of Agrippa Castor (*c.* A.D. 130), or Justin, or Dionysius of Corinth (*c.* A.D. 165), or Melito (*c.* A.D. 175), had been preserved, it would doubtless have been easy to trace in them the recognition of the authority of the Books of the New Testament, which is now first seen in the scattered words of their opponents[1].

The Fragment commences with words which evidently refer to the Gospel of St Mark. The Gospel of 'Luke the physician,' the companion of St Paul, it is there said, stands third. The fourth

---

[1] The first quotation of the Apostolic Epistles as divine Scripture, the first Canon of the New Testament, the first Commentary on an apostolic book (Heracleon *on St John*) are due to heretics. In the fragments from early heretics contained in the *Philosphumena* of [Hippolytus] the Gospels of St Luke and St John, and the Epistles of St Paul to the Romans, Corinthians (1, 2), and Ephesians, are quoted as 'Scripture.' The earliest quotation is in a fragment of Basilides, *c.* A.D. 130.

CHAP. IV.
A.D. 120—170.

place is given to the Gospel of 'John a disciple' of the Lord, which he wrote 'at the request of his fellow-disciples and bishops, in obedience to a revelation given to the Apostle Andrew, aided by the revision of all'......' What wonder is it then,' the author adds, 'that John so constantly brings forward each detail even in his Epistles, saying in his own person, *What we have seen with our eyes, and heard with our ears, and our hands have handled, these things have we written?* For so he professes that he was not only an eye-witness, but also a hearer, and moreover, a historian of all the wonderful works of our Lord.'

1 John i. 1.

Though there is no reference to St Matthew's Gospel, we may assume that this occupied the first place in the enumeration. And at the close of it the writer says: 'And so, though various principles are taught in each of the Gospels, it makes no difference to the faith of believers, since in all of them all things are declared by one guiding Spirit concerning the Nativity, the Passion, the Resurrection, the Conversation [of the Lord] with His disciples, and His double Advent, at first in humility, and afterwards in royal power, as He will yet appear.' Thus clearly does he recognize the unity of the Gospels in contents, in purpose, in inspiration. He notices no doubt as to their authority, no limit as to their reception. They held in his time a position of clear and unquestioned supremacy.

The *Acts* and *Epistles*.

Next to the Gospels the book of the *Acts* is mentioned as containing a record by Luke of what fell under his own observation. Thirteen Epistles are attributed to St Paul, of which nine were addressed to Churches, and four to individual

THE AGE OF THE APOLOGISTS.

Christians. The first class suggests an analogy with the *Apocalypse*. As St John, when writing for all Christendom, wrote specially to seven Churches, so St Paul also 'wrote by name only to seven Churches, showing thereby the unity of the Catholic Church, though he wrote twice to the Corinthians and Thessalonians for their correction.' The second class includes all the books which we receive, 'an Epistle to *Philemon*, one to *Titus*, and two to *Timothy*,' which though written only 'from personal feeling and affection, are still hallowed in the respect of the Catholic Church, in the arrangement of ecclesiastical discipline.'

CHAP. IV.
A.D. 120—170.

'Moreover,' it is said 'there is in circulation an Epistle to the *Laodiceans*, [and] another to the *Alexandrians*, forged under the name of Paul, bearing on the heresy of Marcion; and several others, which cannot be received into the Catholic Church. For gall ought not to be mixed with honey. The Epistle of *Jude*, however, and two *Epistles of John*, who has been mentioned above, are held in the Catholic [Church]......We receive also the *Apocalypses* of John and Peter only, which [latter] some of our body will not have read in the Church.'

Disputed writings.

After this mention is made of the *Shepherd* of Hermas, which is excluded from the collection of Scriptures, in which it appears to have been already placed by some, and of writings of Valentinus, Basilides and others, 'of whom,' the writer says, 'we receive nothing;' and so the Fragment ends abruptly in the middle of an unfinished sentence.

Thus it will be observed, that no mention is made of those Catholic Epistles which are attested by the earliest and most complete evidence,

The omissions of the Fragment.

CHAP. IV.

A.D. 120—170.

1 *John*[1], and 1 *Peter*. The Epistle of *St James, the Epistle to the Hebrews,* and 2 *Peter*, are also omitted. With these exceptions the catalogue includes every book in our New Testament, and adds only one book to it, the *Apocalypse of St Peter*, which, it is said, was not universally admitted.

The Fragment probably a cento of distinct passages.

Various conjectures have been made to explain the omissions of the Fragment. The true explanation of them is probably to be found in the mutilation of the text, which seems to be made up of detached pieces. The first Epistle of *St John* is, in fact, quoted as the work of the Apostle in the notice of his Gospel; and a remarkable allusion to 'the book of *Wisdom* (*Proverbs*) written by the friends of Solomon' was perhaps made originally in explanation of the reception of the *Epistle of the Hebrews*, which was written by a friend of St Paul, and not by the Apostle himself. But it is needless to enter into a discussion of these details. The broad outlines of this earliest list of the Christian Scriptures are clear and full; and doubts, it will be seen, still existed in the next generation, as to the reception of some books, though the Churches of Christendom were then generally agreed as to the contents of their New Testament.

[1] It may be noticed that there is reason to think that two Epistles of St John, and not three, were first popularly received. The two shorter Epistles may have been reckoned together as one. See p. 122.

CHAPTER V.

THE FIRST CHRISTIAN BIBLE.

... *Built upon the foundation of the apostles and prophets, Christ Jesus Himself being the chief corner stone.*—Eph. ii. 20.

IN the last quarter of the second century we emerge at length into the full light of Christian history. From this time the Church stands in open strength, and challenges the power of the empire, lately guided by philosophers, and now hastening to its fall. From this time Christianity leaves its stamp on the schools of heathen thought, and in the contact receives much even where it gives most. It had won the heart of men: it now stood forth to conquer their intellect. From this time Christian writers made good their claim to stand in the first rank among the teachers of their time, for eloquence, for vigour, for grace, for freedom. From this time they speak to us with voices, full and manifold, in which he who wills may follow the simple strains of faith, mingled and at times confounded, yet never wholly lost, amidst strange sounds of strife, of violence, of pride. From this time, as Truth was necessarily bound in ever stricter forms, the sense of a living communion with the Word was more and more withdrawn from the mass of believers, though, by

CHAP. V.

A.D. 170—303.

The progress of Christianity at the end of the second century.

118 *THE BIBLE IN THE CHURCH.*

CHAP. V.
A.D. 170—303.

Retrospect of the earlier history of the New Testament.

the blessing of God, it has never yet wholly ceased to be the noblest heritage of great and humble souls.

Before we enter upon this period of fuller knowledge, the earlier age still demands a brief review. As we look back over it, we can now gather in a few sentences the sum of what it teaches on the formation of the New Testament, and better appreciate the manner in which its testimony is given. In their origin the writings of the Apostles are seen to have been casual and fragmentary. Their authors claim for themselves distinctly the gift of the Holy Spirit, but they nowhere express any design of conveying to their readers a full outline of the Faith. Still less do they indicate any idea of supplementing the Old Testament by a new collection of Scriptures. With the exception of the Apocalypse, no Book professes to contain a direct and complete revelation destined for the use of all Christians. Nor again is there the slightest reason to suppose that the different writers consciously combined to portray various aspects of Christianity. Yet it is equally certain that the New Testament does form a whole. Its different elements are united internally by the closest and most subtle harmonies. No part can be taken away without sensible injury to its unity and richness. Thus in the following generation we find various sections in the Church who followed out one form or other of Apostolic teaching, as it is still preserved in the New Testament, or combined different forms more or less perfectly. But there is no type of doctrine of which the New Testament does not offer a perfect explanation and present the Divine germ. Still, however, the memory of the

THE FIRST CHRISTIAN BIBLE. 119

Apostolic age was too fresh, the anticipation of the Coming of Christ too vivid, to allow of any definite collection of Christian Scriptures being made for the use of future times. An instinctive reverence invested the immediate disciples of the Lord with a natural dignity; and their writings moulded the thoughts of those who succeeded them. Experience soon deepened and defined the impression of this Divine instinct. Controversy brought out the decisive authority of the Apostolic texts. The corruption of the Evangelic tradition placed the simple grandeur of the four Gospels in clear prëeminence. The words of the Apostles were placed more and more frequently by the side of the words of the prophets, as the teaching of Christ had always been placed by that of the Law. Partial collections of the Scriptures of 'the New Testament' were formed without the Church; and as the whole Christian Body realized the fulness of its common life, the teaching and the books which had been in some sense the symbol of a part only, were ratified by the whole. And all this came to pass without any sudden transition or powerful personal influence. During the whole period no single character is marked out by the possession of creative genius. The age of great teachers followed afterwards. As a necessary consequence the evidence which can be adduced, though partial and fragmentary, is always consistent. The movement to which it witnesses was steadily set in one direction towards greater breadth and comprehensiveness. Nor did it cease till the New Testament was approximately, if not absolutely, the same as we receive now.

Such was the Divine process by which during

120 THE BIBLE IN THE CHURCH.

CHAP. V.
A.D. 170—303.
to be judged by reference to the remains of Christian literature.

fifty or sixty years after the death of the last Apostle, or about a hundred and twenty years from the beginning of the Apostolic mission, the Christian Scriptures, were gathered and set apart and at last combined with those of the Old Testament, which meanwhile after a long conflict had been vindicated for the universal Church from the interpretation of Jewish literalism. If the history is obscure in any part, if any details in it are yet uncertain, we may still quiet the impatience of regret by reflecting how little likely it was that the remains of Christian literature, scanty in extent and limited in scope, should have furnished an outline consistent, intelligible, natural, in every respect as this is. The New Testament is itself the truest clue to the investigation of the first half of the second century, the 'dark age' of Church history. For the rest it will be enough to seek in the fuller testimony of the next generation the expression of convictions, which, if they were not current everywhere at the close of the period through which we have passed, must at least have been formed within it.

The first great Fathers the interpreters of an earlier age.

For the Fathers who lived at the end of the second century, however much they were raised above their predecessors in power and range of thought, were trained by that earlier generation which they surpassed. They made no claims to any fresh discoveries in Christian truth: on the contrary they affirmed as their chief glory that they retained unchanged the tradition of the Apostolic age. Their testimony is the clear expression of an earlier faith and not the enunciation of novel deductions. They are the interpreters of the past, and not the mouthpieces of a revolution.

THE FIRST CHRISTIAN BIBLE. 121

By one of those remarkable chances, which so often strike the student of history, if we may not rather call them by a higher name, the three great writers who meet us first represent three great divisions of the Church. The traditions of Asia Minor, Egypt, and North Africa, find fit exponents in Irenæus, Clement of Alexandria, and Tertullian. The testimony of the far East is written in the venerable Syrian Version, the *Peshito;* and that of the Latin-speaking churches is confirmed by the *Old Vulgate* (Vetus Latina), which is of nearly equal antiquity.

CHAP. V.
─────
A.D. 170–303.
These Fathers represent distinct divisions of the Church.

It is uncertain at what time IRENÆUS left Asia Minor on his mission to Gaul. In his early youth he had been trained there under Polycarp, and had heard from him what St John, and others who had seen the Lord, had told of 'the mighty works and teaching, in all things harmonious with the Scriptures.' The recollection of these early lessons was more vivid, he tells us, in his old age than that of events just past; and he appeals with solemn earnestness to them in attestation of the opinions which he held in his latest years. When a presbyter at Lyons (*Lugdunum*) he was commended by the confessors of the Church to Eleutherus, bishop of Rome, as 'zealous for the covenant of Christ'; and when he afterwards became bishop of the city (*c.* A.D. 177—202) he continued to take a watchful regard of 'the sound ordinances of the Church' throughout Christendom. His predecessor in the episcopate, Pothinus, was ninety years old when he died for Christ, so that through him Irenæus was bound yet by another link with the apostolic age. Of his numerous writings one has been preserved, though for the most part only in a very early

IRENÆUS.

Euseb. *H. E.* v. 22.

c. A.D. 177.
Euseb. *H. E.* v. 4.
Euseb. *H. E.* v. 20.

Latin translation, his *Refutation of Knowledge falsely so called*, a treatise against heresies, in five books. In this he deals in passing with the inspiration and authority of Scripure. Nothing can be clearer than his assertion of the equal dignity of the Old and New Testaments, of the permanent spiritual value of every part of them, of their supreme power as 'the rule of truth.' The very form of the Gospels seems to him full of divine mysteries, foreshadowed both in the ancient Law and in nature itself. For, as in the Jewish Church the visible form of God rested on the four-faced Cherubim, 'so Christ, when manifested to men, gave us His Gospel under a four-fold form, though held together by One Spirit,' and on these Gospels He rests. And, again, 'as there are four regions of the world in which we are, and four several winds—as the Church is scattered over the whole earth, and the Gospel is the pillar and support of the Church—we might expect,' he argues, 'that it should have four pillars [and four winds, as it were], breathing on all sides immortality, and kindling [the heavenly spark in] men.'

Elsewhere, he repeats the statement, already quoted from Papias, as to the origin of the Gospels of St Matthew and St Mark, adding that Luke 'committed to writing the Gospel proclaimed by Paul, and that last of all John, the disciple of the Lord, published his Gospel, while living at Ephesus.' Of the remaining books of the New Testament, he quotes repeatedly as Scripture, the *Acts, twelve Epistles* of St Paul, (there is no reference to *Philemon*,) the *Apocalypse* and the *first Epistle of St John*, and 1 *Peter*. In one place he brings forward a passage from 2 *John* as part

THE FIRST CHRISTIAN BIBLE. 123

of the *first* Epistle. But he makes no references CHAP. V.
whatever to the Epistles of *St James, St Jude,* A.D. 170—303.
3 *John,* 2 *Peter.* Eusebius says that in a work
now lost he quoted the *Epistle to the Hebrews;* Euseb. *H. E.*
and a passage from it is found in a fragment v. 26.
attributed to him. On the whole, it is probable
that he was acquainted with the book, but did
not attribute it to St Paul. He also brings forward (as Eusebius noticed) a sentence from the v. 20. 2.
Shepherd as 'Scripture.'

The use which Irenæus makes of the books of His testi-
the Old Testament shows the growing influence Old Testa-
of the LXX. in extending the limits of the collec- ment, and use
tion of Scriptures, as the Jewish element became *crypha.*
less powerful in the Church. This disregard of
the strict limits of the Hebrew Bible has been
already noticed in Barnabas. At a later time it
will be still more apparent wherever the authority of the Greek translation was paramount, whether directly, or in the old Latin Version, which
was derived from it. Thus Irenæus quotes the
apocryphal *additions to Daniel, Baruch* and
Wisdom, side by side with the undoubted books
of Scripture. And though in his account of the
miraculous origin of the Septuagint, he assumes
that its contents were identical with those of the
Hebrew Bible, it is obvious that in the absence
of all power of criticism he, like other Fathers
who were unacquainted with Hebrew, would
receive all the writings which he found in the
ordinary Greek collection as parts of the one
'inspired' translation.

Some, indeed, moved by a more critical spirit, The East
were anxious to gain from others accurate infor- furnished
mation on a subject which they could not examine of the Old
for themselves; and the exigences of controversy Testament

with the Jews must have shown the necessity for accuracy as to the common sources of argument. One most interesting memorial of such an inquiry exists; and this shows beyond doubt that the judgment of the East, or in other words of Palestine, was that which was held to be decisive on the contents of the Old Testament. Onesimus, a Christian of Asia Minor, had frequently expressed a desire 'to learn the exact truth with regard to the Old Books, how many they were in number, and their order.' MELITO, bishop of Sardis—'who directed the whole conduct of his life in the Holy Spirit'—after 'a visit to the East, and even to the very spot where [all which we believe] was proclaimed and done, in which he obtained exact knowledge of the Books of the Old Covenant,' sent a list of them to his friend. 'The names of them are,' he says, 'Five Books of Moses, *Genesis, Exodus, Numbers, Leviticus, Deuteronomy; Jesus*, the son of Naue, *Judges, Ruth;* four *Books of Kings*, two of *Chronicles;* a Book of the *Psalms of David*, the *Proverbs* of Solomon, which is also called *Wisdom, Ecclesiastes*, the *Song of Songs, Job;* the Books of the Prophets *Isaiah, Jeremiah*, the *Twelve* in a single Book; *Daniel, Ezekiel, Esdras* (Ezra).' One important feature of this list has been strangely overlooked. It is evident from the names, the number, and the order of the books, that it was not taken directly from the Hebrew, but from the LXX. revised by the Hebrew. In other words, it appears to be a catalogue of the books in the Palestinian LXX., the Greek Bible which was used by our Lord and the Apostles. Three books of our Old Testament are not mentioned in it, *Lamentations, Nehemiah* and *Esther*. The two former were commonly attached to *Jeremiah* and *Ezra* respectively. It has been supposed that *Esther* also was included in the latter book; but it is more likely that a real difference of opinion existed in Palestine from an early time as to the character of the narrative (of which there are many other traces), and that Melito did not find it admitted by the authorities which he consulted.

The greatest license in the citation of 'Scripture' prevailed at Alexandria. Several causes have been already noticed which tended to obliterate the limits of the Old Testament even among the Alexandrine Jews. Among Christians the confusion of the original books of the Hebrew Bible with the later additions was more rapid and complete. Some of the books of the Apocrypha seemed to the Alexandrine Fathers to foreshadow Christian truths with prophetic power, and the fulness with which they recognized the working of the divine Word in men at all times, inclined them to have little regard for historic data as fixing the boundaries of a written revelation. For they used 'apocryphal' writings of the New Testament no less freely than those of the Old Testament. At times they speak with more critical exactness, but generally it is necessary to interpret their testimony with due regard to their national characteristics.

CLEMENT (Titus Flavius Clemens) is in every respect a true representative of his adopted Church. Of most varied training and extensive knowledge, he was full of wide and generous thoughts, large sympathies, and yet strangely deficient in critical sagacity and chastened judgment. He felt truth rather than found it; and he commends it to the heart more often than to

126   *THE BIBLE IN THE CHURCH.*

the reason. The title of his great work, *Patchwork* (Stromateis or Stromata) *of Hints for Knowledge in accordance with true Philosophy*, reflects a fair image of his character. For about ten years he presided over the Greek Catechetical School of Alexandria, which was famous even in the middle of the second century. Like Irenæus, he succeeded a man (Pantænus) who was removed by one generation only from the Apostles; and he affirms that his writings contain only 'the shadow and outline of what he had heard from men ...who preserved the true tradition of the blessed doctrine directly from Peter and James, from John and Paul' (the connexion is worthy of notice), 'the holy Apostles, from father to son, even to our time...'. Like Irenæus, he dwells on 'the harmony of the Law and the Prophets, of the Gospel and the Apostles, and that under-current of melody which flows on from teacher to teacher through all the changes of persons.' 'The rule of the Church,' he says, 'by which Scripture is interpreted, 'consists in the perfect combination of all the notes and harmonies of the Law and the Prophets with the Testament delivered at the presence of the Lord.' For in all the Scriptures, 'in the Law, in the Prophets, and in the blessed Gospel'— 'which are ratified by Almighty power' —we 'have the Lord as the spring of our teaching, Who, by the various ministrations of His servants *in sundry times and in divers manners*, from beginning to end, guides the course of knowledge,' ruling all their words 'by a wise economy to suit the age and culture of those who heard them.'

The writings of Clement contain no special catalogue of the sacred books. In addition to the

THE FIRST CHRISTIAN BIBLE. 127

books of the Hebrew Bible (including *Esther*) he quotes *Baruch, Wisdom, Ecclesiasticus, Tobit, Judith*, and 2 *Esdras*. Of the New Testament he quotes the *Four Gospels*, the *Acts*, twelve *Epistles of St Paul* (there is still no reference to *Philemon*), the *Epistle to the Hebrews* (as St Paul's), 1 *John*, 1 *Peter*, *Jude*, the *Apocalypse*. There is no express reference in his works to 2, 3 *John*, though the existence of one or both is implied; and it seems certain that he was unacquainted with the *Epistle of James* and 2 *Peter*. On the other hand, he quotes as inspired the *Preaching* (*Apocalypse*) *of Peter*, the *Shepherd*; and also the letters of *Clement* of Rome and *Barnabas* as apostolic. Other apocryphal books, as the Gospels *according to the Hebrews* and *according to the Egyptians*, he uses, but without giving them any place among the Christian Scriptures.

The Churches of Asia Minor were mainly conservative: the Church of Alexandria was liberal, yet subtle and speculative: the Church of North Africa was fervent, impassioned, pitilessly stern. If Clement embodies the spirit of Alexandria TERTULLIAN (Quintus Septimius Florens Tertullianus) is no less fitted to express the genius of Carthage and Hippo. Restless, impatient of control, glowing with unmeasured zeal, bearing down all opposition with the force of impetuous rhetoric, carried even to the heresy of Montanism by his aspirations after a stricter life, he has left writings which will charm as long as the Latin tongue is read, and a name which will live while courage is a Christian virtue. It does not appear that the African Churches had had any great teacher before him. But Tertullian repeats the testimony which we have already heard from

128   *THE BIBLE IN THE CHURCH.*

CHAP. V.
A.D. 170—303.

others. He professes to teach only that which had been taught from the first. The whole record of God's revelation—the collection of Scriptures of the Old and New Testaments—is in his judgment one 'Divine Instrument' (*i.e.* record). He appeals to the historic tradition of the Churches to show the authenticity of the apostolic writings.

adv. Marc.
IV. 5.

'If,' he says, 'it is acknowledged that that is more true which is more ancient, that more ancient which is even from the beginning, that from the beginning which is from the Apostles; it will in like manner assuredly be acknowledged that that has been delivered by the Apostles which has been preserved inviolate in the Churches of the Apostles.' So, he goes on to say at length, the Epistles of St Paul have been preserved in the Churches which he founded: so too the four Gospels have been handed down to us in due succession on the authority of the apostolic Churches. 'These,' he adds, 'are the summary arguments which we employ when we discuss the Gospels with heretics, maintaining both the order of time, which excludes the later works of forgers, and the authority of Churches, which upholds the tradition of the Apostles; because truth necessarily precedes forgery, and proceeds from those to whom it has been delivered.' In the possession of the

de Præscr. 37.

New Testament he proudly says elsewhere 'I am the heir of the Apostles.'

The *Old Latin* Version of the Bible.
Its origin.

The Canon of Tertullian is intimately connected with that of the *Old Latin* Version of the Bible, which he habitually used. The origin of this venerable translation, the 'Peshito,' so to speak, or 'simple' Version of the West, is lost in complete obscurity. Yet it can be affirmed with certainty that it was made in Africa, and that it

THE FIRST CHRISTIAN BIBLE. 129

was so far authorized by popular use even in the time of Tertullian, as to form the theological dialect. It may seem strange that the birth-place of the Vulgate was Africa and not Italy; but all evidence points to this conclusion. Up to the close of the second century Greek was the language of the Christians of Rome. All the Christian writings which were published at Rome were Greek. The names of the bishops with few exceptions are Greek. The first sermons which were preached there were in Greek. And the '*Kyrie*' still remains to witness to the Greek of the earliest Liturgy. On the other hand, the dialect of the version exhibits every peculiarity of African Latin in its rudest form, and, as Greek was little used in Africa, the need of the Version must have been felt as soon as Christianity was firmly planted there. This cannot have been later than the middle of the second century, and to that date we must refer the origin of the *Old Latin Vulgate*. The Jews who were settled in North Africa seem to have spoken Greek exclusively, or it might be supposed that parts of the Old Testament had been rendered into Latin before the introduction of Christianity. On internal grounds the existence of some such a version may be plausibly supported. Its currency would have fixed the outlines of a theological dialect, and would readily explain the substantial similarity of the translation in different parts of the Old and New Testaments. The work, at any rate, whenever it was begun, like the LXX. from which the Old Testament was taken, seems to have been accomplished by successive and 'yet not independent efforts of individuals. The text thus made was afterwards variously altered, and

130   *THE BIBLE IN THE CHURCH.*

CHAP. V.

A.D. 170—303

gradually became so corrupt, by the introduction of glosses and the combination of readings, that at the close of the fourth century Jerome was induced to revise it by the help of the original Greek. His labours, indeed, did not end with that revision, nor were they even thus far universally welcomed. In Ireland and Great Britain especially, the *Old Latin* continued to be used widely for several centuries; and at a later time its influence greatly modified the *New Vulgate*, which was finally accepted as the authorized Version of the Western Churches.

Its Canon.

The translation of the Old Testament in the *Old Latin* was taken from the Alexandrine LXX. It consequently contained the books of the *Apocrypha*, which were added to the Greek Bible, and some others which are not at present found there, as 2 *Esdras*, and perhaps the *Book of Enoch*. In the New Testament it erred by defect and not by excess. From considerations of style it seems certain that the *Epistle to the Hebrews*, the *Epistle of St James*, and 2 *Peter* did not form part of the Version in its original form.

The Canon of Tertullian.

Tertullian's quotations reach generally to the same limits. He uses passages from *Baruch*, *Wisdom*, and *Ecclesiasticus*, without reserve as

de Hab. Mul. 3.

to their authority. The *Book of Enoch* he quotes on the ground of its recognition by St Jude, though he admits that it was not received 'into the Jewish ark.' In addition to the *Four Gospels*, the *Acts*, thirteen *Epistles of St Paul* (*Philemon* is expressly included), 1 *Peter*, 1 *John*, the *Apocalypse*, and *Jude*, he notices the *Epistle to the Hebrews*, under the title of the 'Epistle of

de Pudic. 20.

Barnabas,' and says that it was 'more generally

received in the churches than the apocryphal Shepherd;' but the text which he gives evidently shows that he found no current version of the book, but rendered the passage himself from the Greek. There is nothing in his writings to show that he was acquainted with the *Epistle of James*, *2 Peter*, *2, 3 John*; and he refers to only one 'apocryphal' book besides the *Shepherd*, the *Acts of Paul and Thecla*, which he declares to be a detected forgery. The '*Shepherd*,' he says, was pronounced spurious by every council of the churches; and the presbyter who composed the '*Acts of Paul*' was degraded after confessing his fraud. The two statements are not without interest as showing that in his time at least some criticism was used in discussing the claims of writings which professed to be Apostolic or inspired.

CHAP. V.
———
A.D. 170–303.

de Orat. 12.
de Pudic. 10.

de Bapt. 17.

Of the early Greek literature of the Syrian Church, three books of Theophilus, bishop of Antioch, to Autolycus, on the 'Elementary Evidences of Christianity,' and a few fragments, alone are left. THEOPHILUS quotes the *Gospel of St John* as written by one of those 'who were moved by the Spirit,' and Eusebius mentions that he quoted the *Apocalypse* in a work now lost. One coincidence of language with *2 Peter*—'His word shining as a light in a chamber, enlightened the world'—deserves remark from the great scarcity of even possible indications of the use of the Epistle. SERAPION, the second in succession from Theophilus, shows in a remarkable passage the spirit in which the Apostolic writings were received in his time, and also the tenacity with which some in remote districts still continued to use apocryphal books. Having found the *Gospel*

The *Syrian Church.*

THEOPHILUS
C. A.D.
168—180

H. E. IV. 24
ad Autol. II
18.

SERAPION.

CHAP. V.

A.D. 170—303.

Euseb. *H. E.* vi. 12.

according to St Peter in use at Rhossus, a small town in Cilicia, he allowed the use of it for a time with some cautions, as being on the whole orthodox, though he pronounced it unauthentic. 'We receive,' he says, in writing to the Church there, 'both Peter and the other Apostles as Christ; but as experienced men, we reject the writings falsely inscribed with their names, since we know that we did not receive such from our fathers.'

The *Peshito.*

As a supplement to this meagre evidence the testimony of the Eastern Churches is fully given in their great Version of the Bible, the Syriac *Peshito* (i. e. *simple, literal* version). This was made as far as can be determined in the same manner as the *Old Latin*, but at an earlier date. The Old Testament, no less than the New, was certainly translated by a Christian, and the whole work was probably revised and completed early in the second century, at Edessa, which was at that time the centre of an important Christian school.

The *Old Testament.*

The Version of the Old Testament was taken directly from the Hebrew, yet not without reference to the Palestinian LXX. Its contents are therefore limited to the books of the Hebrew Bible. The Syriac translations of the Apocrypha and of the additions to Daniel were not made till a much later date.

See ch. ix.

The *New Testament.*

The New Testament contains the *Four Gospels*, the *Acts*, fourteen *Epistles of St Paul* (including the *Epistle to the Hebrews*), the *Epistle of James*, 1 *Peter*, 1 *John*. The translations of the *Epistle of Jude*, 2 *Peter*, 2, 3 *John*, and the *Apocalypse*, which are given in the printed editions, were made at a later time, and have found only partial acceptance in the Eastern Churches.

THE FIRST CHRISTIAN BIBLE. 133

Briefly to sum up what has been said, it appears that towards the close of the second century there was little critical consistency in the use of the books of the Old Testament. Where the influence of the Alexandrine LXX. prevailed, all the books which it included were commonly received as Scripture, yet not by any deliberate judgment, but from a natural habit, from inadvertence, and, in part, from the character of some of the apocryphal books themselves. On the other hand when discussion arose, appeal was made to the Hebrew Bible, which was faithfully reproduced in the Version of the Eastern Churches.

CHAP. V.

A.D. 170—303.
Summary.

Of the New Testament, the *Four Gospels*, the *Acts*, thirteen *Epistles of St Paul* (for the partial omission of the *Epistle to Philemon* is obviously accidental), 1 *Peter*, 1 *John*, were universally received in every Church, without doubt or limitation, as part of the written rule of Christian faith, equal in authority with the Old Scriptures, and ratified (as it seemed) by a tradition reaching back to the date of their composition[1].

In the Western and African Churches the *Epistle of St Jude*, 2, (3) *John*, and the *Apocalypse*, were received as parts of the New Testament: in the East the *Epistle of St James* and the *Epistle to the Hebrews*, of which the latter was also known and partially admitted in other

The partial reception of the *disputed* Books of the New Testament.

---

[1] These Books will in future be spoken of as the *acknowledged* Books of the New Testament—*Homologumena* according to the technical term of Eusebius; the remaining books may be described by the corresponding term *Antilegomena*, the *disputed* Books. The same terms may be applied to the *Hebrew Canon* of the Old Testament, and the *Apocrypha* respectively; yet the book of *Esther* occupies an anomalous position.

134   *THE BIBLE IN THE CHURCH.*

CHAP. V.
A.D. 170–303.

Churches. The *Second Epistle of St Peter* alone of the books which we receive appears to have been almost or entirely unused and unknown.

Of other books the *Shepherd of Hermas* obtained a limited authority, but its claims were distinctly set aside by the decisive judgment of those who were best acquainted with its origin.

Testimony of the Fathers of the third century to the *Disputed Books*.

The evidence which can be gathered from the Fathers of the third century confirms completely the results which have been obtained as to the judgment of the different churches upon the 'disputed' books. In the Western Churches (North Africa, Italy) various writers quote as Divine Scripture the *Epistle of St Jude* (an anonymous writer against Novatus), 2 *John* (Aurelius), and the *Apocalypse* (Cyprian, Commodian, Victorinus, Lactantius, Hippolytus); and there is no reason to think that any one of these books was ever rejected there, unless indeed Caius rejected the *Apocalypse*. On the other hand, all direct and indirect evidence combines to show that the Western Fathers unanimously denied the Pauline authorship of the *Epistle to the Hebrews;* and they make no use of the *Epistle of James*, 2 *Peter*, or 3 *John*. In the New Testament they admit no apocryphal books; but, like Tertullian, they use the Apocrypha of the Old Testament freely and without reserve.

The testimony of ORIGEN.
A.D. 186–254.
ap. Euseb. *H. E.* VI. 25.

The judgment of ORIGEN must be noticed a little more in detail. Among all the Fathers of the first three centuries, Origen—the *Adamantine*—stands out with the noblest individuality. Unsurpassed in Christian zeal, unrivalled in universal learning, he devoted a long life to the study of the Scriptures. He believed that the

THE FIRST CHRISTIAN BIBLE. 135

Bible contained all treasures of wisdom, and so he often appears to see mysteries in it which the critic refuses to recognize. He believed that Christianity contained the answer to every human instinct, and so he often presses with unchastened boldness to offer an explanation in its name for that which must as yet be hidden from men. His faults, like the faults of every great man, were themselves great; but his genius is still powerful to warm and to enlighten. No canonization has hallowed his name, but none the less his influence on after ages has been equal to that of the greatest saints—Augustine, Athanasius and Jerome.

The peculiar studies of Origen give additional importance to his statements on the Bible. In his commentary on the first Psalm he gives a list of 'the canonical books' of the Old Testament according to 'the tradition of the Hebrews.' 'They are,' he says, 'twenty-two, equal to the number of letters in their alphabet.' In his enumeration he gives the Hebrew as well as the Greek names of the books. The order is as follows: The *Pentateuch, Joshua, Judges,* and *Ruth, Samuel* (1, 2), *Kings* (1, 2), *Chronicles* (1, 2), *Esdras* (1, 2, *i. e. Ezra* and *Nehemiah*), *Psalms, Proverbs, Ecclesiastes, Canticles, Isaiah, Jeremiah* with *Lamentations* and the Epistle, *Daniel, Ezekiel, Job, Esther.* The twelve *Minor Prophets* (in one book) are omitted by an error of Eusebius or his transcriber, as they are necessary to make up the number. The addition of the Apocryphal Letter (*Baruch,* ch. vi.) to Jeremiah is probably a mistake of Origen, who found the Letter in that position in the LXX. At least there is no reason to believe that it was ever included in the Hebrew Bible. At the close of the

CHAP. V.

A.D. 170–303

His Canon of the Old Testament.

list Origen says, 'the *Books of the Maccabees* are not included in these' [scriptures of the Jews]. In his other writings he uses apocryphal books as Divine and authoritative, yet not without noticing the difference of opinion on the subject. But even in his case the familiar use of the Greek Bible practically overpowered his knowledge of the original Hebrew Canon; and in his famous 'Letter to Africanus' he expressly defends the reception among Christians of the additions found in the Alexandrine LXX.

His Canon of the *New Testament*.

The testimony which Origen gives to the books of the New Testament is more complete than any which has been yet obtained. No one of the writings which we receive escaped his wide research, though he remarks that some were not universally admitted. 'There are,' he says, 'four Gospels only uncontroverted in the Church of God spread under heaven. Peter has left one Epistle generally acknowledged; and perhaps a *second*, for that is disputed. John wrote the *Apocalypse* and an Epistle of very few lines; and, it may be, a *second* and *third*, since all do not admit them to be genuine.' Of the *Epistle to the Hebrews*, he writes, that 'the thoughts are the thoughts of the Apostle Paul;...but who it was who *wrote* the Epistle, God only knows certainly.' Elsewhere he quotes the *Epistles of James* and *Jude*, but at the same time alludes to the doubts entertained as to their right to be classed among the Christian Scriptures.

Quoted by *Euseb.* l. c.

His reference to apocryphal writings.

In various places he refers to 'apocryphal' writings, as the *Epistle of Barnabas*, the *Shepherd of Hermas*, the *Preaching of Peter*, the *Gospel according to the Egyptians*, and more or less decisively questions or rejects their authority.

THE FIRST CHRISTIAN BIBLE. 137

Yet he claims for himself a right of judgment from time to time, and the general principles by which he was guided are set out very clearly in a passage of his 'Commentaries on St Matthew,' which unfortunately is preserved only in a Latin translation. As for the use of apocryphal books, he says, 'it is the part of a great man to hear and fulfil that which is said, *Prove all things: hold fast that which is good.* Still for the sake of those who cannot, "like moneychangers" distinguish whether words are to be held as true or false, and cannot guard themselves carefully, so as to hold that which is true, and yet *abstain from all evil appearance,* no one ought to use for the confirmation of doctrines any books which are not included in the canonized Scriptures. Yet if any one receives the *Epistle to the Hebrews* as the work of Paul'...[he does not ill]. Thus strictly Origen would limit the Bible, in the highest sense, to the *acknowledged* books both in the Old and in the New Testament, that is, the Hebrew Canon and the *Four Gospels,* the *Acts,* 1 *Peter,* 1 *John,* thirteen *Epistles of St Paul,* and the *Apocalypse;* for he seems to have been unacquainted with the doubts which were raised as to the last book. The use of other writings he commits to the discretion of individuals, without suppressing his own opinion as to the very unequal value of different books.

CHAP. V.

A.D. 170–303.

Comm. in Matt. § 28.

In the later Fathers of the Alexandrine Church there is little to notice on the history of the Canon, except the judgment of DIONYSIUS, a scholar of Origen, upon the *Apocalypse.* He fully accepted the book as inspired and divine, but on internal grounds denied that it was written by the author of the Gospel. His arguments

Later testimony at Alexandria.
† A.D. 265.

are full of interest, but he does not attempt to support them by any historic proof. In spite of his influence, however, the earlier opinion continued to prevail, and the usage of Alexandria more and more turned in favour of the disputed books of the New Testament[1].

Asia Minor.

In Asia Minor various writers use as Scripture the *Epistle to the Hebrews* (Gregory Thaumaturgus, Methodius), the *Apocalypse* (Methodius), and perhaps *2 Peter* (Firmilian)[2]; but there is no trace of the acceptance there of any other of the disputed books (*James, Jude*, 2, 3 *John*), or of any apocryphal book of the New Testament. In the Old Testament Methodius uses the Apocrypha (*Ecclesiasticus, Baruch, Wisdom*) without reserve as 'Scripture.'

The first great Christian Library. A.D. 309.

Meanwhile a Christian Library was established at Cæsarea by PAMPHILUS, a devoted admirer of Origen. Manuscripts still exist which claim to have been compared with copies which were preserved there. In one of these the *Epistle to the Hebrews* is placed among the Epistles of St Paul. And Euthalius, who published an edition of the *Acts* and *seven Catholic Epistles* at the close of the fourth century, says that his work

---

[1] Epiphanius places among the heresies which he describes one which he calls that of the *Alogi*—those who deny the Word (the Logos)—which consisted in the rejection of the writings of St John. It seems probable, however, that he only wished to characterize an opinion, and not to describe any actual body of men bearing the name, and professing this tenet as their characteristic mark.

[2] This doubtful reference may deserve more consideration from the fact that MELITO of Sardis, at the conclusion of his Apology, clearly refers to the substance of 2 *Pet*. iii. 10, 12, though not by name.

THE FIRST CHRISTIAN BIBLE. 139

was 'collated with the accurate copies in the library of Eusebius Pamphilus at Cæsarea.'

CHAP. V.

A.D. 170—303.

Thus we stand at length in a position to which existing records extend[1]. The New Testament, though with some reserve, has now been extended at Alexandria to the limits which we allow. In the Western Churches, on the contrary, the *Epistle of St James* and *2 Peter* were still unknown or unused, and the *Epistle to the Hebrews* was not admitted as apostolical. But, with the exception of the Peshito, every authority at present from Alexandria, Africa, Asia and Rome, supports the inspired authority, and, with one exception, the apostolic authorship of the *Apocalypse*. In the Old Testament the enlarged Canon of the Alexandrine LXX. was sanctioned by popular use, but appeals were made to the Hebrew Canon, which alone was universally and formally admitted.

Summary of this date to which existing MSS. go back.

The great heresies by which the Church was disturbed bear witness to the general acceptance of one Bible among all Christians. In the earliest controversies on the Holy Trinity with Praxeas and Theodotus, the Scriptures generally were recognized as the common ground of conflict. Tertullian when he welcomed the outpouring of the Spirit (as he believed) under the teaching of Montanus, yet supposed that it was given to define and explain, and not to supersede the revelations 'in the common records of the ancient Scriptures.' Even Mani, when he claimed the right of reconstructing Christianity, was constrained to admit to some extent the authority of

The testimony of heretical and

c. A.D. 170.

c. A.D 170.

c. A.D. 277.

---

[1] Compare App. B. *The Contents of the most Ancient MSS. of the Bible.*

the apostolic writings which were commonly received.

At the same time heathen writers gained a clearer knowledge of the Christian books. CELSUS quotes 'the writings of the disciples of Jesus' concerning His Life as possessing undoubted authority; and the special facts which he brings forward show that these were our four Gospels. It seems likely also that both he and PORPHYRY were acquainted with the Epistles of St Paul. In other heathen writers there is scarcely anything which bears upon the history of the Christian Scriptures. These have indeed little in harmony with the Stoicism and Scepticism above which the noblest thinkers of the West rarely rose; and the revived Philosophies of Alexandria —the later schools of Plato and Aristotle— claimed to be, as it were, new revelations.

CHAPTER VI.

THE BIBLE PROSCRIBED AND RESTORED.

*Each man's work shall be made manifest: for the day
shall declare it, because it is revealed in fire; and
the fire itself shall prove each man's work of what
sort it is.*—1 Cor. iii. 13.

IF we look back over the last period of our
history, it will be evident by what a wide
interval it is separated from that which immediately preceded it. The influence of great men
succeeded the antagonism of great principles.
A period of speculation followed the struggle for
substantial existence. The heresies which arose,
if not less perilous than those of the earlier age,
were more confined. They sprang more directly
from the interpretation of fundamental records,
than from essential differences in the apprehension of the nature of Christianity. On the other
hand, the great Fathers of the Church were distinguished by larger views of the claims and
destinies of the Truth than their predecessors
had gained. Research and thought were combined with almost boundless freedom. Experience had not yet found out the limits of inquiry,
and the divine instinct of Christendom had not
fixed the range within which it might be exer-

CHAP. VI.

A.D. 303—340.
The Characteristics of
the third
Century.

142 *THE BIBLE IN THE CHURCH.*

CHAP. VI.
A.D. 303—340.

cised. One by one the various sides of Christianity were explored, and its manifold treasures were everywhere exposed to view, but it was not yet exactly defined or reduced to a system.

An appeal always made to antiquity.

Still in every Church, by every writer, an unhesitating appeal was made to the use and judgment of antiquity. The boldest speculator made no claim to novelty. 'The rule of Truth,' 'the rule of the Church,' was the one standard by which each professed to be bound; and this (such was the general belief) found its expression in the words of Scripture, and its embodiment in universal Christian practice. No date was fixed for its origin. It was affirmed to have grown with the growth of the Christian body. However impalpable such a rule may seem to us, it was yet most real and powerful in the third century. And thus though speculation was formally unrestrained, it was tempered by what may be called the tone of Christian feeling, the spirit of Christian life. Already that power was silently working in the whole society which in the next generation moulded the age of Councils.

The importance of this appeal in connexion with the history of the Bible.

This characteristic of the period illustrates a remarkable feature in the history of the Bible. The Bible was received as a heritage secured by prescription. Even controversy failed to raise any spirit of historical criticism. The sacred books generally had been received from the first. Common consent had allowed their authority.

de Pudic. 10.

Tertullian appears to allude once to synodal discussions on the Canon, but with that doubtful exception there is nothing to show that the subject was ever debated by churches. For them it was decided by usage, and single writers only

THE BIBLE PROSCRIBED AND RESTORED. 143

repeat this traditional testimony. Books which were received everywhere were at once admitted without further inquiry as 'acknowledged;' those which were only admitted in some places were reckoned, equally without inquiry, as 'disputed.' No attempt was made to trace the history of the one class, or to determine the critical basis of the doubts which attached to the other. In some cases, as far as we can see, a book was 'doubted' or 'gainsayed' because it was unknown in particular churches; in others, because the apostolical authority of its writer was uncertain; in others, from its internal character. Yet in all alike the doubt was suffered to remain historically indeterminate and undecided. The practical solution of the question, when it was fairly put forward, was left to the judgment of the churches. And we, who receive the Bible which was thus fixed—we *know not how*—may well believe that this judgment was not without the guidance of the Spirit.

CHAP. VI.
A.D. 303—340.

The freedom of inquiry, the power, the outward prosperity which Christians enjoyed during a great part of the third century, bore at last bitter fruit. Eusebius prefaces his account of the persecution of Diocletian with a sad picture of the pride and rivalry and hypocrisy and schism among Christians, which seemed to him to call for divine chastisement. The first gentle visitation, he says, was disregarded, and then 'the Lord covered the daughter of Zion with a cloud in His anger, and cast down from heaven unto the earth the beauty of Israel...'

The persecution of Diocletian.
A.D. 303.
H. E. VIII. 1.
Lam. ii. 1, 2

The persecution of Diocletian offers a singular parallel to that which Antiochus Epiphanes directed against the Jews. Both were specially

Compared with that of Antiochus Epiphanes.

144 *THE BIBLE IN THE CHURCH.*

CHAP. VI.
A.D. 303—340.

designed to effect the destruction of the Scriptures. Both resulted in determining more clearly than before the limits of the Sacred Volume, by giving scope to the practical exhibition of the popular feeling, hitherto vague and wavering. This peculiar characteristic of Diocletian's edict —'that the churches should be razed, and the Scriptures consumed with fire'—was probably due to the suggestions of Hierocles, proconsul of Bithynia, who is said to have originated and guided the persecution. Hierocles himself was well acquainted with the Christian books, and the provision which he made for their destruction shows the position which they held in the Church.

Euseb. *H. E.* VIII. 2.

The effects of the persecution.

One of the first results of the persecution was to create dissensions in the Church itself. Some Christians purchased impunity by the actual sacrifice of 'Scriptures of the Law,' as the Sacred Books were now called. Others availed themselves of the means of escape which were offered by lenient magistrates, and were acquitted on the surrender of 'useless writings.' Others viewed this compromise with reasonable jealousy, and branded as 'traitors' (traditores) those who obtained exemption from persecution by the simulation of guilt. Various causes increased the fierceness of the strife, and the schism of the Donatists witnessed for more than three centuries to its implacable bitterness. Yet good sprang out of persecution and schism. All parties were equally interested in determining exactly the limits of the Bible. The stricter Christians sought clear grounds for the punishment of the 'traditores:' the more lax were anxious not to compromise their faith while they were willing to secure impunity by concession in that which they

THE BIBLE PROSCRIBED AND RESTORED. 145

thought indifferent. Their enemies aimed at a special mark; and from this time the phrase 'Canonical' Scriptures became a familiar title, if it was not now first used.

CHAP. VI.
A.D. 303—340.

Yet even this persecution failed to call out any general decision on the contents of the Bible. The question, which cannot have been left open, was still determined in practice rather than by debate, and we may look for the result in the judgment of those who passed through the ordeal. The persecution, which extended over the whole Roman Empire, with the exception of Gaul, where Constantius Chlorus, the father of Constantine, shielded the Christians, raged with peculiar severity in Africa and Syria. From both these countries a testimony is preserved as to the range of Holy Scripture, when the trial was past.

How its relation to the Canon may be determined.

DONATUS (A. D. 329) headed a party who opposed the appointment of Cæcilian to the bishopric of Carthage, on the ground that he had been ordained by Felix a 'traditor.' In spite of the good offices of Constantine the rupture became complete. Thus the betrayal of the Holy Scriptures was the ground of the Donatist schism, and we may see in the opinion of the Donatists the strictest judgment of the African Churches upon the Canon. Now Augustine in his controversial works against them expressly affirms that Donatist and Catholic alike were 'bound by the authority of both Testaments,' and that they admitted equally 'the Canonical Scriptures.' 'And what are these,' he asks, 'but the Scriptures of the Law and the Prophets? To which are added the *Gospels*, the *Apostolic Epistles*, the *Acts of the Apostles*, the *Apocalypse* of John.' The am-

The Canon of the Donatists in Africa.

Ep. cxxix. 3.

c. Cresc. i. l. xxxi. 3. *New Testament.*

10

146   *THE BIBLE IN THE CHURCH.*

CHAP. VI. biguity of Augustine's language about the Epistle
──────── to the Hebrews leaves some doubt as to the posi-
A.D 303—340. tion which this book occupied in the Donatist
Canon. Otherwise the trial through which they
passed left the African Churches in possession
of a complete and pure New Testament.

Old Testa-   With regard to the Old Testament the influ-
ment.   ence of the LXX. still prevailed, and the Apo-
2 *Macc.* xiv. cryphal books were quoted by Donatists in sup-
37—46.   port of some of their wildest tenets. Augustine,
as we shall see, at times reproached them with
using an authority not admitted by the Jews.
But in spite of occasional protests, persecution
consecrated, as it were, the tradition which reckoned these among the Scriptures. Hitherto the
Churches of North Africa had been wholly shut
off from communication with the East. The
Alexandrine LXX. was for them the original of
the Bible. And even when Augustine gained
clear knowledge of the Hebrew usage, he found
it impossible in the end to exclude from the
Bible books which had been hallowed by the
memories of suffering.

The Canon of   It was otherwise in Palestine. Among the
EUSEBIUS.   witnesses of the persecution there was EUSEBIUS,
† c. A.D. 340. the friend of Pamphilus, afterwards bishop of
Cæsarea, and the historian of the early Church.
H.E. VIII. 2. 'I saw,' he says, 'with my own eyes the houses of
prayer thrown down and razed to their founda-
tions, and the inspired and sacred Scriptures con-
signed to fire in the open market-place.' Among
such scenes he could not fail to learn what books
men judged to be more precious than their lives;
and it may have been what he then saw which
induced him to pay special attention in his history to early notices of the different parts of

THE BIBLE PROSCRIBED AND RESTORED. 147

Scripture. There is, indeed, some obscurity and several apparent contradictions in what he has said in different places on the books of the New Testament. For this and for like faults in other parts of his narrative he has been judged harshly. But he himself pleads justly the character of his work as an excuse for his shortcomings. It was the first comprehensive history of the Church, and his object was to gather from earlier writers all that was of chief interest for his subject. The result is that he made a vast collection of materials for a history, and not a history. He does not pause to weigh or compare his authorities. Frequently he writes under the immediate influence of the author whose judgment he has just recorded, and it is but natural that he has overlooked some facts which have an important bearing upon points which he professes to discuss in detail.

CHAP. VI.
A.D. 303—340.

The manner in which he treats the history of the Canon illustrates the desultory character of his work. After mentioning the succession of Linus to the see of Rome 'upon the martyrdom of Peter and Paul,' he proceeds without further preface to reckon up the writings attributed to those two Apostles. In this passage he notices 1 *Peter* as indisputably genuine; 2 *Peter* as strongly supported, but yet 'not in the Testament.' The Acts, the Gospel, the Preaching, and the Apocalypse of Peter he rejects absolutely, 'because no ecclesiastical writer in ancient times or in our own has made habitual use of the testimonies to be drawn from them.' He then attributes *fourteen* Epistles to St Paul, but notices the doubts as to the authenticity of the *Epistle to the Hebrews* which were still entertained by

The passages in which he treats of the Canon of the New Testament. *H. E.* III. 3.

10—2

148   *THE BIBLE IN THE CHURCH.*

CHAP. VI. some on the authority of the Church of Rome.
A D. 303—340. The mention of St Paul leads to that of Hermas
(Rom. xvi. 14), who was supposed by many to
have been his friend. 'The *Shepherd*,' he says,
'has been gainsayed by some, though it has been
publicly read in the Churches, as most necessary
for those who need elementary instruction in the
faith.' 'The *Acts of Paul* also are not,' he adds,
'indisputably genuine.'

After this Eusebius continues his narrative
to the reign of Trajan, and then while noticing
the last labours of St John, he pauses abruptly
H. E. III. 24. to notice 'the indisputable writings of this apostle also.' First he names his Gospel 'clearly
recognized in all the churches under heaven.'
This leads him to speak of its place as last of
the four, of its relation to the other Gospels, of
the scantiness of the Apostolic writings; he then
adds that 1 *John* is also universally acknowledged; 2, 3 *John* gainsayed; and that 'about
the *Apocalypse* men's opinions are very generally
divided. Though in due course [the authority of]
this book also will be decided by the testimony of
the ancients.'

H. E. III. 25.   Then follows the great passage in which he
gives his general opinion on the whole subject,
only leaving the character of the *Apocalypse* to
be determined by the evidence which he will ad-
duce later. This passage must be given at length.

Acknow-   'Now we have come to this point,' he writes,
ledged Books. 'it seems reasonable that we should give a summary catalogue of the writings of the New Testament which we have indicated. And first then
we must place the holy quaternion of the *Gospels*,
which are followed by the narrative of the *Acts
of the Apostles*. After these we must reckon the

[fourteen] *Epistles of Paul;* and next to them we must ratify the Epistle circulated as the *former of John*, and in like manner that of *Peter*. After these books we must place—if at least such a view seem correct—the *Apocalypse*, the judgments on which we shall set forth in due course. And these are reckoned among the books "acknowledged."

'Among the controverted books which are nevertheless well-known [and used] by most, we class the Epistle circulated under the name of *James*, and that of *Jude*, as well as the second Epistle of *Peter*, and the so-called second and third of *John*, whether they really belong to the Evangelist or possibly to another of the same name.

'We must rank among the spurious the account of the *Acts of Paul*, and the so-called *Shepherd*, and the *Apocalypse of Peter*. And besides these the Epistle circulated under the name of *Barnabas*, and the so-called *Teachings of the Apostles;* and moreover, as I said, the *Apocalypse of John*, if such a view seem correct, which some, as I said, reject, while others reckon it among the books "acknowledged." We may add that some reckoned in this division also the *Gospel according to the Hebrews*, to which those Hebrews who have received [Jesus as] the Christ are especially attached. All these then will belong to the class of "controverted" books.

'It has been necessary for us to extend our catalogue, even to these latter works [in spite of their questionable authority], having distinguished the writings which, according to the tradition of the Church, are true and genuine and universally acknowledged, and the others besides these

CHAP. VI.

A.D. 303—340.

Controverted Books.

Spurious (i.e. Uncanonical) Books

which though they are not in the Testament (Canonical), but in fact controverted, are yet constantly recognized in most of the ecclesiastical writers, that we might be acquainted not only with these but also with the writings brought forward by heretics in the name of the Apostles as containing the Gospels of Peter and Thomas and Matthias and some others, or the Acts of Andrew and John and the other Apostles, which no one in the different successions of ecclesiastical writers has deigned to mention. And further also, the character of the language which varies from the Apostolic spirit, and the sentiment and purpose of their contents, wholly discordant with true orthodoxy, clearly prove that they are forgeries of heretics; whence we must not even class them among the spurious books, but set them aside as every way monstrous and impious.'

A careful examination of the classification here made leaves no doubt that Eusebius divided all the writings which claimed to be apostolical into three principal divisions—the Acknowledged, the Controverted, the Heretical. The terms are used in a modified sense, and must be explained with reference to the immediate purpose of the arrangement. That a book should be 'acknowledged' as Canonical, it was requisite that its authenticity should be undisputed, and that its writer should have been possessed of apostolic authority; if it were supposed to fail in satisfying either of these conditions it was 'controverted,' though it might confessedly satisfy the other; if it failed absolutely either in authenticity or apostolic sanction, then it was 'spurious.'

This definition of the words of Eusebius clears the way to a satisfactory explanation of his judgment. As to the class of 'acknowledged' Books, one remark only is necessary. He speaks generally of '*the* Epistles of Paul,' without noticing the *Epistle to the Hebrews* specially in any place. But both from his general usage and from his former mention of '*the fourteen* Epistles of Paul,' it seems certain that he looked upon it himself as 'acknowledged.' In other words, for him, like Origen, the uncertainty was simply as to 'who wrote it;' but whoever wrote it, he received the book as stamped with the spirit and sanction of the Apostle[1].

CHAP. VI.

A.D. 303—340.

How the *Epistle to the Hebrews* is 'acknowledged.'

The second class of 'controverted' Books includes all those which claiming inspiration or apostolicity had obtained a partial reception in the Church[2]. This class is again subdivided. Some were popularly admitted, though their claims were not beyond question either as to authenticity (2 *Peter*) or as to apostolicity (*James, Jude,* 2, 3 *John*). If 2 *Peter* were written by the author whose name it bore, then it was canonical. On the other hand, it was allowed that *James, Jude,* 2, 3 *John,* were written by men of that name, but it was doubted whether they were Apostles or possessed of Apostolic authority. These formed the first group. They were controverted, but yet used. The second group was made up of books, which, in the opinion of Eusebius, were positively deficient in one or other of the conditions of a

The classification of 'controverted' Books.

---

[1] Such a sense of the word 'acknowledged' is implied also in its application to the *Apocalypse* below.

[2] The *Epistle of Clement*, though used in the Church, made no claims to apostolical authority; and hence, it appears, Eusebius omits to mention it here, though in other places he calls it a 'controverted' book: *H. E.* VI. 13.

152 *THE BIBLE IN THE CHURCH.*

CHAP. VI.
A.D. 303—340.

canonical writing. Two of these still remain, the *Shepherd* and the *Epistle of Barnabas;* the others have been lost, and it is impossible to form any opinion as to their character. With regard to these two, it might have been plausibly urged that if the *Shepherd* was an authentic work of a friend of St Paul, its internal claims to inspiration must be admitted: that if the *Epistle* was by the 'Apostle' then it also was canonical. But Eusebius decided that both were certainly not works of Apostolic men, and therefore, in his sense, spurious.

Acts xiv. 14.

The anomalous position of the *Apocalypse*.

The *Apocalypse* alone remains. The objections to this were based, as we have seen, not on historical data, but on the criticism of its style. If then it were allowed that its style certainly shewed that it was not written by the author of the fourth Gospel, a division of opinion might yet arise. Some, like Dionysius himself, would look upon it as Apostolic in the same sense as the *Epistle to the Hebrews*, and so still call it 'acknowledged:' others would regard the disproof of direct Apostolic authorship as a mark of 'spuriousness.' The peculiarity of the position of the Book followed from the peculiarity of the evidence adduced against its claims. Its authority was questioned from its internal character, and not from the deficiency of external support, as in the case of 2 *Peter*. It could not, therefore, remain in the same group with books of which history was almost silent; and, it must be added, Eusebius himself seems to have been absolutely undecided as to the position in which it should be placed.

Eusebius' quotations of New Testament.

The usage of Eusebius in the quotation of the books of the New Testament generally agrees

THE BIBLE PROSCRIBED AND RESTORED. 153

with his summary judgment which we have just examined. He cites the *Epistle to the Hebrews* constantly, as being substantially St Paul's, though he inclined to the belief that it was actually written by Clement of Rome. He mentions a collection of 'the *seven*, so called, Catholic Epistles,' and constantly quotes *St James*, but appears to make no use of *St Jude*, 2 *Peter*, 2, 3 *John*. The *Apocalypse* he quotes rarely, and simply as the 'Apocalypse of John;' and in one passage in his History he leaves the alternative open, that 'it was seen by the presbyter and not by the Apostle.'

Eusebius has left no express judgment on the contents of the Old Testament. In three places he quotes from Josephus, Melito and Origen, lists of the books (slightly differing) according to the Hebrew Canon. These he calls in the first place 'the Canonical Scriptures[1] of the Old Testament, undisputed among the Hebrews;' and again, 'the acknowledged Scriptures of the Old Testament;' and, lastly, 'the Holy Scriptures of the Old Testament.' In his Chronicle he distinctly separates the *Books of Maccabees* from the 'Divine Scriptures;' and elsewhere mentions *Ecclesiasticus* and *Wisdom* as 'controverted' books. On the other hand, like the older Fathers, he quotes in the same manner as the contents of the Hebrew Canon passages from *Baruch* and *Wisdom*. On the whole, it may be concluded that he regarded the Apocrypha of the Old Testament in the same light as the books in the New Testament, which were 'controverted and yet familiarly used by many.' The books of the Hebrew Canon alone were in his technical language 'acknowledged.'

[1] Literally 'Scriptures in the Testament.'

154   *THE BIBLE IN THE CHURCH.*

CHAP. VI.
A.D. 303—340.

His judgment based on ancient testimony.

One general characteristic of his judgment must not be neglected. It is based expressly on the collective testimony of antiquity expressed in the works of the chief ecclesiastical writers. There was no combined decision of any number of Churches to which he could appeal; no definite catalogue of sacred books of the New Testament supported by anything more than individual authority. According to Eusebius the only method by which the contents of the Bible could be determined was that of a simple historical inquiry into the belief and practice of earlier generations, and this did not appear to him to lead to a certain conclusion in every case. He could not feel, as those of a later age can do, the complete unity and fulness of the New Testament, which had but lately assumed its final shape, nor grasp the real difference between the books of the Hebrew Bible and the later additions to the Alexandrine LXX. in relation to the divine teaching of the Jews. Yet even thus his limited investigation led to results generally identical with those which wider experience has confirmed.

His connexion with Constantine.

The part which Eusebius had to fulfil in regard to the history of the Christian Bible was not limited to the investigation of ancient testimonies. It was to his single judgment that Constantine committed the preparation of fifty copies of Holy Scripture for public use in his new capital. The commission was given when Eusebius had completed his History; and thus his private opinion found a public, and, in virtue of the imperial sanction, an authoritative expression.

General consent on Scripture in the time of Constantine.

It is said that at the time when Constantine's imagination was moved by the sight of the heavenly cross he 'devoted himself to the reading of

THE BIBLE PROSCRIBED AND RESTORED. 155

the divine Scriptures' that he might find there the interpretation of his vision; and in later times he professed the deepest reverence for the Christian 'Law.' At the Council of Nicæa, which he summoned immediately after he became sole Emperor, the Holy Scriptures of the Old and New Testaments were silently admitted on all sides to have a final authority[1]. And no better proof could be wished of the general uniformity of opinion as to the contents and character of the Bible, than that it was not made the subject of discussion in any of the four great Councils[2]. It underlay all controversy as the sure and known source and support of Truth.

CHAP. VI.

A.D. 303—340.

A.D. 325.
A.D. 324.

After the close of the Council, Constantine continued to exercise with no less zeal than before the power with which he felt himself invested as 'bishop in outward matters, appointed by God.' According to Eusebius he 'studied the

Constantine's commission to Eusebius to prepare a Bible for public use.

---

[1] Some of the Arians rejected the *Epistle to the Hebrews*. Too little is known at present of the *Gothic* Version which was made by ULPHILAS (†A.D. 388) to allow of any certain conclusion as to its contents. It is said that it contained 'all the Scriptures except the *Books of Kings*,' which were omitted as being likely to inflame the warlike spirit of the Goths (*Philostorg*. II. 5). The reason alleged seems to be ridiculous, but the fact may be true. Of the Old Testament very scanty fragments remain of *Psalms, Ezra,* and *Nehemiah*. Of the New Testament a large part is preserved; but at present there are no traces of the *Acts*, the *Catholic Epistles*, or the *Apocalypse*. A supposed reference to the *Epistle to the Hebrews*, in a fragment of a Commentary on St John, is somewhat doubtful.

[2] Jerome's statement that "the Synod of Nicæa is said to have reckoned the book of *Judith* in the number of the Sacred Scriptures" (*Præf. in Judith*), can only refer to some use made of the book there, if it be not entirely erroneous.

Bible in his palace,' 'giving himself up to the meditation of the Inspired Oracles,' and persuading 'multitudes to receive rational support for rational souls by divine readings.' It cannot be by a mere figure of rhetoric that the Scriptures are brought thus prominently forward in the record of his life. They doubtless appeared to him as the Code of the Faith which he had adopted, the Law—to use the term which he constantly applies to them—of the imperial religion. The founding of Constantinople furnished him an occasion for giving marked expression to his judgment. It was then that he applied to Eusebius to provide a number of copies of the Bible in a manner suited to the importance of his object. His words are full of interest. 'In the city which bears our name,' he writes, 'by the help of the providence of God our Saviour, a very great multitude of men have attached themselves to the most holy Church. Since everything there is increasing most rapidly, it appears very fitting that more churches should be constructed in the city. Wherefore welcome with all zeal the judgment which we have formed. For it appeared becoming to us to signify to your wisdom that you bid fifty copies of the divine Scriptures (of which you judge the preparation and use to be most necessary for the purpose of the Church) to be written on prepared skins, by skilled scribes who are well acquainted with their craft.' 'For this purpose,' he adds, 'orders have been issued to the governor of the province to furnish everything required for the work'; and authority was given to Eusebius to employ 'two public carriages for the speedy conveyal of the books, when finished, to the Em-

THE BIBLE PROSCRIBED AND RESTORED. 157

peror.' Everything was designed to give importance to the commission. The copies were for the service of the churches of the new capital; they were to be executed with the greatest care; and every part of the work was to be marked by the sanction of imperial authority.

CHAP. VI.
A.D. 303—340

Eusebius simply adds that he fulfilled the charge. How he fulfilled it can only be gathered from what he tells us elsewhere on the subject. Thus we are led by what has been already stated to the belief that the first complete Greek Bible issued by authority for public use contained the Books of the Hebrew Canon in the Old Testament, with the Alexandrine Apocrypha as an appendix. But one Book must be left in a doubtful position. The Catalogues which Eusebius himself quotes and later Greek usage differ as to the canonical authority of *Esther;* and there is nothing to show certainly where Eusebius himself placed it. For the rest, the Constantinopolitan Bible included all the Books of the New Testament which we now receive, with the exception of the *Apocalypse*, which may have been added as an appendix. The 'controverted' Epistles in the New Testament seem to have been arranged with the others, and not separately; but the whole group of the seven *Catholic* Epistles stood after the *Epistles of St Paul*, and not, as in the Alexandrine lists, immediately after the *Acts*. The Old Testament Apocrypha more probably was placed separately, as in the best MSS. of Jerome's Vulgate, and in our own Bible, and not, as in the copies of the Alexandrine LXX., among the 'acknowledged' books according to their contents.

The contents of the Eusebian Bible.

None of the most ancient MSS. present these

No copy at present known.

CHAP. VI.
A.D. 303—340.

characteristics. The attempts to identify any one of the four great copies with the Bible of Eusebius fail at first sight[1]. But though this fact shows how great must have been the perils to which the most jealously-guarded MSS. were exposed, recent discoveries hold out the hope that an original monument of his labours may yet reward the zeal of some future scholar. But whether this be so or not, his work was not without fruit. He furnished a standard which had a powerful influence on those who came after him. The apocryphal books of the Old Testament fell definitely into a second rank in the Greek Church, though they were quoted with respect from time to time, and resumed in the copies of the LXX. the places which they had long held in the old Alexandrine Bible. The difference between the 'controverted' and 'acknowledged' Epistles of the New Testament was done away. Only on the *Apocalypse* there were still doubts: some received and some rejected it. But on this a judgment clear and weighty was soon given, supported by the prescription of primitive tradition.

ATHANASIUS.

†A.D. 373.

In the knowledge of Christian antiquity Eusebius was without a rival among his contemporaries; but there was one among them—ATHANASIUS of Alexandria—far greater in grasp of mind and clearness of conception, who completed as far as his authority reached the work which Eusebius began. It may have been that Athanasius viewed with some jealousy the decisive influence of Eusebius, whose orthodoxy was not beyond suspicion, in such a matter as the deter-

---

[1] See Appendix B.

THE BIBLE PROSCRIBED AND RESTORED. 159

mination of a common Bible, or still more probably he felt that the act required ecclesiastical rather than imperial sanction. At any rate, after the fall of the house of Constantine he availed himself of an opportunity furnished by his position as metropolitan of Egypt to publish a list of the Sacred Scriptures. It had long been the custom of the Bishop of Alexandria to announce by letter to the different churches of his province the date of Easter from year to year, on which the other moveable festivals depended. These Paschal or Festal Letters, as they were called, gradually assumed the character of Pastorals, and were received with great respect. Large extracts from the Festal Letters of Athanasius have been preserved in the original Greek ; and a considerable part of them has been found also in a Syriac translation among the treatises brought from the Nitrian desert. In the 39th, which was written in the year A.D. 365, Athanasius, after contrasting the relation of heretics and true believers towards Holy Scripture, prays his reader to bear with him if he touches on a subject with which they were familiar, and seeks to avert the danger which might arise from the use of apocryphal books. The passage occurs both in the Greek and Syriac texts, and alike from its form and from its substance is of the highest interest. 'As I am about to speak of the [divine Scriptures],' he says, 'I shall use for the support of my boldness the model of the Evangelist Luke, and say as he does, *Forasmuch as* some *have taken in hand to set forth in order* for themselves the so-called Apocrypha, and to mix these with the inspired Scripture *which* we *most surely believe, even as they delivered* it to our

CHAP. VI.

A.D. 303—340.

fathers *which from the beginning were eyewitnesses and ministers of the word; it seemed good to me also*, having been urged by true brethren, and having learnt [the truth] *from the first*, to publish the books which are admitted in the Canon and have been *delivered* to us and are believed to be divine, that if any one has been deceived he may condemn those who led him astray, and he that has remained pure from error may rejoice in being again reminded [of the truth].

The *Old Testament*.

'All the Books then of the Old Testament are in number twenty-two; the number, as I have heard, of the Hebrew letters. In order and name they are as follows: *Genesis...Joshua, Judges, Ruth* (separately)...*Psalms*...then *Isaiah, Jeremiah*, and with him *Baruch, Lamentations* and the *Letter;* and after him *Ezekiel* and *Daniel*...Again, we must not shrink from mentioning the Books of the New Testament, which are these: *Four Gospels*...After these the *Acts of the Apostles* and the so-called *Catholic Epistles* of the Apostles, seven in number, in the following order: *James...Jude*. In addition to these *fourteen Epistles of the Apostle Paul:* to the *Romans...Thessalonians* (1, 2); and that *to the Hebrews* and in succession to *Timothy* (1, 2)... and last one to *Philemon*. And again the *Apocalypse* of John. These are the fountains of salvation, so that he who thirsts may satisfy himself with the oracles in these. In these alone the lesson of piety is proclaimed. Let no one add to these nor take anything from them. It was of these that the Lord reproached the Sadducees, saying: *Ye err, not knowing the Scriptures;* and it was of these He charged the Jews:

The *New Testament*.

Search the Scriptures, for they are they which testify of me. But for the sake of greater accuracy I add this also, writing of necessity, that there are also other [ecclesiastical] books not included in these, nor admitted in the Canon, which have been framed by the fathers to be read for the benefit of those who are just approaching [Christianity], and wish to be instructed in the word of piety: the *Wisdom of Solomon*, and the *Wisdom of Sirach* [i. e. *Ecclesiasticus*], and *Esther* and *Judith* and *Tobias*, and the so-called *Instruction of the Apostles*, and the *Shepherd*. And yet, beloved, neither among those included in the Canon, nor in those which are read, is there anywhere mention of the Apocryphal books; but they are a device of heretics...'

In the New Testament this list gives exactly the books which we receive, in the order in which they stand in the oldest Greek MSS. In the Old Testament it offers several points of difference from our Bibles. *Baruch* and the *Letter* are added to Jeremiah; *Esther* is placed among the Apocrypha; and the *Books of Maccabees* are omitted altogether. It is unnecessary to dwell on these details. Other authorities omit *Esther* from the Old Testament, and include *Baruch* and the *Letter*. The language of Athanasius shows that he had no knowledge of Hebrew, and it is obvious how easily errors might arise as to the exact contents of the Hebrew Bible. At least there can be no doubt that Athanasius intended (like Melito and Origen) to give the Books of the Old Testament which were received by the Jews. In spirit his judgment agrees completely with the judgment of our own Church; and he professes to repeat only what he had himself received. If we revert to the testimony of Origen we shall see that his appeal to antiquity is essentially confirmed, though his wider experience enabled him to speak with greater confidence on some points than Origen could do. The judgment which was originally laid down by the help of almost universal learning was confirmed by the voice of a tried and subtle champion of truth; and we may rejoice that we receive our Christian Bible, with solemn and significant warning, from the hands of that Christian Father first, who, by God's help, saved Christianity from degenerating into mere philosophy or polytheism, in the greatest crisis through which it has ever passed.

CHAPTER VII.

THE AGE OF JEROME AND AUGUSTINE.

Let each man be fully assured in his own mind.
*Let us not judge one another any more: but judge ye
    this rather, that no man put a stumbling-block in
    his brother's way or an occasion of falling.*—Rom.
    xiv. 5, 13.

IT does not fall within our scope to examine in detail the causes which led to the rapid growth of the power of the Latin Churches towards the end of the fourth century. Some of them lie upon the surface. On the one side the characteristic work of the Greek Church was drawing to a close. The broad outlines of 'orthodoxy' were marked out, and already the spirit of the Church was turned with restless subtlety towards those metaphysical speculations which multiplied sects, and at last prepared the way for the future desolation of the East. The unity which Constantine had endeavoured to centre in the control of the imperial supremacy had been rudely broken. Antioch, Alexandria, and Constantinople were rivals for power; and the precedence which was yielded to Constantinople was more than counterbalanced by the influence which a corrupt court exercised upon the Church of the capital. At Rome all was otherwise.

CHAP. VII.
A.D. 340—450.
The growth of the power of the Roman Church.

From the first the Roman Church had chosen 'catholicity' rather than 'orthodoxy' for its symbol; and the time was come when it could exhibit with imposing dignity the framework of that society which embodied the idea. The transference of the seat of government to Constantinople gave free range for the outward extension of an ecclesiastical system which had already caught something of the majesty of Old Rome. The same spirit which had organized the Empire remained to inspire the Church, powerful to subdue and to incorporate all which fell within its reach, slow to innovate but resolute to retain every position which it had once taken. Rome could not abdicate her sovereignty though she might change her throne. It has been said that 'Papal Rome is the ghost of imperial Rome sitting crowned upon the grave thereof.' The saying is as true as it is noble; but there was a time when the monuments of ancient grandeur were falling but not fallen, and the genius of Rome still lingered among them to consecrate her last treasures of law and order to the service of Christianity. It was too at this crisis that the two greatest of the Latin Fathers —wholly different in temper, in genius, in education—were raised up to complete the glory of the Latin churches by adding the distinctions of thought and learning and eloquence to the triumphs of organization. There have been other men in the West with larger hearts, subtler intellects, bolder originality than Jerome and Augustine, but none have ever equalled them in the extent and permanence of their influence. The one gave a Bible to all the Western Churches: the other drew out at length that doctrine of original sin which has lain at the foundation of all Western theology.

Before we consider the history of the Bible in the West at this momentous epoch, we must trace its history yet a little further in the East. There were, as it has been seen, three distinct forms in which the Bible was circulated there shortly after the middle of the fourth century; and each was supported by grave authority. The *Constantinopolitan* Bible, as determined by Eusebius, either omitted the *Apocalypse* altogether, or placed it only in a second rank. The *Alexandrine* Bible, determined by Athanasius, expressly included the *Apocalypse* among the Canonical Scriptures. With regard to the Old Testament, the Constantinopolitan and Alexandrine Bibles were apparently in complete accordance. Eusebius, as far as can be determined, and Athanasius expressly, admitted the Apocrypha of the Old Testament (to which Athanasius added the *Instruction of the Apostles* and the *Shepherd* in the New Testament) as an appendix to the Canonical Scriptures, but denied to them any original or final authority. On the other hand, the *Syrian* Bible, determined by the old translation, differed from both as well in the Old Testament as in the New. This excluded from the New Testament the *Apocalypse* and the Epistles of *St Jude*, 2 *Peter*, and 2, 3 *John;* and gave no place to the Apocrypha of the Old Testament. Thus not one of the Eastern Bibles contained exactly the Books which we receive and those only, though their variations are included within very narrow limits, and the Bible of Athanasius is essentially identical with our own.

The characteristic differences of the Constantinopolitan, Alexandrine and Syrian Bibles, continued to exist for some time in the Canon of Holy Scripture which was generally admitted in the districts with which they were naturally connected. The first was used chiefly in Asia Minor and Palestine: the last at Antioch and in the far East. The Alexandrine Canon was for a time confined to Egypt. The differences which were thus locally sanctioned were not, as will be seen in a later chapter, ever formally discussed or removed. Usage alone in process of time introduced a general uniformity; and in this case, as in all similar divergences of opinion, the broadest range of books was that which was sanctioned by popular consent.

Two Fathers of Asia Minor have left Catalogues of the Books of Holy Scripture. One of these was written by GREGORY of Nazianzus, Bishop of Constantinople. It is in the form of a set of verses, in which metres and quantities are strangely confused. 'In order,' he says, 'that you may not be cheated by strange books...receive, my friend, this my approved (or exact) enumeration.' He then gives a list of the Hebrew Canon of the Old Testament, reckoning twelve Books as historical, five as metrical, and five as prophetical, 'together equal in number to the Hebrew letters;' but in doing this he counts *Ruth* as a distinct Book, and omits *Esther*. In the New Testament he enumerates the four *Gospels*, the *Acts*, fourteen *Epistles of St Paul*, seven *Catholic Epistles;* and then adds, 'You have all [the Books]: if there be any besides these, it is not among the genuine [Books].' The catalogue of AMPHILOCHIUS, Bishop of Iconium, which is often included in the writings of his

THE AGE OF JEROME AND AUGUSTINE. 167

friend Gregory of Nazianzus, is also written in CHAP. VII.
verse, but with greater regularity and correct-
ness than that of Gregory, and not without some A.D. 340—450.
vigour. It is also fuller and more explicit, 'You
may not,' Amphilochius writes, 'safely believe
every book which claims to be Scripture...Some
are of intermediate value, and near (so to speak)
to the words of truth; some, again, are spurious
and very perilous...Therefore I will enumerate
separately the inspired Books...' He then gives a
list of the Books of the Old Testament exactly
the same as that of Gregory; but continues,
'some add *Esther* to these.' The order of the
Books of the New Testament which he gives is
the same as before, but he adds three important
notes to the 'controverted' Books. 'Some affirm,'
he says, 'that the *Epistle to the Hebrews* is spurious, speaking not well, for the grace [i. e. the
revelation which it gives] is genuine.' Further,
'some say that we ought to receive seven *Catholic Epistles*, but others three only, one of
James, one of *Peter* and one of *John*. Some
again include the *Apocalypse* of John [in the
Bible], but the greater number, on the other
hand, say that it is spurious. This,' he concludes,
'will be the most truthful Canon of the Inspired
Scriptures, which if you shall obey you will escape
the snares of the world...'

In both of these Catalogues the influence of The Relation
Eusebius is obvious. The list of Amphilochius is of these Cata-
little more than a rhythmical version of his judg- Eusebius.
ment. With one exception the same points are
left open by both; but Amphilochius reckons the
Epistle of James as an 'acknowledged' Book,
following in this respect the opinion of the Syrian
Churches. On the other hand the definiteness of

the list of Gregory perhaps indicates that it was taken directly from a copy of the Constantinopolitan Bible. The incidental evidence which can be gathered from the writings of Gregory and Amphilochius, and from those of their contemporories GREGORY of Nyssa and his brother BASIL of Cæsarea, adds something to the evidence of the Catalogues. All agree in using the *Epistle to the Hebrews* as essentially St Paul's: all (except Amphilochius) use the *Apocalypse* with marked respect, or as Scripture; but no one of them (as it appears) uses any of the 'controverted' Catholic Epistles except that of *St James* (Gregor. Naz., Basil). On the other hand, several of the books of the Apocrypha are quoted in the same manner as the Canonical books: *Baruch* (Amphilochius, Basil), *Wisdom* (Basil), Additions to *Daniel* (Basil, Gregory of Nazianzus).

The influence of Eusebius was not limited to Asia Minor: it extended naturally also to Palestine. CYRIL, who died Bishop of Jerusalem, has left a series of Instructions designed for the use of those who were being trained in the Christian Faith. The subject of one of these is 'the Divine Scriptures,' in which he defines the extent and the foundation of the Canon, mainly after the model of Eusebius. The need of clear teaching on the Sacred Books seems to have become urgent from the wide circulation of the Apocryphal writings which were brought into use by the Manichees, a supposition which derives some weight from the precision with which Cyril forbids the use of all Books not included in the Canon under any circumstances. 'Learn from the Church,' he says, 'what are the Books of the Old Testament, and what of the New, and I pray

THE AGE OF JEROME AND AUGUSTINE. 169

you read nothing of the Apocryphal books... Read the Divine Scriptures, the twenty-two Books of the Old Testament, which were translated by the seventy-two translators'...' For the translation of the Divine Scriptures which were spoken by the Holy Spirit was accomplished through the Holy Spirit. Read the twenty-two Books which these rendered, but have nothing to do with Apocryphal writings. Study these only with diligence, which also we read with confidence in the Church. The Apostles and the ancient bishops, the heads of the Church who delivered these [to us] were much wiser than thou. Do thou, then, being a child of the Church, not violate her laws.' After this preface Cyril enumerates of the Old Testament twelve historical books—including *Esther*, without remark, and adding *Ruth* to *Judges* as one book—five metrical books, and five books of the Prophets, adding *Baruch* and the *Letter* to *Jeremiah*: of the New Testament the four *Gospels*, the *Acts*, the seven *Catholic Epistles*, and the fourteen *Epistles of St Paul*. 'But let all the rest,' he concludes, ' be placed without [the Canon] in a second rank; and whatever books are not read in churches, neither do thou read in private.'

CHAP. VII.

A.D. 340—450.

The prominence which Cyril gives to the account of the contents of the Bible in his Instructions, no less than the metrical Catalogues of Gregory and Amphilochius, shows the popular interest which was excited in the subject in some provinces about the middle of the fourth century. But as yet no decision had been made by any council or synod upon the Bible. Every one who dealt with the question appealed to tradition, to usage, to antiquity, but not to any definite

The Council of Laodicea.

decree. At last, however, a decree was made upon the Sacred Books at the Synod of Laodicea, a small gathering of clergy from parts of Lydia and Phrygia, which was held about A.D. 363. After other disciplinary ordinances the last Canon runs: 'Psalms composed by private men must not be read in the Church, nor books not admitted into the Canon, but only the Canonical [books] of the New and Old Testaments.' To this decree in the printed editions of the Canons and in most MSS., a list of the Holy Scriptures is added, which is absolutely identical with Cyril's, except as to the position of *Esther* and *Job*, adding *Baruch* and the *Letter* to *Jeremiah*, and omitting the *Apocalypse*. But this list is without doubt a later addition. It is omitted in good Greek MSS., in two distinct Syriac versions, preserved in MSS. of the sixth or seventh century, in one of the two complete Latin versions, and in the oldest digests of the Canons. Yet it was in all probability a very early gloss, derived either directly from Cyril, or from the usage of the Churches which Cyril himself followed.

The authenticity of the list is really a question of very little moment. Even if it were authentic, it could in itself have no binding authority for the Church at large. The Synod was small and (as it seems) unorthodox. But the genuine decree has none the less considerable historical interest. For the first time the Canonical Books of Scripture were invested with a special and exclusive ecclesiastical authority. Cyril, in opposition to Athanasius, had already marked out the same law, though general usage still sanctioned a wider range of ecclesiastical books. The change was called for by the circum-

THE AGE OF JEROME AND AUGUSTINE. 171

stances of the Church; and as the Arian party, CHAP. VII.
of whom the Synod appears to have been com-
posed, were always inclined towards the stricter A.D. 340—450.
view of the Canon, it was natural that they
should touch upon the subject in a series of disciplinary rules. But if the origin of the Laodicene decrees is not above suspicion, they were
fully ratified at a later time by the Eastern
Church at the Quinisextine Council of Constan- A.D. 692.
tinople, and sometimes with the appended list of See Ch. ix.
the sacred books, sometimes without it, passed
into the general code of Christendom.

No special list of the Books of Holy Scripture ii. The
has been given by any Alexandrine writer of the Church of
fourth or fifth centuries in addition to that of Alexandria.
Athanasius. DIDYMUS, who probably wrote be- †c. A.D. 395.
fore Athanasius' Festal Letter was issued, published a commentary on the Seven *Catholic
Epistles*, but especially remarked that 2 *Peter*
'was [accounted] spurious, and not included in
the Testament, though it was publicly read.' The
statement is preserved only in a translation, and,
like the corresponding remark of Eusebius upon
the Epistle of *St James*, probably refers to the
doubts entertained by some as to the Book
and does not express the judgment of Didymus
himself. At least it is evident from the range of
his Commentary that the *seven* Epistles were
popularly reckoned as forming a complete whole;
and he uses the *Second Epistle of Peter* himself
frequently and without reserve. This is also
shewn by the later work of EUTHALIUS, who c. A.D. 450.
published an edition of fourteen *Epistles of
St Paul* and of seven *Catholic Epistles* by the
help of ancient MSS. The incidental quotations
of CYRIL of Alexandria († A.D. 444), ISIDORE

CHAP. VII.
A.D. 340—450.

(† A.D. 440), and MACARIUS († c. A.D. 390) bear witness generally to all the disputed books of the New Testament.

Use of the Apocrypha at Alexandria.

The usage of these later Alexandrine Fathers with regard to the books of the *Apocrypha* agrees with that of Origen and Athanasius. They cite them habitually as Scripture; and though they use them less frequently on the whole than the books of the Hebrew Canon—the references to *Maccabees* and *Judith* are extremely rare—yet in other respects they treat them in the same way as the Canonical Scriptures. *Baruch* and *Wisdom* in especial were placed in practice on the same footing as the undoubted works of Jeremiah and Solomon. To take one Father only, Didymus quotes *Wisdom, Baruch*, the additions to *Daniel*, and *Ecclesiasticus* as Scripture. The example of Athanasius himself shows how this custom must be interpreted.

EPIPHANIUS.
† A.D. 404.

The testimony of EPIPHANIUS, bishop of Constantia (Salamis) in Cyprus, may be connected with that of Athanasius, though the narrow spirit of the mere disciple of tradition had little real sympathy with that of the great teacher whom he professed to follow. Epiphanius has left three partial Catalogues of the Books of the Bible. In these he expressly reckons the Books of the Old Testament as twenty-two (including *Esther*), according to the Hebrew Canon. In one place he adds to Jeremiah 'the *Letters* of Jeremiah and Baruch:' in another he remarks that 'the Letters of Baruch' are not found in the Hebrew Bible. He is equally inconsistent or uncertain with regard to *Wisdom* and *Ecclesiasticus*. 'These,' he says, 'occupy a doubtful place. They are useful, and still they are not reckoned

Hær. VIII. 6.
Hær. LXXVI.
p. 941.
De Pond. et Mens. 4.
Hær. VIII. 6.

De Pond 4.

among the acknowledged Books, nor were they ever placed in the Ark of the Covenant (i. e. received as Scripture by the Jews).' Yet again after enumerating summarily all the Books of the Old and New Testaments, he adds, 'and the *books of Wisdom*, that of Solomon, and of the son of Sirach, and generally all divine writings[1].' It is evident that he wishes to combine the practice of the early Fathers with their direct teaching. He will sacrifice nothing which had even the appearance of authority; and this characteristic of the man gives weight to his repeated statement that the Books of the Old Testament 'were twenty-seven, counted as twenty-two.' The Hebrew Canon was that which he, like all the other Greek Fathers, wished to mark as definitely authoritative; though he admitted to a second place the books which had been sanctioned in some measure by Christian usage[2].

CHAP. VII.
A.D. 340—450.

Hær. p. 941.

---

[1] Augustine (*De Doctr. Christ.* II. 12. See p. 187) distinguishes between 'divine' and 'canonical' writings. The 'canonical' writings are one class only of the 'divine' writings.

[2] It may be well to mark the differences with regard to the Old Testament.

Esther is omitted by *Gregory of Nazianzus, Amphilochius* (doubtfully): is admitted by *Cyril of Jerus.* (*Council of Laodicea*), *Epiphanius.*

Baruch and the *Letter* are admitted by *Cyril of Jerus.* (*Council of Laodicea*), *Epiphanius* (once): *Baruch* is omitted (silently) by *Gregor. Naz., Amphilochius;* and, as not in the Hebrew canon, by *Epiphanius* (once).

But it may be added that the writers who omit *Baruch* also omit *Lamentations,* which was reckoned with it as an appendix to Jeremiah; and there can be little doubt that from a mistake as to the extent of the Hebrew book of *Jeremiah,* dating from the time of Origen (p. 135), *Baruch* and the *Letter* were generally received in the Greek Church in the 4th and 5th

174　　　*THE BIBLE IN THE CHURCH.*

CHAP. VII.

A.D. 340—450.

iii. The Churches of Syria.
† A.D. 407.

Tom. VI. ed. Bened.

The Churches of Antioch and Eastern Syria remained for some time faithful to the Canon of the Peshito at least in the New Testament. In the works of CHRYSOSTOM, a presbyter of Antioch and afterwards patriarch of Constantinople, a *Synopsis of the Old and New Testament* has been preserved which is probably genuine and certainly a Syrian Catalogue of Chrysostom's time. In this the contents of the Old Testament are described somewhat indistinctly. The enumeration of the *historical* books contains only those of the Hebrew Canon (except *Esther*) though reference is made to the Maccabæan war. *Ecclesiasticus* (the Wisdom of Sirach) is added to the moral books; and the *Psalter* is reckoned among the Prophets. In the Synopsis itself, *Esther*, *Tobit*, *Judith*, *Wisdom* and *Ecclesiasticus* are analysed without any note as to their character.

† c. A.D. 458.
A.D. 428.

The order in which the Books of the New Testament are cited is remarkable: the fourteen *Epistles of St Paul*, the four *Gospels*, the *Acts*, and three of the *Catholic Epistles* (i. e. *James*, 1 *Peter*, 1 *John*). The quotations in Chrysostom's voluminous writings confirm the same Canon. He never uses the *Apocalypse*, nor the four *Catholic Epistles* which are omitted in the Peshito. THEODORET also has nowhere quoted these 'controverted' books. THEODORE of Mopsuestia appears to have gone further. He rejected the Epistle of *James ;* and in the Old Testament *Job*, *Canticles* and *Chronicles*. But his judgment is that of an independent critic, and not a record of that of his age and country. The

centuries. Didymus (*De Trin.* I. p. 80) expressly says that the book 'of Jeremiah and Baruch is one.'

evidence of EPHREM SYRUS, deacon at Edessa, 'the prophet of the Syrians,' is unfortunately ambiguous. In his Syriac writings he refers (I believe) once to the *Apocalypse*, and once to 2 *Peter*, from among the books omitted by the Peshito, but in his works, which are preserved only in Greek, he appears to use all the books of our New Testament.

With regard to the Old Testament, the usage of the Syrian fathers coincides with that of the Greek fathers generally. They use the books of the Apocrypha freely, and without distinguishing them from the books of the Hebrew Canon. Thus Chrysostom, to take only one example, quotes passages from *Baruch*, *Ecclesiasticus* and *Wisdom* as Divine Scripture.

One remarkable testimony of Eastern origin yet remains to be noticed. In the *Apostolical Constitutions*, a collection of Ecclesiastical Laws of various dates, which probably assumed its present form in the 5th century, is a description of the celebration of public worship in which the reading of Holy Scripture occupies a prominent place. The passage itself is in all likelihood as old as the third century. When the congregation is gathered in silence, 'Let the Reader,' it is said, 'standing upon some raised place, read the *Books of Moses*, and *Joshua* the son of Naue, the Books of *Judges* and of the *Kings*, the Books of *Chronicles*, and those of the Return [*Ezra, Nehemiah*]: in addition to these the Books of *Job* and of *Solomon* and the Books of the 16 *Prophets*. But as the readings are made two at a time, let another chant the Hymns of *David*, and let the people chant in response the close of the verses. After this let our Acts (*the Acts of the Apostles*, in

CHAP. VII.

A.D. 340—450.
† A.D. 578.

Use of the *Apocrypha*.

The *Apostolical Constitutions*.

Const. Ap. II. 57.

CHAP. VII.
A.D. 340—450.

whose name the passage is written) be read, and the *Epistles of Paul*, our fellow-worker, which he enjoined on the Churches, according to the guidance of the Holy Spirit; and after these books let a deacon or presbyter read the Gospels which we *Matthew* and *John* gave to you, and which the fellow-workers of Paul, *Luke* and *Mark*, having received, left to you. And whenever the Gospel is being read, let all the presbyters and the deacons and all the people stand in complete silence, Deut. xxvii. 9. for it is written, Be silent and hear, O Israel.' Unless the Book of *Esther* be omitted, the Canon of the Old Testament is exactly that of the Jews. In the New Testament the *Catholic Epistles* are probably included in the *Acts*[1]. But however the omission may be explained, the glimpse which is here opened of the Bible in an early Christian gathering is full of interest. Above all, the solemn silence and standing when the Gospel was read— a custom which has descended even to our own times—seems to mark the description as belonging in spirit to the earliest age[2].

---

[1] This opinion is strongly supported by the subscription of a Syrian (Karkaphensian) version, in which at the close of the *Catholic Epistles*, which follow the *Acts*, it is said 'The end of the *Acts*' (Wiseman, *Horæ Syriacæ*, p. 217. See ch. IX).

[2] The List of the Books of the Bible in the 85th of the *Apostolical Canons* was introduced into its present place at a much later date. Yet the List itself is remarkable, and probably Alexandrine in origin. It contains the Books of the Hebrew Canon with *three books of Maccabees* (*Judith* is a later insertion). Besides these, the *Wisdom of Sirach* (*Ecclesiasticus*) is recommended for the instruction of the young. In the New Testament are enumerated 'the four *Gospels*, 14 *Epistles of St Paul*, two of *Peter*, three of *John*, one of *James*, [one of *Jude*]; *two of Clement;* and our (i. e.

THE AGE OF JEROME AND AUGUSTINE. 177

From the East we now turn to the West. It will have been seen that the love of outward order and uniformity which prevailed there, and the tenacity with which the Western Churches held to all which they had once received, had already prepared the way for a great change in the Bible of a large section of Christendom. The old Latin version, which was current in North Africa, was based upon the Alexandrine LXX. and included the Apocrypha as an integral part of Holy Scripture. The use of the same version extended to Spain and Northern Italy; and in the fourth century also to Rome. But as yet no formal decision was made upon the contents of the Bible in the Latin Churches. Usage alone and popular tradition fixed its contents. In the New Testament this continued unfavourable to the Apostolic authority of the *Epistle to the Hebrews*, but the earlier doubts as to the 'controverted' *Catholic Epistles* seem to have been practically set aside after the persecution of Diocletian.

CHAP. VII.
A.D. 370—450.
The Bible of the West.

See p. 130.

The first Italian writer who gives any account of the Canon is PHILASTRIUS, bishop of Brescia. This he does in his 'Treatise on Heresies,' but both the text of his book and the style of its composition are very unsatisfactory. In one place he writes: 'It has been determined by the Apostles and their successors that nothing else ought to be read in the Catholic Church except the *Law* and the *Prophets*, and the *Gospels* and the *Acts of the Apostles*, and thirteen *Epistles of St Paul*,

PHILASTRIUS.
† A.D. 387 (?).

Hær.
LXXXVIII.

the Apostles) *Constitutions* in eight books.... and the *Acts* of the Apostles.' This Canon, together with the Canon of Carthage, was ratified at the Quinisextine Council, and had a powerful influence on many of the Eastern Churches. See Chap. IX.

and seven others, two of *Peter*, three of *John*, one of *Jude*, and one of *James*, which seven are joined with the *Acts*. Secret, i.e. Apocryphal writings, although they ought to be read for moral instruction by the perfect, ought not to be read by all.' In this list, which appears to give the ecclesiastical usage which he followed, no mention is made of the *Epistle to the Hebrews* or the *Apocalypse;* but elsewhere he marks as 'heretics' those who rejected these books; and notices an 'Epistle to the Laodicenes' which was read privately 'by some, but not read in the Church, in which only thirteen Epistles of St Paul were read, and the *Epistle to the Hebrews* sometimes...' The latter book, he adds, was used with reserve on account of its teaching on repentance and the Person of Christ. With regard to the Apocrypha of the Old Testament, he notices that one sect 'used the Book of the Wisdom of Sirach (*Ecclesiasticus*), who wrote after Solomon, that is, after a long interval, a Book of Wisdom;' yet he himself quotes *Wisdom* as the work of 'a prophet.'

RUFFINUS gives a much clearer account of the Canon than his fellow-countryman Philastrius. His experience was much larger. While still young he spent many years at Alexandria and in Palestine, and devoted himself with special zeal to the writings of Origen. After his return to Italy he composed an 'Exposition of the Apostles' Creed' at the request of a bishop Laurentius. In this he treats of the Books of the Bible with singular precision. Having discussed some points in our belief in the Holy Spirit, he continues; 'This then is the Holy Spirit Who inspired the Law and the Prophets in the Old Testament, the Gospels and the Apostles in the New,'—the complete parallelism is worthy of notice—'...and therefore it seems fitting in this place to mark by a clear enumeration what are the Books of the Old and New Testaments, which according to the tradition of the ancients are believed to have been inspired by the Holy Spirit, and delivered to the Churches of Christ, as we have received them from the records of the Fathers.' Then follows a catalogue exactly agreeing with our own, except in order; and he concludes: 'These are the Books which the Fathers included within the Canon, and from which it was their will that the dogmas of our faith should be maintained. Yet it must be known that there are other books which have been called by the ancients not Canonical but Ecclesiastical, that is, the *Wisdom* (as it is called) *of Solomon*, and the other *Wisdom of the Son of Sirach*...The Book of *Tobit* is of the same class, and *Judith*, and the *Book of the Maccabees*. In the New Testament the book which is called the 'Shepherd,' or 'Hermas,' [and] that which is called 'The two ways, or the Judgment of Peter,' [are of the same order]. All which [the Fathers] willed should be read in churches, but not alleged to support any article of faith. The other Scriptures they called apocryphal, and these they did not allow to be read in churches.' The close connexion of this list with that of the Alexandrine Church (Athanasius) is evident at once; and the remarkable order in which Ruffinus arranges the *Catholic Epistles* (*Peter, James, Jude, John*) agrees with that of Origen in a Homily which he translated. His testimony, therefore, is from the East and not from the West, but is full of

180 THE BIBLE IN THE CHURCH.

CHAP. VII.
A.D. 370—450.

interest as marking the growth of the literary influence of the Greek on the Latin Church, and of the division on the Canon between the conservative (African) party, and the critical party of trained scholars.

HILARIUS.
† A.D. 368.

The earliest instance of this influence is offered by HILARY, Bishop of Poitiers, the champion and fellow-confessor of Athanasius, who died in exile in Asia. In the Prologue to his 'Commentary on the Psalms,' in which he is said generally to have followed Origen very closely, he gives a free rendering of the list of the Books of the Old Testament which Eusebius

See p. 135.
Prol. in Ps. § 15.

has preserved from Origen in the original Greek. At the end he remarks: 'Some, however, have thought fit, by the addition of *Tobit* and *Judith*, to reckon twenty-four books, according to the number of the Greek letters; the Roman language [with its alphabet of twenty-three letters] being comprised between the Hebrew and the Greek. Because it is in these three languages especially that the Sacrament of the will of God, and the expectation of the blessed kingdom, is preached.' The passage is interesting and characteristic. The insertion of *Tobit* and *Judith*

See p. 29.

in the place of *Ruth* and *Lamentations* shows the natural introduction of an error into the list from imperfect knowledge; and though the evidence of Hilary cannot be held to possess independent authority, it is at the same time a record of the readiness of the literary chiefs of Western Christendom to abide by the decisions of the Eastern Church on the contents of the Bible.

JEROME (Hieronymus).
A.D. 329—420.

Hilary adopts in France the same standard which Ruffinus adopted in Italy.

But the great representative of Western

THE AGE OF JEROME AND AUGUSTINE. 181

learning, its true head and glory, and the rich CHAP. VII.
source from whom almost all critical knowledge ─────────
of Holy Scripture in the Latin Churches was A.D. 370—450.
drawn for ten centuries, was JEROME (Sophro-
nius Eusebius Hieronymus). Jerome was born at
Stridon in Dalmatia, A.D. 329. After long and
zealous studies in the East and West he went to
Rome in 382, and from the next year to his death
at Bethlehem in 420, devoted himself with concentrated energy to the study of Holy Scripture.
In the course of his labours he revised the Old
Latin Version of the New Testament with the
help of Greek MSS. (383), and also the Old Latin
Version of the Old Testament by the help of the
Greek Versions and the collations of Origen and
the original text, (c. 383 —390). In 391 he began
his new translation of the Old Testament from
the original Hebrew, which was finished about
404. By slow degrees his work, variously modified, became the 'Vulgate,'—the *common* Version—of the Latin Churches; and all the verna-
cular versions of Europe are indebted more or
less to his toil and judgment[1].

Jerome prefaced his great work—the new *The Helmed*
translation of the Old Testament—with what he *Prologue.*
styled 'a Helmed Prologue' (*Prologus Galeatus*)[2],

[1] The 'Gallican' Psalter (one of Jerome's revisions
of the Old Latin) was almost universally substituted
in MSS. of the Vulgate for his Version from the
Hebrew; and many of its characteristic readings are
found in our own Prayer-Book Psalter: *e.g.* i, 5;
vii, 12; xiv, 5—7, 9; xxii, 1; xxix, 1; &c.

[2] The exact meaning of this remarkable phrase
has been variously given; yet it seems tolerably certain that Jerome intended to signify that this Preface
was to be his general apology for limiting his special
work to the books of the Hebrew Canon, a limitation
which would expose him to the assaults of many in
the African Churches. At the close of the Preface, fol-

CHAP. VII. in which he gave an account of the Canonical
Scriptures of the Hebrew Bible. These he enumerates exactly, noticing the double numbering of twenty-two and twenty-four Books, according as *Ruth* and *Lamentations* were reckoned separately, or added to *Judges* and *Jeremiah*, and then adds: 'This Prologue to the Scriptures may suit as a helmed preface to all the Books which we have rendered from Hebrew into Latin, that we may know'—my readers as well as myself—'that whatever [book] is beyond these must be reckoned among the Apocrypha. Therefore the *Wisdom of Solomon*, as it is commonly entitled, and the book of the Son of Sirach [*Ecclesiasticus*] and *Judith* and *Tobias* and the *Shepherd* are not in the Canon.' Jerome, it is clear, deliberately wished to make the formal distinction between the Hebrew Canon and the Apocrypha as clear in the Latin as it was in the Greek Churches. 'We follow,' as he says elsewhere, speaking of the New Testament, 'by no means the custom of this time, but the authority of ancient writers.' Again and again he insists on the difference between the 'canonical' and 'ecclesiastical' books. 'As the Church,' he writes, 'reads the books of *Judith*, and *Tobit* and *Maccabees*, but does not receive them among the Canonical Scriptures, so also it reads *Wisdom* and *Ecclesiasticus* for the edification of the people, not for the authoritative confirmation of doctrine.' At the same time he was careful to explain distinctly that the apocryphal additions to *Esther*, *Daniel* and *Jeremiah* (*Baruch*) had no

A.D. 370—450.

Ep. ad Dard.
129, § 3.

*Pref. ad
Libros Sol.*

lowing out the image, he prays Paula and Eustochium, to whom it was addressed, to 'oppose the shields of their words against the detraction' of his enemies.

THE AGE OF JEROME AND AUGUSTINE. 183

place in the Hebrew Canon, and therefore no claim to be included in the Christian Bible as Canonical Scripture. So strongly did he desire to emphasize the distinction which he drew, that he resolved to 'correct only the Canonical Scriptures,' but afterwards, yielding to the importunity of friends, he made a hasty version of *Tobit* and *Judith*. The rest of the Apocrypha in the modern Vulgate have been added to Jerome's work from the Old Latin.

CHAP. VII.
A.D. 370—450.

But while Jerome thus drew a clear line between the books of the Hebrew Bible and the later additions to it, he still reserved for the Apocrypha an ecclesiastical use, quoting them, as Hilary did before him, with marked respect, and even as 'Scripture.' In this he followed the example of Athanasius, and furnished a rule which it were to be wished that the Western Churches had universally followed.

Jerome's use of the *Apocrypha*.

In the New Testament he accepted the complete Canon of the Greek Church, though he mentions from time to time the doubts which had been entertained as to the 'controverted' books. In his revision the *Epistle to the Hebrews* was still placed after the undoubted Epistles of St Paul; and he appears to have questioned at least its Pauline authorship, though he made no scruple as to its canonical authority. 'If,' he writes, 'the custom of the Latins does not receive it among the Canonical Scriptures, neither do the Greek Churches (using the same freedom) accept the *Apocalypse* of John; and still we accept both, by no means following the custom of this time, but the authority of ancient writers.' The Epistles of *James* and *Jude* were doubted, he says, at first, but in course of time came to

His Canon of the New Testament.

Ep. ad Dard. 129, § 3.

De virr. illustr. 2, 4.

be reckoned among the Holy Scriptures; and according to him the contrast of style between the First and Second Epistles of *St Peter* is to be explained by the supposition that the Apostle employed different 'interpreters' in writing them. In addition to these canonical books Jerome notices many apocryphal writings claiming to be of apostolic origin, but never attributes to them any ecclesiastical authority.

AUGUSTINE (Aurelius Augustinus), in spite of his logical power, his passionate devotion, his moving eloquence, was not endowed with critical sagacity or historical learning. He had very little knowledge of Greek, and fully shared the common prejudices which were entertained against a new translation of the Old Testament from the original Hebrew. His life was spent in action and controversy, and not (like Jerome's) in the student's cell. Born at an inland town of Numidia, in A.D. 354, he had much of the fiery nature of his countryman Tertullian. For some time he was attached to the Manichees, but was converted to the Catholic Church by Ambrose in 387. In 395 he became Bishop of Hippo Regius in North Africa, and died there in 430. The vigour and fulness of his polemical writings, the fearless vigour of his deductions, the symmetry of his doctrinal system, not to speak of his higher graces of faith, spirituality, submission to the Divine Will, made him the evangelical master of the middle ages, and even of our own. His acknowledged claims as a profound reasoner gave him authority even in matters of criticism; and his judgment on the Canon (falling in with popular usage in form though not in spirit) furnished the occasion for the definite equalization of the Apocrypha of the

THE AGE OF JEROME AND AUGUSTINE. 185

Old Testament with the Books of the Hebrew Bible, which was completed by the Council of Trent. CHAP. VII.
A.D. 354—430.

Augustine's attention seems to have been directed towards the attainment of a conciliar determination of the contents of the Bible soon after his conversion. His former connexion with the Manichees, who were especially addicted to the use of 'apocryphal' Gospels and Acts, probably impressed him keenly with the sense of the necessity of some such decision. The wide circulation of the Manichæan books had already moved Cyril of Jerusalem to write upon the subject, and afterwards led the Spanish bishops to seek the assistance of the Roman Church in checking their spread. The fact is important, for it explains the motive which may have led Augustine to hold the distinction between the 'controverted' and 'acknowledged' books of the Old Testament as of comparatively little moment. It might have seemed well to him if both could be placed in a position wholly and for ever separate from the pernicious writings which had been turned to heretical uses. Their mutual relations might be determined when the pressing danger was averted. The motive which led him to seek a determination of the Canon.

The first discussion on the Canon in which Augustine took part was at a Council at Hippo in A.D. 393. The decision which was then made is lost, but the statutes of the Council were revised and confirmed by the Council of Carthage in A.D. 397. In the mean time Augustine wrote his essay, 'On Christian Doctrine,' in which he treats of the Books of Scripture, and the mode in which he handles the subject justifies the The decrees of Hippo.

Augustine's treatise 'On Christian Doctrine.'

view which has been given of his purpose. 'He will be,' he says, 'the wisest student of the divine Scriptures who shall have first read and learnt... those which are called canonical. For the rest he will read with greater security when furnished with faith in the truth, [as there is danger] lest they preoccupy a mind as yet unstable, and instil some ideas contrary to sound understanding by perilous fictions and fancies. In [judging of] the Canonical Scriptures let him follow the authority of as many Catholic Churches as possible, among which assuredly are those [like Rome] which were deemed worthy to be apostolical sees, and to have Epistles addressed to them. He will therefore hold this course in [judging of] the Canonical Scriptures, that he prefer those which are received by all Catholic Churches to those which some do not receive; of those again which are not received by all, those which more and more influential Churches receive to those which are held by Churches fewer in number or inferior in authority. If, however, he find some writings maintained by more Churches, others by more influential Churches (though this case can hardly be realized), I fancy that they must be held to be of equal authority. The whole Canon of Scriptures in which we say that this question turns is made up of these books: *Genesis*...[*Joshua* the son of] Naue...*Chronicles; Job, Tobias, Esther, Judith, Maccabees* (2), *Ezra* (2)...; then the prophets, among which is the *Psalter* of David, three books of Solomon. For those two books, which are inscribed *Wisdom* and *Ecclesiasticus*, are said to be Solomon's from a certain resemblance [which they bear to his writings], for it is a most certain tradition that Jesus the Son of Sirach wrote them[1]; and still since they have been deemed worthy to be received into authority, they must be reckoned among the prophetic books. The remaining books are of those who are properly called prophets...In these forty-four books the authority of the Old Testament is closed. Of the New Testament, four *Gospels*... fourteen *Epistles of St Paul*...(that to the *Hebrews* last), *Peter* (2), *John* (3), *Jude, James, Acts, Apocalypse*. In all these books those who fear God and cherish humble piety seek the will of God.'

CHAP. VII.
A.D. 354—430.

The whole tone of the passage shows that he was contemplating a definite danger from apocryphal books used by heretics, and other religious writings claiming to be of authority, which he called generally 'divine Scriptures,' and distinguishes from 'canonical Scriptures.' His object was to mark distinctly those books which had any ecclesiastical authority. The authority itself was admitted to vary in an indefinite degree. In accordance with the liberty which he thus gave, Augustine himself admitted a distinction between the Hebrew Canon and the Apocrypha. In one place he even limited the term '*Canonical*' in its strict sense to the Books which were received by the Jews. The Jews, he says frequently, are our librarians, our witnesses. He allowed that objections might fairly be urged to passages quoted from *Wisdom* and *Ecclesiasticus* in support of doctrine, as the books were not of unquestioned authority, though long custom had entitled them to respect. When the

The spirit of Augustine's judgment.

Comp. p. 173, n. 1.

De Civ. Dei, XVIII. 36.

---

[1] Augustine in his 'Retractationes' corrects this strange mistake.

CHAP. VII.
A.D. 354—430.

De Civ. Dei, l. c.

The decree of Carthage.

Can. 39 (47).

Donatists urged a passage from 2 *Maccabees* in defence of suicide, he disparaged their proof by showing that the book was not received into the Hebrew Canon to which Christ bore witness, though it had 'been received by the Church not unprofitably, provided it were read or heard judiciously...' 'These books (the *Maccabees*),' he elsewhere says, 'the Church, and not the Jews, holds for canonical on account of the marvellous sufferings of some martyrs which they relate;' and in the context distinguishes them from the 'Holy Scriptures.'

So far the teaching of Augustine, if interpreted by his practice, does not differ essentially from that of Jerome. But his Canon was soon separated from his gloss upon it. At the Council of Carthage, A.D. 397, at which Augustine was present, a decree was ratified which determined the list of 'Canonical Scriptures' in accordance with his opinion. ['It is decreed] that nothing except the Canonical Scriptures be read in the Church under the name of divine Scriptures. The Canonical Scriptures are *Genesis* .... *five* books of Solomon [*Proverbs, Ecclesiastes, Canticles, Wisdom, Ecclesiasticus*] .... *Ezechiel, Tobias, Judith, Esther, Esdras* (2), [*Maccabees*, 2][1]. Of the New Testament the four *Gospels, Acts*, thirteen *Epistles of St Paul*, the Epistle of the same to the *Hebrews, Peter* (2), *John* (3), *James, Jude, Apocalypse.* Note. Let the transpontine (Roman) Church be consulted about the confirmation of that Canon. Also let it be allowed that the Passions of Martyrs be read on the celebration of their anniversaries.'

[1] The two books of *Maccabees* are wanting in many authorities.

THE AGE OF JEROME AND AUGUSTINE. 189

It will be observed that the object of this decree was to limit the ecclesiastical use of books, and that it contains nothing formally to exclude the liberty for which Augustine pleaded. Indeed, as the council was ruled by his influence, he probably contemplated such an interpretation of the decree. But in this he forgot the natural inaptitude of men for critical labour. The books were all placed together without distinction, and it was inevitable that they should all be considered popularly as exactly equal in authority.

The confirmation which was sought from Rome seems not to have been obtained. At another Council of Carthage in 419, at which also Augustine presided, the decree was renewed[1], and again a note added: 'Let this also be notified to our brother and fellow-priest Boniface, Bishop of Rome, or to other bishops of those parts, for the purpose of confirming that Canon.' It does not, however, appear that anything more was done. Yet already a revolution was wrought. The question of the Canon had been taken, so to speak, out of the domain of criticism. A provincial assembly had decided upon it, as a subject to be settled by the authority of the Christian Church. And from this time no new element was introduced into the History of the Bible till the Council of Trent. As a general rule popular usage and the judgment of scholars were at variance in the West till the era of the Reformation. Usage received

---

[1] In this revised decree one significant change was made. In place of the strange circumlocution by which the *Epistle to the Hebrews* is described separately as St Paul's, the Epistles of St Paul are reckoned together as *fourteen*.

190 *THE BIBLE IN THE CHURCH.*

CHAP. VII.
A.D. 354—430.

all the books of the enlarged Canon more and more generally as equal in all respects; learned tradition kept alive the distinction between the Hebrew Canon and the Apocrypha which had been drawn by Jerome.

The Bibles of the West in the 5th century.

The decree of Carthage was framed with reference to the Old Latin Version. In 397 Jerome's New Version was not finished, much less generally received. But from the beginning of the fifth century three different Bibles were circulated in the West, of which no one had paramount authority. The first was the Old Latin Bible, containing all the books included in Augustine's Canon, and often 2 *Esdras* and the *Shepherd:* the second, Jerome's New Translation of the Old Testament according to the Hebrew Canon, with his revised New Testament; the third was Jerome's Translation (except the Psalter) of the Hebrew Canon, with the addition of the Apocrypha, arranged in the manner of the Old Bible. The Old Bible gradually fell into disuse. No complete MS. of it has yet been discovered; but in England and Ireland it was found till the eighth and ninth centuries, and probably later. Manuscripts of Jerome's Bible, to which the books of the Apocrypha are sometimes added as an appendix, or a separate section, are rare. From the ninth century the mixed Bible was almost universally current, and 2 *Esdras*, which was not included in Augustine's Canon, was very frequently added to the Apocrypha of the Old Testament, and the Epistle to the Laodicenes to the New Testament. How widely these differences extended will be seen in the next Chapter.

CHAPTER VIII.

THE BIBLE OF THE MIDDLE AGES IN THE WEST.

The kingdom of heaven is like unto leaven, which a woman took, and hid in three measures of meal till it was all leavened.—Matt. xiii. 33.

AFTER the death of Jerome the study of Greek rapidly declined in the West. A few scholars, especially in the great Irish monasteries, still kept alive a faint knowledge of the language, and retained at the same time something of that generous freedom which it seems to confer as its constant gift; but the intellectual commerce of the East and West was broken. The Latin Churches were speedily left alone to do their appointed work, to preserve civilization from the wreck of the Roman Empire; to subdue new races; to mould a Christian society; to vindicate the majesty of Divine Law in the face of barbarous despotism; to witness to the reality of the eternal and the unseen in the face of rude passion and brute force. It is no part of our object to discuss how the work was performed, where it failed, what it accomplished. Enough was done to form the sure basis of our modern life: enough was left undone to call for a Reformation, when Greece again claimed her

CHAP. VIII.

The work and character of the Western Churches in the Middle Ages.

intellectual sovereignty. But it is necessary to mark distinctly the general character of the work of the Western Churches from the sixth to the fifteenth century, that it may be seen why all original investigation of the Bible would have been well nigh impossible in that period. It was not a time for historical criticism, but for law and discipline and logical analysis. Men were content to receive without question 'the books which the authority of the Catholic Church delivered.' Scholarship very rarely amounted to more than the quotation or adaptation of a note of Jerome on the Hebrew or Greek text. Verbal interpretation, with very rare exceptions, was the mere reproduction of opinions already recorded. The brief critical commentaries (*Correctoria*) which began to be written in the twelfth century were almost exclusively made up of old materials. Thus the history of the Bible till the fifteenth century is the history of a tradition, or rather of a tradition in conflict with usage. Its interest lies in the distinctness with which the Hieronymian Canon was maintained by all the greatest teachers against the (supposed) authority of the papal decretals and common practice.

For the sake of clearness it will be convenient to take each division of the Western Church separately; and for the present the Apocrypha of the Old Testament alone will claim our attention. The New Testament was received by all in its present shape. The last trace of any division of opinion upon it is found in a decree of the fourth Council of Toledo (632) which forbade under pain of excommunication the rejection of the *Apocalypse*, or the refusal to read it in the public service in due course.

THE BIBLE OF THE MIDDLE AGES. 193

SECT. I. *The Church of North Africa.* CHAP. VIII.

The dissensions by which the African Church was torn during the time of Augustine were multiplied afterwards by the introduction of new elements of strife. To the fierceness of the Donatist schism was added the equal fierceness of an Arian controversy. Christianity was almost exhausted by the conflicts through which it passed, and when the Arabian invaders appeared, the oldest Latin Churches—the Churches of Tertullian and Cyprian—fell helplessly before the concentrated power of Islam.

The fall of the African Churches.

Yet the meagre remnants of later literature show that the decree of Carthage was not held to be binding even in Africa, so far at least as it has been taken to affirm the absolute equality of the books which it pronounced to be 'canonical.' PRIMASIUS, Bishop of Adrumetum, repeats the mystical interpretation which Jerome attached to the twenty-four wings of the four living creatures of the Apocalypse, and the twenty-four elders round the throne of God. 'They are,' he says, 'the books of the Old Testament which we receive of that number as possessing canonical authority.' Another contemporary African bishop, Junilius, diverges yet further from the letter of the Carthaginian Canon, though, in point of fact, he only carries out in detail the theory of Augustine, by distinguishing books as possessed of 'complete' and 'intermediate' authority, according as they were severally received by all or very many. But in doing this he follows a very remarkable tradition. He divides all the books of the Bible into books of history, prophecy, proverbs, and simple doctrine. In history

PRIMASIUS. *c.* A.D. 550.

In Apoc. 4.

JUNILIUS. *c.* A.D. 550.

13

CHAP. VIII.

De part. legis, I. 3—7.

he reckons the *Pentateuch, Joshua, Judges, Ruth, Samuel* (2), *Kings* (2), and the four *Gospels* and the *Acts*, as of 'perfect' authority; *Chronicles* (2), *Job, Ezra* (2), *Judith, Esther, Maccabees* (2), as of 'intermediate' authority. 'They are not,' he says, 'included among the Canonical Scriptures, because they were received among the Hebrews only in a secondary rank' (such appears to be his meaning), 'as Jerome and others testify.' In prophecy, *Psalms* and the sixteen prophets are of perfect authority. 'As to the *Apocalypse*, there are,' he adds, 'great doubts in the East.' In proverbs, the *Proverbs* of Solomon and *Ecclesiasticus* are of perfect authority, 'to which some join *Wisdom* and *Canticles*.' In simple doctrine, 'sixteen are canonical, *Ecclesiastes*, fourteen *Epistles of St Paul*, 1 *Peter*, 1 *John*. Very many add five others which are called "Canonical Epistles of the Apostles," *James*, 2 *Peter*, *Jude*, 2, 3 *John*[1].' This, he says, was the judgment of the teachers of Nisibis, where biblical criticism was made a subject of professed study, like rhetoric; and this judgment he feels himself free to adopt and promulgate among his countrymen. No other proof is needed to show that a distinction in authority between the 'Canonical' Scriptures (improperly so called) was not supposed in his time to be excluded by the decision of the Council of Carthage.

Sect. II. *The Churches of Italy.*

The decretal of INNOCENT I.

The earliest alleged judgment of the Roman Church upon the Canon of Scripture is found in

[1] *Tobit* is omitted entirely. It seems difficult to believe that the list is free from corruptions.

THE BIBLE OF THE MIDDLE AGES.

a letter of INNOCENT I. addressed to Exsuperius, CHAP. VIII.
Bishop of Toulouse, in A.D. 405. Among other
questions, of a very miscellaneous character, Exsuperius is said to have enquired of Innocent
what books were to be received in the Canon.
In reply Innocent gives a list identical in contents with that of the Council of Carthage, but
differing in the arrangement of the books. In
addition to this there is a second papal list attributed most commonly to GELASIUS, who was The decretal
pope A.D. 492—496, and in other forms to DA- of GELASIUS.
MASUS (A.D. 366—384), and HORMISDAS (A.D. 514—
523). This list also includes the Apocrypha
(with some variations in different copies) among
the books of the Old Testament.

But it must be admitted that both these lists
are open to the gravest suspicion. It is impossible to point out in detail here the grounds on
which they appear to belong to a later age. It
must be enough to notice that the lists themselves are African, and not Italian, in form,— See p. 197.
that they were unknown to Cassiodorus, who
carefully collected the different lists of Holy
Scripture current in his time, and at a still
later time to Isidore of Seville,—that the text
of the Gelasian list varies considerably in different copies, and in such a way as to indicate that
the variations were not derived from one original. The earliest historical traces of the decretals of which they form a part are found in the
eighth century[1]. The letter of Innocent was sent
to Charlemagne in A.D. 774 by Hadrian I. in the

[1] The letter of Innocent is found in the collection
of Decretals of the Popes attributed to Dionysius
Exiguus (c. A.D. 500); but this collection is very different in character from Dionysius' genuine collection

196 *THE BIBLE IN THE CHURCH.*

CHAP. VIII. Code of Ecclesiastical Law, and from that time it exercised some influence upon the judgment of the Church. The list of the Canonical Books in the decree of Gelasius does not distinctly appear till about the tenth century; and even in later times was comparatively little known.

These lists regard only ecclesiastical use.

But however interesting the question of the authenticity of these lists may be in a critical aspect, it has little bearing on the history of the Canon in the strictest sense. Both lists simply repeat the decision at Carthage, and determine the Ecclesiastical Canon, the books, that is, which might be publicly used in the Church services. They do not touch upon the character of the books as sources of dogmatic teaching, and are in fact perfectly reconcileable with the more exact judgment of Jerome and the Eastern Churches on their doctrinal authority. The ecclesiastical use was practically the matter of chief moment from the sixth to the twelfth century; and a remarkable monument of the rapidity with which it prevailed over the critical arrangement of the books of the Old Testament is found in the oldest and most precious MS. of the Vulgate. This MS., known as the *Codex Amiatinus*, was written *c.* A.D. 541, about a hundred and thirty-five years after Jerome's version was completed, and in it the books of the Hebrew Canon (in Jerome's translation) are partially mixed with the books of the Apocrypha; and the compound book is called by Jerome's name[1].

Codex Amiatinus.

A yet more signal proof of the indifference

of Conciliar Canons, and cannot be accepted as authentic without further examination. The biblical catalogue of Gelasius is not found in the collection.

[1] See Appendix B.

THE BIBLE OF THE MIDDLE AGES.

with which the question of the Canon was viewed, CHAP. VIII.
apart from its ecclesiastical value, is given by
the writings of CASSIODORUS. This distinguished CASSIODORUS
statesman and scholar, after enjoying the highest †*c.* A.D 565.
civil honours under Theodoric and his immediate
successors, retired in A.D. 537 to a monastery
which he founded in Calabria, and devoted himself to literary labour with the object of raising
the character of the clergy of Italy. Among
other works designed for this end he wrote
(*c.* A.D. 556) an 'Introduction to the Study of
Holy Scripture,' in which he gives a threefold
enumeration of the sacred books, first according *Instit. ad div.*
to Jerome, next according to Augustine, and *lect.* 11—14.
lastly according to 'the old translation and the
Septuagint.' The first list is of course confined
to the books of the Hebrew Canon and the books
of the New Testament as they are commonly
received. The Apocrypha are passed over in
silence. The second list is substantially identical
with that already quoted from Augustine, with
some differences in order. The third gives the
Augustinian Canon of the Old Testament, but
differs widely from Augustine in the New Testament. In this it reckons four *Gospels*, the *Acts*,
the (1) Epistle of *Peter* 'to the Gentiles,' the
Epistle of *James*, the 1 Epistle of *John* 'to the
Parthians,' fourteen Epistles of Paul, and the
Apocalypse[1]. But though Cassiodorus records
these wide differences of opinion both in the Old
and New Testaments, he does not dwell upon
them for a moment. The question of the Canon
was for him an open question, and he nowhere

[1] In the editions the Epistle of *Jude* is added, but
this is omitted in all the MSS. (four) which I have
examined.

indicates that it had been made the subject of any final and binding decision at Rome.

Gregory the Great.
† A.D. 604.

The same conclusion may be drawn from the language of GREGORY the Great, who apologises for quoting a passage from 1 *Maccabees* on the ground that the book was 'put forth for the edification of the Church, though it was not canonical.' It is evident that he could not have spoken in these terms if he had been acquainted with the decretals of Innocent and Gelasius, or at least if he had placed that construction upon them which was enforced afterwards.

In Job. c. xxi. § 34.

Later Italian writers contribute little to the history of the Canon, but that little tends to show that the critical side of the question was still open within certain limits, though the ecclesiastical usage was fixed. Thus ANASTASIUS, the 'Librarian' of the Roman Church, when he translated into Latin the Ecclesiastical History of Nicephorus, gave without question or comment the remarkable list of the books of Holy Scripture which it contains, though this excludes the *Apocrypha* and *Esther* from the Old Testament, and the *Apocalypse* from the New Testament. GRATIAN in his collection of Decretals (A.D. 1151) gives the catalogues of Innocent and Carthage, but not that of Laodicea, nor the Biblical Catalogue of Gelasius. THOMAS AQUINAS recognizes the doubts which attach to the authority of *Ecclesiasticus*, and appears to exclude *Wisdom* definitely from the Canonical Scriptures. JOHANNES BALBUS of Genoa, in his *Catholicon*, a Latin Glossary, gives as a definition of an 'apocryphal' book in a good sense (with a direct reference to Jerome) 'a book whose author is unknown, but whose truth is patent, which the

Anastasius Biblioth.
† c. A.D. 880.

See Ch. IX.

GRATIAN.

THOMAS AQUINAS.
† A.D. 1274.

JOHANNES GENUENSIS.
c. A.D. 1280.

Church receives for instruction of manners and not for the proof of faith;' and this definition was frequently quoted from him in later times. Among others ANTONINUS, Archbishop of Florence, makes use of the definition, and affirms in the plainest manner the judgment of Jerome.

On the other hand is alleged a decree of the *Council of Florence*, which was held in A.D. 1439 for the purpose of effecting a union between the Greek and Latin Churches, in which the books of the Old and New Testament, 'received and venerated' by 'the Holy Roman Church,' are enumerated after the order of the common copies of the Vulgate and Augustine, the Apocrypha being inserted among the other Scriptures. But there is not the slightest evidence to show that this list was the result of any joint discussion of the question at the Council, or that it was ratified by the Council in any way. Even from the form in which it is written it appears clear that it emanated directly from the pope Eugenius IV., and was a mere repetition of the earlier lists of Innocent and Gelasius, which in his time were generally received as authentic.

CHAP. VIII.

ANTONINUS FLORENT. c. A.D. 1460.

The decree of the *Council of Florence*.

SECT. III. *The Church of Spain.*

The question of the Canon continued to be of considerable moment in Spain till the final conversion of the Goths to the Catholic faith in A.D. 589. During the fifth century the Priscillianists, following in this the example of the Gnostics and Manichees, from whom they derived much of their doctrine, had introduced a vast multitude of apocryphal writings into common use, which usurped the place of the Scriptures. To collect and destroy these was one of the

The condition of Spain in the 6th century.

200   *THE BIBLE IN THE CHURCH.*

CHAP. VIII. chief cares of the orthodox bishops. The Goths, again, as Arians probably rejected the *Epistle to the Hebrews* and the *Apocalypse* no less than the *Apocrypha* of the Old Testament. On their conversion they bound themselves to submit to the decision of the papal rescripts generally, and so also on the subject of the Holy Scriptures.

The decretal of *Hormisdas.* See p. 195.
It is to this concession that the origin of the peculiar recension of the Gelasian decree which bears the name of Hormisdas, Bishop of Rome 514—523, must be attributed. The list of 'Books to be received and not to be received,' which seems to have been the genuine substance of the earlier recensions of the decree, is in this case prefaced with a list of the Books of Scriptures, and the decree thus supplemented appears to have been addressed to Spain. The Books of the Bible are given according to the enlarged Canon

† A.D. 636. of Augustine. The same Canon is given by ISIDORE of Seville, who follows Augustine expressly in dealing with the Old Testament Apocrypha. 'These which constitute a fourth class with us,' he says, 'are not in the Hebrew Canon.' 'The Hebrews do not receive them, but the Church reckons them among the Canonical Scriptures.' Yet elsewhere he speaks of Ezra arranging 'the whole of the Old Testament in twenty-two Books;' and says that 'the edition of Jerome' (which properly included only the Books of the Hebrew Canon) 'was generally used by all the Churches[1].'

† A.D. 657.
† A.D. 667.
The Augustinian Canon is also given by EUGENIUS, Bishop of Toledo, and HILDEFONSUS his

[1] Alcuin does not hesitate to quote Isidore (though, as it seems, unfairly) as agreeing with Jerome in regard to the inferior authority of *Ecclesiasticus.* Compare p. 202.

successor. The latter simply transcribes Augustine's words, with his explanation of the unequal authority of different books.

The connexion of Africa and Spain.

This close adherence of the early Spanish Church to the opinion of Augustine is of interest and importance as showing its intimate connexion with the Church of North Africa. Not only were the churches closely united by language, by feeling and by history, but even the circumstances under which the canonical contents of the Bible were determined in both were the same. Augustine, as we have seen, embodied the custom and tradition of the old Latin Churches in a decree directed to meet a special danger from the wide use of Apocryphal books. The same danger existed in Spain, and the same decision was adopted there. But the decision in both cases was not absolute, but relative. The decree separated all the books which it enumerated for exclusive ecclesiastical use, but left the question of their equality untouched.

The judgment of the later Spanish Church. A.D. 1450. Quoted by Hody, p. 659

In the later Spanish Church the judgment of Jerome was expressly maintained. One example will suffice. ALPHONSUS TOSTATUS, Bishop of Avila, 'the marvel of the world' for his learning, discusses the authority of the Apocrypha at length. 'They are reckoned,' he states, 'among the books of Holy Scripture, but set without the Canon.' ' No one of them, even though they are read among the other books of the Bible, and read in the Church, is of so great authority that the Church argues from it to maintain any truth.' The same, we shall see afterwards, was the opinion of a yet greater man, Cardinal Ximenes, to *Chap. x.* whom belonged the glory of first printing the complete Bible in the original languages.

Sect. IV. *The Transalpine Churches.*

The French Church.
p. 187.

Aug. *Ep.* ccxxvi.

CHARLE-MAGNE.

ALCUIN.
† A.D. 804.

c. *Elipand.* i. 18, p. 883.

c. A.D. 802.

The Church of Spain was originally connected with Africa, that of France was connected with Asia Minor. Thus we have already seen that French divines demurred to receiving a passage from *Wisdom* quoted by Augustine 'as not canonical,' while Hilary reproduced Origen's judgment on the Old Testament. But the development of the national Church was checked as rapidly by invasion and war in France as in Britain. When order was at length restored to the desolated provinces, CHARLEMAGNE fully recognized his ecclesiastical allegiance to the see of Rome; and the code which he established at Aix for the government of the Church was moulded in a great measure upon that which he received from pope Hadrian. It was enjoined in this, that 'the canonical books only be read in the Church;' but it appears that no definite list of these was given, though in the editions the list of *Laodicea* is added.

ALCUIN, a British scholar, the pupil of Bede, was the chief literary adviser of Charlemagne. In controversy with a Spanish bishop he distinctly affirmed (on the authority of Jerome and Isidore) that *Ecclesiasticus* was a 'doubtful Scripture,' and not to be alleged for the proof of doctrine. But in common practice he suffered the ordinary ecclesiastical usage to remain unchanged. Towards the close of his life he was commissioned by Charlemagne to undertake a revision of the Latin Bible for public use. The simultaneous use of the old Latin and Jerome's new Version had led to great corruption of the text. Alcuin restored the original readings of

Jerome in a great measure in the books which CHAP. VIII.
he had translated or corrected, but he made no
endeavour to separate the Apocrypha as Jerome
had done. Several magnificent MSS. remain
which claim to be directly derived from Alcuin's
own revision. One of the finest of these (known
as 'Charlemagne's Bible') is among the chief or-
naments of the Library of the British Museum;
and it is a singular proof of the small interest
which attached in the ninth century to the exactness of the Canon, that it contains the Apo- See p. 209.
cryphal *Letter to the Laodicenes* as a fifteenth
letter of St Paul.

Elsewhere there are abundant proofs of the
uncertainty which prevailed as to the exact contents of the Bible. The Augustinian Canon is
confirmed for ecclesiastical purposes by RABANUS † A.D. 856.
MAURUS, who transcribes Isidore, and by IVO, † A.D. 1115.
Bishop of Chartres, who follows the list added
to the decretal of Gelasius. PETRUS DE RIGA c. A.D. 1170.
in his metrical paraphrase of Scripture uses the Hody, p. 655.
books of the Apocrypha, but distinguishes them
from the twenty-four books of the Hebrew Canon; yet though they are distinguished, he says,
'the usage of the Church declares them authentic.' This wavering opinion is illustrated by the
language of HUGO DE S. CARO, who gives a metri- † A.D. 1260.
cal catalogue of the books of the Hebrew Bible, Hody, p. 656.
in which 'the whole ancient Law is completely
contained,' and then adds the Apocrypha, according to the enumeration of Jerome. 'These
books,' he continues, 'because they are doubtful
are not reckoned in the Canon; but because their
strain is true the Church receives them.'

Meanwhile there was a great increase of
learning, if not of historical criticism, in Europe,

consequent upon that intellectual impulse from the East, which found its characteristic expression in Scholasticism. One result of this is seen in the growing clearness of the teaching of the most celebrated French doctors on the Canon. RADULPHUS FLAVIACENSIS expressly separates *Tobit, Judith* and *Maccabees* from the other historical books of the Bible. 'Although they are read,' he says, 'for the instruction of the Church, yet they have not perfect authority.' PETER of Clugny in a controversial passage enumerates all the books of the Hebrew Bible as necessary to be received and of equal authority. He then adds, 'After these authentic books of Holy Scripture there remain six books which I must still mention, *Wisdom, Ecclesiasticus, Tobit, Judith, Maccabees* (2), which, although they have not been able to reach the sublime dignity of the preceding Books, yet on account of their praiseworthy and very necessary teaching, have been held worthy to be received by the Church.' HUGO DE S. VICTORE[1] is even more decided. After

---

[1] The testimony of Hugo de S. Victore is peculiarly interesting from the form in which it is given. He follows Jerome in dividing the Scriptures of the Old Testament into three classes; but he evidently regards the classes as indicating a difference of rank as well as a difference of character in the books themselves. The first class (Ordo) contains the *Pentateuch;* the second the *Prophets;* the third the *Hagiographa*. Hugo then applies the same arrangement to the New Testament. The first class includes the four *Gospels;* the second class the *Acts*, the *Pauline Epistles*, the *Catholic Epistles*, the *Apocalypse* ('also four books'); the third class, the Decretals in the first place, and then, in the second place, the writings of the Fathers; 'but,' he adds, 'these writings of Fathers are not reckoned in the text of Divine Scriptures; since in the Old Testament (as we have said) there are certain

enumerating the twenty-two Books, as Jerome does, he subjoins the six Apocrypha, with the note that these 'are read, but not reckoned in the Canon;' and in a later passage of the context he appears to place them in the same rank with the decretals and the works of the Fathers. It is needless to quote at length the evidence of RUPERT, Abbot of Deutz († A.D. 1135), of JOHN BELETH of Paris (c. A.D. 1162), of PETRUS COMESTOR of Troyes († A.D. 1198), to the same effect. It is more worthy of notice that HONORIUS of Autun (c. A.D. 1130) repeats the old ecclesiastical Canon (of Augustine) with some singular criticisms, describing the books as 'those to be read in the sacred offices[1].'

The 'Ordinary Gloss,' a brief marginal or interlinear commentary on the Bible, dates probably, for the most part, from the twelfth century, though parts of it are much earlier. In

The Ordinary Gloss.

books which are not written in the Canon, and still are read, as the *Wisdom of Solomon*, and the rest.' Thus he appears to wish to make a complete parallel between the three classes in the two Testaments, adding the Apocrypha to the Old Testament and the patristic writings to the New Testament as appendices. But still, in conclusion, he reckons the 'whole body of Scripture as consisting properly of thirty books, twenty-two of the Old Testament, and eight of the New Testament. The other writings being, as it were, added and flowing from these.'

How completely the papal decretals were placed by the Canonists on the same footing with Scripture, may be seen from the heading of Gratian, *Part* I. *Distinct.* 19, *c.* 6. "The Decretal Epistles are reckoned among the Canonical Scriptures." Compare p. 222, *n.*

[1] In a Gallican service-book (Hody, *Col.* 74) a list of the canonical books is given in which 'the book of the Sacraments' (that is probably the selections of Scripture used in the offices) is reckoned among them.

CHAP. VIII.

this notes are added to *Judith*, *Tobit*, and *Maccabees*, to the effect that they are 'not in the Canon.'

NICOLAUS DE LYRA.
† A.D. 1340.

Of later commentators, NICOLAUS DE LYRA (Lyranus) was one of the greatest and most popular. He was a Fleming of Jewish descent, and was consequently able to apply an independent judgment to the criticism of the Old Testament. After he had completed his commentary on 'the canonical books of Holy Scripture from *Genesis* to the *Apocalypse*,' he undertook one, as he says, on those which are 'not of the Canon.' 'It must be known,' he goes on to say, 'that the books which are called canonical are of so great authority, that whatever is contained there is held to be certainly true...The books which are not of the Canon have been received by the Church that they may be read for moral instruction; yet their authority is considered less adequate to prove points which are debated ...'

SECT. V. *The Churches of Britain.*

The old Latin Version continued to be commonly used in the Irish, Welsh, and Northumbrian Churches till the eighth and ninth centuries, and even later[1]. The memorials of this which still remain in rich abundance have not yet been thoroughly examined, nor can anything be said accurately with regard to the ancient British Canon. The only complete MS. of the New Testament—the famous Book of Armagh—written at the beginning of the ninth century,

---

[1] One minute trace of this is preserved in the order of the Pauline epistles. In the oldest Saxon MSS. the *Epistle to the Colossians* is placed after those *to the Thessalonians*, as by Augustine.

contains the *Epistle to the Laodicenes*, but with the note that 'Jerome says that it is not St Paul's.'

In the absence of direct and immediate evidence from our own islands, the opinion of *Notker*, abbot of St Gall († A.D. 912), may be taken as the expression of the judgment of the ancient Irish church, from which the monastery of St Gall derived its origin, and with which it maintained a close literary connexion. Notker gives a summary of 'the Interpreters of the Holy Scriptures.' In doing this he passes in review the various books. First he notices the '*Pentateuch, Joshua* and *Judges, Samuel* and *Kings* and the Prophets;' next the '*Psalter, Proverbs, Ecclesiastes, Canticles*;' he then comes to *Wisdom*, 'which,' he says, 'is wholly rejected by the Hebrews, and held uncertain among us; still because our forefathers were accustomed to read it for the usefulness of its teaching, while the Jews have it not, it is called an ecclesiastical book also among us. It is right too that you should hold the same opinion about the book of Jesus the Son of Sirach (*Ecclesiasticus*), except that that is held and read by the Hebrews.' He then notices *Job* and *Tobit* and *Ezra*, observing that Bede wrote 'a commentary on the two last books, rather pleasing than necessary, because he endeavoured to turn simple history into allegory. What shall I say,' he continues, 'of *Judith* and *Esther* and *Chronicles*...since their letter is not considered as having authority, but only as possessing a historical and literary value? You will be able to guess that the same is the case with the *Books of Maccabees*.' On the Books of the New Testament he makes no remarks, though he places them in

CHAP. VIII.

NOTKER.

De Int. SS. §§11 ff. ed. Migne.

an order somewhat unusual in the West, *Gospels*, epistles of *St Paul, Acts*, the *Seven 'Canonical' Epistles*, the *Apocalypse*.

Anon. ap. August.

Another anonymous writer, who probably belonged to the Irish Church, and lived towards the end of the seventh century, is still more explicit in limiting the title of Canonical Scripture to the Hebrew Books. In a treatise 'On the Marvels of Holy Scripture' he gives a summary of the chief events in both Testaments. The second book closes with the return from Babylon, and the writer adds: 'In these two books I have given a historical summary of the marvels of the Holy Scripture of the Old Testament...Although some incidents are found in the books of *Maccabees* suitable to be inserted in the list of marvels, yet I shall not distress myself with any care about these; because I have only professed to touch on ...the marvels of the Divine Canon[1].'

De Mirab. S. Scr. II. 34 (ap. S. August. *Opera*, III.).

BEDE, the great father of English learning, who connects historically the British and Saxon Churches, distinctly recognizes Jerome's division of the Hebrew Canon. On the other hand, he wrote an allegorical exposition of Tobit, referred to by Notker, though he never claims for it the rank of authoritative Scripture. The first Saxon writer who expressly treated of the Canon was ALFRIC, a distinguished Benedictine scholar, who

BEDE, † A.D. 735.

ALFRIC

---

[1] As an illustration of the absence of exact knowledge on the subject of the Canon, it may be observed that this writer quotes one part of the Apocryphal additions to Daniel (iii. 49, 50), but says shortly afterwards 'the history of the den and the carrying of Habbacuc to Babylon in the legend of *Bel and the Dragon (Dan.* xiv.) is not set in this synopsis, because [those legends] are not held to possess the authority of Divine Scripture.' (c. XXXII.)

THE BIBLE OF THE MIDDLE AGES. 209

died Archbishop of Canterbury in A.D. 1005. In CHAP. VIII.
an interesting little treatise, 'On the Old and New
Testaments,' he gives a summary account of the
sacred books. After mentioning the earlier writings, he comes to those of Solomon: 'Solomon,' Translation
he says, 'by his wisdome wrote 3 bookes, one is by W. De L'Isle, p. 14.
Paraboles, that is *Proverbs*. His second booke
is called *Ecclesiastes*. The third is called *Cantica
Canticorum* (*Canticles*)...And these bookes are
still in the Bible...Now there are two bookes p. 17.
more placed with Solomons workes, as if he made
them: which for likenesse of stile and profitable
use have gone for his; but Jesus the son of Sirach
composed them. One is called...the *Booke of
Wisdome;* and the other *Ecclesiasticus*. Very
large bookes, and read in the Church, of long cus-
tome, for much good instruction.' As the last
books he notices *Tobit, Esther, Judith* and *Maccabees* (2), which are reckoned in the number of
the books of the Bible as 'tending to the glory of
God.' In the New Testament he enumerates all
the books in detail, but assigns *fifteen* epistles to
St Paul 'as loud as thunder to faithful people,' of
which the last is that *to the Laodicenes*.

The introduction of this spurious epistle into The Latin
the Latin Bible is one of the most remarkable *Epistle to the Laodicenes*.
episodes in the history of the Canon. It was pro-
bably of African origin, and first appears, as far
as can be traced, in the sixth century. The two
earliest documents in which it appears contain
also the famous interpolation of 'the three hea- 1 John v. 7.
venly Witnesses.' At the close of that century,
Gregory the Great noticed that St Paul 'wrote
fifteen epistles, though the Church received only
fourteen;' and this partial recognition of the
epistle gave it increased currency. In England

14

210 *THE BIBLE IN THE CHURCH.*

CHAP. VIII. and France it seems to have been especially pŏpular. It is contained in the two finest MSS. of the Vulgate in the library of the British Museum (of the ninth century), and in very many later MSS. John of Salisbury, in the twelfth century, expressly affirms that it was 'written by St Paul, though it was the common and almost universal opinion that St Paul wrote only fourteen.' The insertion of the epistle in the Bible is instructive. It offers a clear proof, if any proof were needed, of the utter absence of the power of historical criticism at the time, and of the unwillingness even of the learned to give up anything which came with the seeming sanction of adequate authority. St Paul says that he wrote to the Laodicenes—such is the argument of John of Salisbury—therefore this epistle which purports to be addressed by him to them is genuine.

JOHN OF SALISBURY. †1180.

Ep. 143

This testimony of JOHN of SALISBURY is the more remarkable, because he treats of the Canon in the context with some independence. 'I have been asked,' he writes, 'what I believe to be the number of the books of the Old and New Testaments...Because then I read manifold and different opinions of the fathers as to the number of the books, following Jerome, the teacher of the Catholic Church, whom I consider to be the most approved authority....I believe that there are twenty-two books of the Old Testament, arranged in three classes... *Wisdom* and *Ecclesiasticus*, *Judith, Tobit* and the *Shepherd* are not reckoned in the Canon, nor the book of *Maccabees*...As for the book called the *Shepherd*, I do not know whether it exists anywhere...To these are added eight volumes of the New Testament: (1—4) four Gospels, (5) fifteen epistles of St Paul (the 15th

to *the Laodicenes*)..., (6) **seven** Canonical (i. e. CHAP.VIII.
Catholic) epistles, (7) *Acts*, (8) *Apocalypse*. And
that this is the number of the books which are
admitted into the Canon of Holy Scripture, is the
current and undoubted tradition in the Church.'

The language of WILLIAM OCKHAM, the repre- W. OCKHAM.
sentative of a very different literary school, is not † *c.* A.D. 1347.
less distinct as to the subordinate position of the
Apocrypha. He compares with them the expository writings of the Fathers of the Church, and
says that these are of no *greater* authority than
the Apocrypha, 'which are read for the edification of the people, but not for the establishment
of doctrine.'

The contemporary evidence of ANDREW HORNE, A. HORNE.
a great jurist, may be added as coming from a † *c.* A.D. 1345.
witness of another character. All Law, he argues,
is based upon Holy Scripture. Thus for him the
Canonical books had a binding legal value; and
he limits them strictly. Of the Old Testament he
enumerates the books of the Hebrew Canon, and
adds: 'Besides these there are other books in the
Old Testament, although they are not authorized
as Canonical, as *Tobit, Judith, Maccabees, Ecclesiasticus.*'

Towards the close of the fourteenth century The *Wycliffite*
the great Wycliffite versions of the Bible were Bible.
made, which formed a new epoch in the history
of the Bible in England. The first version which
was completed under Wycliffe's care, and, probably, in part by his hand, contains all the books
of the *Apocrypha* except 2 *Esdras;* but, like
the contemporary MSS. of the Vulgate from
which it was translated, it gives Jerome's Prefaces, in which he affirms the exclusive authority
of the Hebrew Canon of the Old Testament, and

separates the Apocrypha from it. In the revised version which was afterwards put forth by Purvey, these prefaces are omitted in the Old Testament, at least in most copies, and a general Prologue is added in their place. This opens with an account of the Canon, which may be transcribed at some length for the sake of its interest as the first English discussion of the contents of the Bible:

'Fyue and twenty bookis of the olde testament ben bookis of feith, and fulli bookis of holy writ; the first is *Genesis*...and these fyue ben the bookis of Moises, whiche ben clepid propurly the law; the vi book *Josue*, the vii book is *Judicum*, that enclosith the story of Ruth...the xiiii book is *Esdre*, that comprehendeth *Neemye*, and al is o bok anentis Ebreyes, as Jerom seith, but anentis Grekis and Latyns these ben twey bookis ...the xvi is *Joob*...the xxi...xxiiii ben the foure grete prophetis...the xxv book is o book of xii small prophetis. And what euer book in the olde testament is out of these fyue and twenty byfore seid, shal be set among apocrifa, that is, with outen autorite of bileue; therefore the book of *Wisdom* and *Eclesiastici* and *Judith* and *Tobie* be not of bileue. The first book of *Machabeies* was founden write in Ebreu and the ii book of *Machabeyes* was writen first in Grek. Jerom seith al this sentence in the prologe on the first book of Kyngis. Also the book of *Baruc* and the *pistle of Jeremye* ben not of the autorite of the bible anentis Ebreyes, ne the *preyer of Manasses*, as Jerom witnessith, and how mich of the book of *Hester* and of *Daniel* is of autorite anentis Ebreyes, and in Ebreu lettre, it is told in the same bookis by Jerom hym

self...Therefore as holy chirche redith *Judith* CHAP.VIII.
and *Tobie* and the bookis of *Machabeies* but
resceyveth not tho among holy Scripturis, so the
Chirche redith these ii. bookis *Eclesiastici* and
Sapience (Wisdom) to edifying of the people, not
to conferme the autorite of techingis of holy
Chirche; Jerom seith this pleynly in the prologe
on Proverbis...But sothely alle the bookis of the
newe Testament, that is foure gospelleris.. xii
[so in the MSS.] pistelis of Paul, vii smale pistils,
the *Dedis of Apostlis*, and the *Apocalips* ben
fulli of autorite of bileue.'

In the translation itself the books of the
Apocrypha are placed among the other books, as
in the common Latin Bibles. In the New Testament the order is remarkable, *Gospels, Epistles
of St Paul, Acts, Catholic Epistles, Apocalypse*.
In many MSS. the Epistle to the *Laodicenes* is
added after the *Colossians* with a note: 'But
this Epistle is not in common Latin books, and
therefore it was but late translated into English
tongue.' The Epistle however had been excluded
both by Wycliffe and Purvey, and the MSS. in
which it is found are not earlier than about the
middle of the fifteenth century.

Nor was this distinction of the Canonical and THOMAS OF
Ecclesiastical Books any peculiarity of the follow- WALDEN.
ers of Wycliffe. THOMAS of WALDEN, in a work
written against them, quotes Jerome in the
'Helmed Prologue' in support of the opinion,
that there were twenty-two Books of Canonical
authority in the Old Testament.

Popular use
But while the critical judgment of the an- disregarded
cient churches was thus kept alive, general use tion of the
placed all the books of the Ecclesiastical Bible books of the
on the same footing. The manuscripts of the ment.

214   *THE BIBLE IN THE CHURCH.*

CHAP. VIII. Latin Bible rarely made any distinction between the apocryphal books and the books of the Hebrew Canon; and it was scarcely possible that those who used them should habitually distinguish elements which were always offered to them without distinction[1]. One example may suffice. ROBERT GROSSETESTE, Bishop of Lincoln A.D. 1235—1253, was justly regarded as one of the most accomplished scholars of his age. He had even some acquaintance with Greek and Hebrew, but it does not appear that he was led to examine specially the exact limits of Holy Scripture, and consequently his usage falls in with the popular custom of his age. He quotes *Wisdom*, 1, 2 *Maccabees*, and especially *Ecclesiasticus*, in his Letters as books of Scripture; and it is a singular illustration of the strange want of critical skill in the time at which he lived, that he quotes also a passage from the apocryphal *Testament of the twelve Patriarchs* as an authentic prophecy. This is the more remarkable, as in the letter which immediately precedes he insists on the supreme importance of the study of the Old and New Testaments. 'Let your morning lectures,' he says, writing to the regents of Oxford, 'be taken exclusively from these. In the morning the foundation of after teaching is best laid. And that foundation must be sought in Scripture.'

R. GROSSE-
TESTE.

Ep. cxxiv.
(Ed. Luard)

This usage as yet ratified by no specific judgment.

Thus slowly in the different churches of Europe usage was setting aside the distinction be-

[1] Of the large number of Latin Bibles in England which I have examined, one only contains the Hebrew Canon separate from the Apocryphal books, which are placed in a distinct class. This MS., which is in the British Museum, was brought from the Netherlands.

tween the books of the Bible which was still preserved by scholars. But this usage was ratified by no public or general authority: it was not affirmed to imply any dogmatic estimate of the value of the writings to which it extended: it coëxisted with the most explicit recognition of the Athanasian Canon, and even of still narrower collections of the sacred books. In a word, it was simply an ecclesiastical usage answering to the current copies of the Bible, and not an ecclesiastical judgment[1]. Before examining the conflict which arose in the sixteenth century, when this usage was exalted by some into an absolute law of complete doctrinal force, it will be necessary to trace in rapid outline the history of the Bible during the corresponding period in the Eastern Churches.

[1] Pecock in his *Repressor* (p. 251) gives an interesting explanation of the addition of the Apocrypha to the Canonical Scriptures on account of 'the great scarceness of devout books' in early times.

CHAPTER IX.

THE BIBLE OF THE MIDDLE AGES IN THE EAST.

Jerusalem shall be trodden down of the Gentiles, until the times of the Gentiles be fulfilled.—St Luke xxi. 24.

CHAP. IX.

Decay of Eastern Churches.

THE history of the Eastern Churches from the sixth century offers a melancholy picture of decay and ruin. Exhausted by internal divisions, hampered by the civil power, blindly tenacious of ancient customs, they could offer but little effectual resistance to the desolating invasion of Mahommedanism, when at last that new scourge was directed against them. At the time when the Latin Church was moulding the barbarian conquerors of the old empire by a new civilization and gathering strength from their allegiance, the Churches of Egypt and Syria and Asia Minor were reduced, first in one province and then in another, to mere remnants, which were barely able to preserve the name and tradition of their past glory. All vigorous and independent life was crushed out of them. They lived and live still, in virtue of the past, till the time shall be fulfilled, that the divine germ which they preserve may be quickened to some new activity.

THE BIBLE OF THE MIDDLE AGES. 217

SECT. I. *The Greek Church.*

CHAP. IX.

Even in the midst of this general desolation the Greek Church has vindicated its claim to its chosen title, and preserved an 'orthodox' faith through successive revolutions. In one respect, indeed, the Greek Church offers a favourable contrast to that of the West. The spirit which forbad Bishops to read Gentile books never found a welcome there, and learning had a home at Constantinople as long as it remained a Christian city. But while the Greek fathers cherished learning with true devotion and refused to change or add to the dogmas of antiquity, they brought little more critical sagacity to the solution of historical questions than Western scholars. The one conciliar decision on the Canon, which was made (by implication and not directly) at Constantinople, involves the ratification of two absolutely inconsistent lists of the sacred books, those of Carthage and the Apostolical Canons; and neither of these lists is supported by the independent evidence of any Greek Fathers.

The Greek Church learned but not critical.

Conc. Carthag. iv. *Can.* XIV.

This decision of the so-called Quini-Sextine Council is remarkable on many grounds. No disciplinary Canons had been enacted at the fifth and sixth Councils of Constantinople—the so-called fifth and sixth general councils—which were occupied with the condemnation of the errors of Origen and the Monothelites. To supply this deficiency a Council of 227 bishops was held in A.D. 692 (691) in a hall of the imperial palace (*Trullus*, i.e. the *Cupola*), who enacted a large and comprehensive code of laws, which is still valid in the Greek Church. The first canon is occupied with the assertion of the orthodox

The *Quini-Sextine* Council of *Constantinople.*

A.D. 553.
A.D. 680.

faith in the Blessed Trinity against the various errors which had been condemned in successive councils. The second contains an enumeration of those canons already enacted, which 'from henceforth are to be held sure and certain for the nurture and healing of souls.' In these are included the 'eighty-four Canons of the holy and glorious Apostles,' and especial reference is made to the catalogue of Holy Scriptures which they contain by a notice of the *Apostolical Constitutions.*

See p. 176, n. 2.

This book, as we have seen, was included in the *Apostolic Canons* among the books of the Bible, but now, it is said, it must no longer be received as part of 'the genuine teaching of the Apostles,' owing to the interpolations of heretics. Thus the *Epistles of Clement,* which are also contained in the Apostolic Catalogue, are absolutely ratified as Holy Scripture. Yet further the Canons of Carthage are confirmed, and consequently the enlarged Bible of Augustine; and to make the confusion still more complete, the Canons of Athanasius, Gregory of Nazianzus, and Amphilochius, who expressly exclude the Apocrypha from the Old Testament, are also admitted among those which it is unlawful 'to change or subvert.'

The exact determination of the Canon of Scripture was not regarded as of serious moment.

It may be argued that the ratification of these various decrees does not descend into every detail, that the ecclesiastical list of sacred writings formed at Carthage is not inconsistent with the critical list of Athanasius, that the object of the Quini-Sextine decree was disciplinary and not doctrinal; but when every allowance is made on these or other grounds, it is obvious that the decree is a signal proof of the indifference with which the exact determination of the contents of the Bible was regarded at Constantinople in the seventh century. The Catalogues of Holy Scripture were prominent parts of the codes which were authorized; in one case at least they were revised; and yet the large residuum of discrepancies which they contained elicited no discussion or remark.

Individual writers exhibit the same absence of all desire for a precise determination of the limits of the Bible. Even where they give a formal opinion, they do not hold themselves bound by it in practice. Thus the later Greek fathers universally exclude the Apocrypha from their lists of the books of the Bible, and still constantly use them with respect in their own writings. In this respect their evidence forms an instructive commentary on that of earlier writers. Citation alone, with whatever marks of reverence it may be accompanied, cannot be confidently accepted as a test of the admitted canonicity of a book.

Later fathers equally inexact in usage.

The judgment of LEONTIUS of BYZANTIUM, who has been called by an impartial judge 'the most accomplished theologian of his age,' will help to connect the catalogues of the fourth century with the decision of the Quini-Sextine Council. It is singularly explicit and complete. Leontius prefaces his discussion of the opinions of different sects by an enumeration of 'the ecclesiastical books,' as the natural basis of his inquiry. 'Of the Old Testament there are,' he says, 'twenty-two books...The historical books are twelve...The first five, called the *Pentateuch*, are according to universal testimony the books of Moses : those which follow are by unknown authors, namely *Joshua...Judges...Ruth...Kings* (in two books)...

LEONTIUS OF BYZANTIUM. *c.* A.D. 600.

De Sectis, II.

CHAP. IX. *Chronicles...Ezra...*The prophetic books are five, *Isaiah, Jeremiah, Ezekiel, Daniel,* the twelve Prophets...The didactic books are four, *Job,* which some thought to be a composition of Josephus (?), *Proverbs, Ecclesiastes, Canticles*...These three books are Solomon's. The *Psalter* follows. [In these] you have the books of the Old Scripture. Of the New there are six books. Of these two contain the four Evangelists, the first *Matthew* and *Mark,* the second *Luke* and *John.* The third is the *Acts of the Apostles.* The fourth the *Catholic Epistles,* in number seven...They are called catholic or general, because they are not written to one nation, as those of St Paul, but generally to all. The fifth is the fourteen *Epistles of St Paul.* The sixth, the *Apocalypse* of St John. These are the books reckoned as canonical in the Church, both old and new; of which the Hebrews receive all the old.'

Cosmas Indicopleustes.

c. A.D. 535.

Top. Christ. v. p. 242

p. 243.

The testimony of the Egyptian monk COSMAS, who was surnamed *Indicopleustes* (the Indian voyager), from his original profession of a merchant, belongs to an earlier period; but this must be regarded rather as a bold expression of personal opinion than as a reflection of a popular or current view. 'There is joy and exultation,' he says, 'to those who are really Christians, who obey all the Divine Scripture—the Old and the New Covenant...Who will not reverence...the harmony of the Old and New Covenants?...All [the sacred writers] as guided by One Spirit signified the same things by words and by deeds or types, and all look forward to the future constitution of the world.' So far he repeats the old catholic belief; and in the pursuit of this harmony he examines passages from the prophets (sixteen) of the Old Testament, and the Evangelists and Apostles in the New. But with this remarkable omission, that he neglects altogether the *Catholic Epistles* and the *Apocalypse*. In a later passage he notices the objection which had been brought against his views from 2 Pet. iii. 12; and after urging other reasons against its conclusiveness, he goes on to state that the *Catholic Epistles* were held as of doubtful authority by the Church from ancient times. 'And of all those who have commented on the Divine Scriptures, not one has taken account of the Catholic Epistles. And yet more, all those who have drawn up lists of the canonical books of the Divine Scripture have reckoned them as debateable; I mean Irenæus,...Eusebius, Athanasius, Amphilochius...who plainly declared that they were of doubtful authority. And in like manner Severian, bishop of Gabala...rejected them. For most say that they are not the works of the Apostles, but of some others, simple presbyters.' Wherefore, he continues, Eusebius and Irenæus agree in reckoning only the first of St John and the first of St Peter as genuine. Others reject these also. 'Others receive the Epistle of James with these two: others receive all. Among the Syrians, only the three above-mentioned are found, 1 *Peter*, 1 *John*, and *James;* for the rest are not admitted among them.' The evident exaggeration with which Cosmas writes, and the unfairness with which he transfers to all the Catholic Epistles what Eusebius and others say only of some of them, detract from the value of his evidence as to the rejection of *all* the Catholic Epistles by some in his time. Yet whatever may be his historical inaccuracy, his argument still

CHAP. IX.

Top. Christ. VII. p. 292.

222   *THE BIBLE IN THE CHURCH.*

CHAP. IX. remains a conspicuous proof of the freedom of opinion which was still considered to be permissible in the sixth century with regard to some of the books of the New Testament[1].

JOHANNES DAMASCENUS.
† after v. 754.

JOHN of DAMASCUS (JOHANNES DAMASCENUS), the last of the great Greek fathers, whose writings are still regarded with the deepest reverence in the Eastern Church, treats the question of the Canon very summarily; or rather he adopts opinions which he found expressed in earlier writings, without submitting them to any independent examination. For the Old Testament, he transcribes almost verbally one of the lists of Epiphanius, which gives only the books of the Hebrew Canon as of primary authority. To these *Ecclesiasticus* and *Wisdom* are subjoined as an appendix, 'being noble and good books, though not prophetical.' The other books of the Apocrypha are not specially noticed; but even in this case usage prevailed so far, that Damascenus quotes *Wisdom* as the work of Solomon; and *Baruch* as 'Divine Scripture.' In the New Testament, he gives all the books commonly received with the addition of the *Apostolic Canons*. To these one MS. adds the two *Epistles of Clement*, but the clause has been introduced without doubt from the last of the Apostolic Canons.

De Fide Orth. IV. 18.

De Imag. I. p. 325. *De Fide Orth.* IV. 6.

See p. 176, *n.*

His general views on Holy Scripture.
l.c.

The preface with which Damascenus introduces this catalogue gives force to the judgment which he expresses. 'The Law and the Prophets,

[1] A remarkable proof of the converse wish to extend the limits of the absolutely authoritative sources of doctrine is found in a decision of Justinian (after A.D. 535), enacting that 'the dogmas of the first four General Councils are to be honoured as the divinely-inspired Scriptures' (Voellii et Justelli *Bibl. Jur. Can.* II. 1346).

THE BIBLE OF THE MIDDLE AGES. 223

Evangelists and Apostles, and Shepherds and teachers spake,' he says, 'by the Holy Spirit. *All inspired Scripture*, therefore, is wholly *profitable*[1]. So that it is best and most profitable for the soul to search the Divine Scriptures... Let us then knock that we may enter that fairest paradise...But let us not knock carelessly, but rather with zeal and steadfastness. Let us not faint in knocking ; for thus it shall be opened to us...Let us draw from the fountain of Paradise perennial and most pure streams springing up into eternal life...But if we can gather anything useful from other sources without, it is not forbidden. Let us show ourselves tried moneychangers, storing up the genuine and pure gold, but declining the base...' Thus clearly and fully is the spirit of Origen reproduced by the last father who used his language.

CHAP. IX.

The later Greek Commentators on the Conciliar Decrees add nothing of importance to the evidence which has been already adduced. In their case the power of exact criticism was practically extinct ; and they seem to have been incapable of realizing the discrepancies between the different lists of the Sacred Books which the Ecclesiastical Code included.

The Greek Canonists.

Thus PHOTIUS, patriarch of Constantinople, in his summary of the Laws of the Church, refers for the list of Canonical Books to the Catalogue of the Apostolic Canons, the Council of Carthage and the Council of Laodicea. ZONARAS, one of the chief Byzantine historians and theologians of the twelfth century, in a note on the Catalogue of

† c. A.D. 891. *Biblioth. Jur. Can.* (Voellius et Just.) II. p. 898.

---

[1] The best MSS. of Damascenus omit the conjunction (inspired *and* profitable) with several versions.

224   THE BIBLE IN THE CHURCH.

CHAP. IX. the Apostolic Canons, remarks that 'some admit
besides those which were there enumerated the
Beveridge, *Wisdom of Solomon*, and *Judith*, and *Tobit*, and
Synodicon, the *Apocalypse* of [John] the Divine.' Again, in
I. 56.
another note he appeals to 'the exact enumeration of the books of the Old and New Testaments
which ought to be read' made by Athanasius,
Gregory of Nazianzus, Amphilochius and the
Beveridge, *l.c.* Council of Carthage. ALEXIUS ARISTENUS (a
c. A.D. 1165. distinguished ecclesiastical officer of Constantinople) gives as a list of 'the only books which
ought to be judged venerable and holy by clergy
and laity' the Hebrew Canon, with the addition
of *three books of Maccabees*, and the received
New Testament with the *two Epistles of Clement*,
and the *Apostolical Constitutions*. *Wisdom* and
Ecclesiasticus are added as an appendix to the
Old Testament; and notice is also taken of the
decision of the Quini-Sextine Council against the
See p. 176, n. Apostolical Constitutions. With this exception,
Alexius accepts in the most complete manner the
Beveridge, *l.c.* Catalogue of the Apostolic Canons. THEODORUS
c. A.D. 1180. BALSAMON, who became patriarch of Antioch,
c. A.D. 1255. and ARSENIUS, patriarch of Constantinople, both
Justellus, *l. c.* refer generally to the chief Greek Catalogues, and
that of Carthage, without any attempt to reconcile them.

The '*Sixty*   Among other titles which were given to the
Books.'   Bible in the Greek Church was that of 'The Sixty
Books.' The enumeration which suggested this
title has been preserved in a list of the Holy
Scriptures which is still found in some ancient
Montf. *Bibl.* MSS. The list is styled 'Of the Sixty Books
Coislin.   and those which are without (*i.e.* not included
p. 193 f.
Hody, p. 649. in) them.' It contains the Pentateuch (5); the
Historical Books (7); the *Poetical* Books (5),

THE BIBLE OF THE MIDDLE AGES. 225

and *Ezra* (1); the *Lesser Prophets* (12); the CHAP. IX.
Greater Prophets (4); the *Gospels* (4), the *Acts* (1),
the *Catholic Epistles* (7), the *Epistles of St Paul*
(14). 'Those which are without the Sixty are,'
the list continues, 'the *Wisdom* of Solomon, the
Wisdom of Sirach (*Ecclesiasticus*), *Maccabees* (4),
Esther, Judith, Tobit. Those which are Apocryphal: Adam, Henoch...the Psalms of Solomon
..the Revelation of Esdras [2 *Esdras*]...the Revelation of Peter...the Epistle of Barnabas...(in
all 25).'

It is possible that the number (sixty) may Omission of
not always have been made up in the same way, *Esther* and
but under any circumstances the list is a remarkable monument of the permanence of the doubts
entertained from an early time in the Eastern
Church as to the canonicity of *Esther*. The total
omission of the *Apocalypse* is yet more worthy of
notice. Nothing could more significantly express
the division of opinion about the book than the
fact that the author of the Catalogue does not
place it among the apocryphal or the acknowledged books.

The catalogue which has been just quoted is The *Sticho-
sometimes ascribed to ANASTASIUS SINAITA, pa- metry* of
triarch of Antioch. The evidence in support of † A.D. 599.
this opinion as to its authorship is wholly untrustworthy; and though it may possibly have
been derived from some Syrian source, it is perhaps more natural to refer its origin to Asia
Minor. There is, however, another important list
of the Holy Scriptures which is referred with
great probability to Antioch. This is found in a
short Compendium of History (Chronographia)
compiled by NICEPHORUS, patriarch of Constan- A.D. 828.
tinople, in which it occurs after the list of the

15

patriarchs of Antioch. To the title of each book is added the number of lines (*stichoi*) which it contained according to the ancient mode of writing. From this circumstance the list is known as the Stichometry of Nicephorus, but its contents and arrangement show that it must be assigned to a very early date, probably in the 4th century. The books are ranged in three classes, (1) 'The Divine Scriptures received (or used) in the Church and which have been canonized,' (2) 'Those which are disputed,' (3) 'The Apocryphal.' To the first class belong all the books of the Hebrew Canon except *Esther* with the addition of *Baruch* (22 in all); and all the received books of the New Testament except the *Apocalypse*. The second class comprises in the Old Testament *Maccabees* (3), *Wisdom*, *Ecclesiasticus*, the Psalms of Solomon, *Esther, Judith, Susanna, Tobit;* and in the New Testament: the *Apocalypse* of John, the Apocalypse of Peter, the Epistle of Barnabas, and the Gospel according to the Hebrews. The third class includes among other books Enoch...the Ascension of Moses...and in the New Testament...the Epistles of Clement, Ignatius, Polycarp and the Shepherd.

This Stichometry of Nicephorus appears to have been widely circulated. It was translated into Latin by Anastasius of Rome in an ecclesiastical history, and was combined with the Festal Letter of Athanasius in the Synopsis of Holy Scripture, which commonly passes under the name of that great father. When viewed in connexion with the other catalogues of the biblical books which were sanctioned by the Greek Church, it completes the picture of the confusion which was allowed to remain within it as to the exact limits of the canonical writings. No less than six different lists of the Scriptures were received there more or less widely in the 10th century: that of Laodicea and Cyril, which adds *Baruch* in the Old Testament and omits the *Apocalypse* in the New: that of Carthage which includes all the *Apocrypha* of the Old Testament: that of the Apostolical Canons which adds the two Epistles of Clement to the New Testament, and omits the *Apocalypse:* that of Gregory Nazianzen, which omits *Esther* and the *Apocalypse:* that of Amphilochius, which reckons *Esther*, 2, 3 *John*, 2 *Peter*, *Jude* and the *Apocalypse* as doubtful: that of Nicephorus, which reckons only *Esther* and the *Apocalypse* as doubtful. At a later time still another catalogue was added. Nicephorus Callistus, in a metrical catalogue, based on those of Gregory and Amphilochius, reckons up the books of the Bible, in which he includes all that we receive as canonical except Esther. 'Some,' he says, 'add *Esther*, *Judith* and *Tobit*.' Of the other Apocrypha of the Old Testament he makes no mention; nor does he notice the doubts which had been entertained as to the *Antilegomena* of the New Testament; and at the close of his list he adds, 'besides these every writing is spurious.'

Quoted by Hody, p. 648. c. A.D. 1333.

The later history of the Bible in the Greek Church exhibits the same uncertainty and vacillation as to its exact contents which was involved in the Quini-Sextine decree. CYRIL LUCAR, the reforming patriarch of Constantinople, in his *Confession of Faith*, gives a definition and list of the Canonical Books which reflect the protestant opinions with which he was imbued. 'We call by the name Holy Scripture,' he writes, 'all the

Later history of the Bible in the Greek Church.

CYRIL LUCAR.

Kimmel, *Libri Symb.* 1. p. 42.

CHAP. IX. Canonical books which we receive and keep as the rule (Canon) of our faith; especially because the teaching which they set before is given by Divine inspiration and sufficient to instruct, to illuminate and to perfect him who comes to the faith. These Canonical books we believe to be so many in number as the synod of Laodicea declared, and the Catholic and Orthodox Church enlightened by the most Holy Spirit confesses. But those which we call Apocryphal, have this name for this reason, that they do not possess the same ratification from the most Holy Spirit, as the books which are properly and indisputably canonical.' Then follows a list shortly describing the twenty-two books of the Old Testament (without *Baruch*) and all the Books of the New Testament which we receive, including the Apocalypse, though this was not contained in the Laodicene Catalogue. The judgment of Cyril Lucar is confirmed by that of his friend METROPHANES CRITOPULUS, in whose *Confession of the Catholic and Apostolic Eastern Church* a list of the books of the Old Testament is given, according to the Hebrew Canon, and also of the New Testament as they are commonly received; 'but the remaining books,' it is added, 'which some wish to include in the Holy Scripture, such as *Tobit*, *Judith*, the *Wisdom of Solomon*, the Wisdom of Jesus the son of Sirach [*Ecclesiasticus*], *Baruch*, and the books of the *Maccabees*, we do not hold to be worthy to be entirely cast aside, for many moral precepts, worthy of the greatest praise, are contained in them; but the Church of Christ never received them as canonical and authentic; as many others bear witness, but especially St Gregory the Divine, and St Amphilochius, and last of

Kimmel, II. p. 105.

THE BIBLE OF THE MIDDLE AGES. 229

all, St John of Damascus. Wherefore we do not endeavour to establish our doctrines from these, but from the thirty-three canonical and authentic books, which we also call inspired and Holy Scripture.'

This opinion of Metrophanes is quoted with approbation by Platon, formerly Metropolitan of Moscow, in his *Orthodox Teaching*; and in the authorized Russian Catechism, the Hebrew Canon is quoted and supported by the authority of the fathers; though in this the Apocrypha are recommended, after the example of Athanasius, as forming a useful study preparatory to the study of the Bible.

On the other hand, in the Synod of Jerusalem, in 1672, which was directed against 'the Calvinists' (*i.e.* the party of Cyril Lucar), under the pressure (as it is said) of Latin influence, the books of the Apocrypha were distinctly reckoned as 'genuine parts of the Scripture,' even though it is allowed that they had not always been received. But this judgment appears to be isolated. In the contemporary Synod of Constantinople notice was taken of the variations in the lists of Laodicea, Carthage and the Clementine Constitutions. And it was then added that 'those books which are not embraced in the enumeration of the Holy Writers, are not rejected and treated as pagan and profane; but styled good and excellent.'

SECT. II. *The Nestorian Churches.*

The disastrous controversies which were brought to an issue at the Councils of Ephesus and Chalcedon left the orthodox Eastern Church crippled in power and narrowed in range. The

230   *THE BIBLE IN THE CHURCH.*

CHAP. IX. regions of the far East retained or adopted with characteristic fervour the doctrines of Nestorius, which were extended from the banks of the Euphrates through Arabia, Persia and India, and in China in viith and viiith cent. The teaching of the Monophysites (Jacobites) on the other hand, found a firm support in Egypt, Abyssinia, Western Syria and Armenia. Both the Nestorian and Monophysite Churches retained for a long time their early vigour, even in the face of Mahommedanism, and a noble series of scholars gives lustre to their history. It does not appear that the question of the Canon of the Bible was ever brought forward as a subject of discussion in the controversies which thus divided the East. Nestorians and Monophysites alike wished, as far as can be seen, to retain the original Bible of the Churches from which they sprang ; or if they differed, the difference was the result of habit and not of design. At Nisibis alone a remarkable (Nestorian) school of biblical criticism cherished the ancient freedom of Syrian thought.

The School of Nisibis.

See p. 193.

The judgment of the school of Nisibis has been already quoted from Junilius. According to this, the books of the Bible were divided into two classes as possessed of 'complete' or 'intermediate' authority, and it is worthy of special remark that the former class in the Old Testament did not include all the books of the Hebrew Canon. The books of perfect authority are the *Pentateuch, Joshua, Judges, Ruth, Samuel* (2), *Kings* (2), *Proverbs, Ecclesiasticus, Ecclesiastes, Psalms,* sixteen *Prophets;* the *Gospels* (4), *Acts,* fourteen *Epistles of St Paul,* 1 *Peter,* 1 *John.* On the other hand *Chronicles* (2), *Job, Ezra* (2), *Judith, Esther, Maccabees* (2), *Wisdom, Canti-*

cles; James, 2 *Peter, Jude*, 2, 3 *John, Apocalypse* are reckoned as of doubtful or intermediate authority, as being received only partially. Thus *Ecclesiasticus* is raised to complete canonical dignity; and *Chronicles* (2), *Job, Ezra, Nehemiah,* and *Esther* are placed on the same level with the additional books of the Alexandrine Bible. In the New Testament, the *Epistle to Hebrews* alone of the 'disputed' books is allowed to possess complete authority.

It is impossible to determine on what evidence or at what time this classification was made. In part at least it seems to be the result of internal criticism, and probably it was confined to scholars. In the New Testament it differed from the usual judgment of the Syrian Churches by the exclusion of *St James* from the books of perfect authority. In the Old Testament it appears to stand alone in the peculiarities which it presents; but even this fact scarcely lessens the interest which attaches to it.

The second testimony on the Nestorian Canon, which is derived from a later Metropolitan of Nisibis, is very different in character. EBED JESU, one of the most accomplished of Nestorian theologians, was raised to that dignity *c.* A.D. 1286; and in a poetical catalogue of ecclesiastical writers he has given a list of the books of the Old and New Testaments. This list indeed forms the opening paragraphs of his work, but it is written in such a form that the account of the books of the Old Testament can only be received with the greatest caution. This[1] commences with the *Pentateuch,* and then enumerates without break *Jo-*

CHAP. IX.

Peculiarities of the Canon of Nisibis.

EBED JESU.

† A.D. 1318.

Assemani, III. 1. 4 ff

Badger, *Nestorians and their rituals,* II. 361 ff.

[1] I have followed the translation of Assemani.

232   *THE BIBLE IN THE CHURCH.*

CHAP. IX. *shua, Judges, Samuel, Kings, Chronicles* and *Ruth, Psalms, Proverbs, Ecclesiastes, Canticles,* Bar-Sira (*i. e. Ecclesiasticus*), *Wisdom, Job,* sixteen *Prophets, Judith, Esther, Susanna, Esdras,* and the lesser *Daniel* (*i. e.* Bel and *the Dragon*), the *Epistle of Baruch,* and the Book of the tradition of the Elders (*i.e.* the *Mishnah*). 'Of Josephus there remain Proverbs, and the history of the Sons of Samona (*i.e. Maccabees,* 4). Another Book of Maccabees (Book 1 or 2?), and the history of Herod the King, and the book of the last destruction of Jerusalem by Titus; and the book of Asenath the wife of Joseph the Just, son of Jacob; and the book of *Tobias and Tobit,* just Israelites.' Having completed this list, which is evidently intended to be a complete list of all Jewish literature, Ebed Jesu continues, 'Now having completed the Old let us approach the New Testament,' just as if he had confined himself to an exact enumeration of the Sacred Books. His list of the writings of the New Testament includes the four *Gospels,* the *Acts,* fourteen *Epistles of St Paul,* 'three Epistles assigned to the Apostles in every copy and tongue, *James* and *Peter* (1), and *John* (1).'

See p. 238.

The later Nestorians appear to have paid no attention to the discussion of the contents of the Bible. Their ecclesiastical books recognize both the Catalogue of the Apostolic Canons and also the Canon of the Alexandrine LXX. And the only complete modern Nestorian MS. of the Syriac Old Testament in the British Museum gives the books in the following order: *Pentateuch, Joshua, Judges, Kings* (4), *Wisdom of Solomon, Ecclesiastes, Ruth, Canticles, Ecclesiasticus, Job, Isaiah,* twelve *Minor Prophets, Jeremiah,*

Badger, II pp. 81 ff. B. M, Rich, 7149.

Lamentations, Ezekiel, Daniel, Bel and the Dragon[1].

[1] There is a MS. of the Syriac Bible in the University Library, at Cambridge, which 'was found in one of the Churches of the Syrian Christians in the interior of Travancore, at the foot of the mountains,' and presented to Dr Buchanan, by a Syrian bishop. This is written in the Estrangelo character, without points, but its date has not yet been accurately determined. With the exception of a copy at Milan, it is probably the only complete ancient MS. of the Syriac Bible in Europe; and offers a complete example of the enlarged Syriac Canon. The order of the books is remarkable; and the number of lines (*Stichoi*, see p. 309) in each book is given at the end.

Genesis, 4509 lines.   *Exodus*, 3626 lines.
Leviticus, 2454 lines.   *Numbers*, 3521 lines.
Deuteronomy, 2796 lines.

Job ('The book of Job the Just was written by the Prophet Moses, but it was not inserted among his other books because Job was a Gentile and not of the sons of Jacob...'), 2553 lines.

Joshua and *Judges*, 4233 lines (i. e. *Joshua* 2167, *Judges* 2066).

1, 2 *Samuel*, 3436 lines.

Psalms, 150 in five books, 4830 lines.

1, 2 *Kings*, 5327 lines. (At the end the number is 5326).

Chronicles, 5603 lines.

Proverbs, 1863 lines.

Ecclesiastes, 627 lines.

Canticles ('Solomon's Wisdom of Wisdoms'), 296 lines.

Wisdom ('The book of the Great Wisdom of the same Solomon; concerning which it is doubtful whether some other wise man of the Hebrews did not compose it by the spirit of prophecy, though he wrote it in the name of Solomon; and it has been so received'), 1236 lines.

Isaiah, 4801 lines.   *Jeremiah*.
Lamentations (subscription mutilated).
Prayer of Jeremiah (Lam. v.).
The first Epistle of Baruch.
The second Epistle of Baruch (*Baruch*).

CHAP. IX. SECTS. III—VI. *The Monophysite Churches.*

SECT. III. *The Coptic Church.*

The Monophysite heresy, which was an exaggeration and distortion of the great truth to which Athanasius bore a life-long witness, found a speedy acceptance in Egypt; and the rivalry between the Monophysites and the orthodox is

The Epistle of Jeremiah (Baruch vi.).
Ezekiel, 4154 lines.
The twelve Minor Prophets, 3021 lines.
Daniel with *Bel and the Dragon,* 2263 lines.
Ruth. Susannah. Esther. Judith.
Ezra with *Nehemiah,* 2361 lines.
Ecclesiasticus (subscription mutilated: 2500 in *Bodl.*).

1 *Maccabees,* 2766 lines.

2 *Maccabees* (apparently 1600 lines).

3 *Maccabees,* 1400 lines.

Josippon, i.e. 4 *Maccabees* ('The history of Josippon concerning Eleazer and his seven sons').

1 *Esdras* ('This first book of Ezra we have written according to the LXX., because we could not find it in the Simple Version').

Tobit (imperfect at the end).

Four Gospels, 9938.

XIV Epistles of St Paul (*Hebrews* last).

Acts.
James.
1 *Peter.*
1 *John.*
2 *Peter,* 195 lines.
2 *John,* 40 lines.
3 *John,* 47 lines.

Jude, 97 lines. ('Thus conclude these seven Catholic Epistles of the Holy Apostles'.)

The Clementine Constitutions in eight Books. (The last two books are lost, and the whole is much mutilated.) For the description of this MS. I am indebted to Mr R. L. Bensly, M.A. of Caius College. Very similar notes and numbers are given by Prof. Payne Smith from Bodleian MSS. in his account of the Syriac MSS. of that collection.

THE BIBLE OF THE MIDDLE AGES. 235

said to have contributed greatly to the success of the Arabian invasion. This division, however, led to no difference as to the authority or contents of the Bible. Translations of the Sacred Writings into the dialects of Upper and Lower Egypt had existed from the third century; and one of these, the *Memphitic (Coptic)*, still remains in use in the native Church, though the language is at present unintelligible to the congregation. The translation of the Old Testament in these Versions was made from the LXX.; but so little is known of them that at present it is impossible to say whether they contained all the books of the Apocrypha, or whether the whole work was completed at once or only by successive efforts. The oldest Version in the dialect of Upper Egypt (*Sahidic*, or *Thebaic*), which was probably made early in the third century, contained all the books of the New Testament which we receive, of which fragments still remain. The Memphitic Version of all is preserved entire.

At a later time (thirteenth century) the Apostolic Canons were adopted as part of the Ecclesiastical Code of the Coptic Church, and consequently the Catalogue of Scriptures which they contain, including 'the two Epistles of Clement and the eight books of the Apostolic Constitutions,' received an authoritative sanction. But this fact did not hinder some at least from accepting the books of the Apocrypha, which were omitted in the Apostolic Catalogue, as Canonical Scripture; and on the other hand there is not, as far as appears, any evidence that the Clementine writings were added to the Coptic New Testament.

CHAP. IX.

See p. 176, *n.*

Assemani, *Bibl. Or.* III. 1. p. 6, *n.*

SECT. IV. *The Abyssinian Church.*

The history of the Canon in the Abyssinian Church offers some points of interest. The earliest evidence as to the extent of the Abyssinian collection of Sacred Books is found in the Æthiopic translation of the Bible, which was made about the fourth or fifth century from the Alexandrine Greek text. By whom this translation was made is wholly unknown. Indeed from internal evidence it appears that it was made by various hands and at various times. It contains at present not only all the canonical books with the Apocrypha of the Old Testament, but also several other books, as *Enoch*, the *Ascension of Isaiah*, the *Book of Jubilees*, &c. which are not now found elsewhere, but different copies and lists present very great discrepancies. No MS. contains the whole Bible; but from the connexion in which the acknowledged and disputed or apocryphal books are found in the several smaller collections of sacred writings, it appears certain that the books of different ranks were intermingled from a very early time, as in the Alexandrine LXX. The different classes may have been distinguished originally, but the evidence of this distinction is now entirely lost.

The Abyssinian Ecclesiastical Code.

After the establishment of the Mohammedan supremacy in Egypt, a new literary æra commenced in Abyssinia. The influence of Greek, which had been paramount up to that epoch, gave way to that of the Arabian conquerors. In process of time this was exhibited in revisions or additions to the Æthiopic Bible; and at a later period still more directly in an authorized definition of its contents. Shortly after the thirteenth

THE BIBLE OF THE MIDDLE AGES. 237

century a code of canon law which was originally compiled for the Arabo-Coptic Church of Egypt was introduced into Abyssinia, and under the name of the Royal Code was accepted as the authoritative basis of spiritual and civil right. In this code a statement is made as to the 'number of the books which are or ought to be received in the Church.' This is derived from that contained in the Coptic recension of the Apostolic Canons. The Coptic Catalogue itself is found in two forms; and the Æthiopic Catalogue differs widely from the Greek Catalogue which has been already quoted, and on which it was based. Altogether the number of the sacred books is reckoned as eighty-one. In the Old Testament *Tobit, Maccabees* (1, 2) and *Wisdom* (the so-called 'Wisdom of Bozor' is *Prov.* xxx. xxxi.) are added to the Hebrew Canon. Besides these the *Wisdom of Sirach* and 'the book of Josephus ben-Gorion' are noticed as suited for the instruction of the young. The New Testament contains all the received books without apocryphal additions. But it will be observed that the books thus enumerated will not make up the required number; and it seems probable that the sum was originally completed by the addition of the 'two Epistles of Clement and the eight books of the Constitutions' which are contained in the Catalogue of the Apostolic Canons. In process of time the 'Synodus,' a collection of early conciliar and other canons, was substituted for the Constitutions, and like that reckoned as eight books; by which means, with the addition of the two appended books, the sum of eighty-one books was again made up. But in fact while the number of Sacred Books was held firmly and without variation,

238   *THE BIBLE IN THE CHURCH.*

CHAP. IX. the books by which it was completed varied considerably. The New Testament remained fixed as containing our twenty-seven books with the eight books of the Synodus; but the forty-six books of the Old Testament were reckoned now in one way and now in another, though some of the *Apocrypha* are always found among them.

An Æthiopic Catalogue of Scripture. Dillmann, *Cat. MSS. Æth.* p 4.

One Catalogue which is contained in a MS. in the British Museum, may be given as an example: 'The number of the Scriptures: of the Law of *Moses* 5, *Judges* 3, Jubilees 1, *Kings* 4, *Chronicles* 1, *Job* 1, *books of Solomon* 5 (*Proverbs* is divided into two), *Isaiah* 1, *Jeremiah* 1, *Ezekiel* 1, *Daniel* 1, the Minor *Prophets* 12, *Ezra* 2, *Maccabees* 1, *Tobit* 1, *Judith* 1, Assenath 1, *Esther* 1, *Ecclesiasticus* 1, *Psalms* 1, Ozias 1. The sum of the Old Testament is forty-six. The *Gospels* 4, *Epistles of Paul* 14, *Epistles of the Apostles* 7, *Acts* 1, the *Vision of John* 1, the Book of Clement with the *Synodus* 8[1].'

The list without any critical value.

In this it will be observed that there are the Books of *Wisdom, Ecclesiasticus, Maccabees* (1), *Judith* and *Tobit*, which belong to the Greek Apocrypha; and besides these are reckoned the

See p. 232.

Apocryphal story of Asenath the wife of Joseph, the Book of Jubilees, a strange Judaic commentary on Genesis, and an unknown apocryphal writing 'Ozias.' The list, as all the other Æthiopic lists, is indeed a curiosity and nothing more. It expresses no critical or exact traditional judgment on the canon. As far as it has any historical value it is to show the powerlessness of an

---

[1] A second Catalogue is given by Dillmann (l. c. p. 40) which is found in another MS. which differs both in contents and order. *Baruch* is very rarely found.

isolated and rude Christian Society to preserve CHAP. IX. a pure Bible, and to place in a clear light the function which literary criticism has to exercise in preserving the treasures once committed to the Church.

SECT V. *The Armenian Church.*

The Armenian Version of the Bible, which has been called by competent scholars 'the Queen of Versions,' was made by Miesrob, the real founder of Armenian literature, in the fifth century. The version was made from the Hexaplaric revision of the LXX. and not from the Hebrew. The New Testament was translated directly from the Greek. Moses Choronensis, who was himself a nephew of Miesrob, states that the translation included originally 'all the twenty-two books' (that *Hist. Arm.* is the Hebrew Canon), 'and the New Testament.' III. 53. But in process of time the other books of the Alexandrine Greek Bible were added. These, however, are said generally to be distinguished from the first work by their diffuse, inexact and ambitious style.

The printed editions of the Armenian Bible The printed differ considerably as to their contents. The Bibles wholly Latin in most important copies have been published under form. Latin influence; and if this has not affected their text, it has certainly affected their contents. Even the edition which was printed at St Petersburg (A. D. 1817) 'for the Jacobite Church under the patriarch of Etchmiazin,' which may be supposed to represent the authorized collection of the Armenian Scriptures, is a mere reflex of the Latin Vulgate. The volume is styled 'the Divinely inspired Books of the Old and New Testaments according to our ancient and pure Armenian Version.' The index prefixed to it contains all the Books of the Hebrew Canon and the Apocrypha with the addition of 3 *Maccabees;* and after the *Apocalypse,* the *Prayer of Manasses* and 4 Ezra (*i.e.* 2 *Esdras*) are added, 'that they may not be altogether lost, as they are sometimes quoted by the Holy Fathers and are found in some *Latin* Bibles both manuscript and printed.' It is further noticed that 1, 2 *Esdras,* the *Prayer of Manasses* and 3 *Maccabees* are 'out of the order of the Canonical Books which the Council of Trent adopted and declared to be canonical[1].' The list of books therefore has evidently no independent value; and on the other hand the Epistle of the Corinthians to St Paul and an Epistle of St Paul's in reply to it, which are sometimes added to the Armenian Version of the New Testament, are merely apocryphal additions which have no canonical authority in the Church.

Sect. VI. *The Jacobite (Monophysite) Churches of Syria.*

It is wholly uncertain at what time the Syriac translations of the Apocrypha of the Old Testament, which are added to the Peshito, were first made. Some of the books—as *Maccabees*—seem not to have been translated in the time of Ephraem Syrus; but as the intercourse between the Syrian and Greek Churches increased, it could not be but that all the books which had any ecclesiastical dignity as parts of the current Greek

[1] For the collation of this edition of the Armenian Bible I am indebted to the kindness of M. Deutsch of the British Museum.

Bible would be rendered into Syriac. A MS. of the recension of the Peshito which was made for the Monophysite (Jacobite) Church (called the *Karkaphensian*) may be taken as exhibiting a good specimen of the later Syrian Bible which was thus formed. This MS. gives the books of the Old Testament in the following order, the *Pentateuch, Joshua, Judges, Job, Samuel, Psalms, Kings; Isaiah,* the *Minor Prophets, Jeremiah, Lamentations, Baruch,* the *Epistle of Jeremiah, Ezekiel, Daniel* (with the additions); *Proverbs, Wisdom, Ecclesiastes, Canticles; Ruth, Esther, Judith; Ecclesiasticus.* The New Testament is divided into three sections, the *Acts* and three *Catholic Epistles;* the fourteen *Epistles of St Paul;* the four *Gospels.* Thus in the Old Testament *Chronicles, Ezra, Nehemiah,* as well as *Tobit* and *Maccabees,* are wanting. In the New Testament those books only are omitted which are excluded from the Canon of the Peshito.

The Karkaphensian Version.

Wiseman, *Horæ Syriacæ*, p. 213.

In the seventh century a new version was made from Origen's revision of the LXX. (called the Hexaplar Greek text) by a Monophysite, Paul of Tela. A considerable part of this has been preserved, and among other books *Wisdom, Ecclesiasticus* and *Baruch,* so that it seems certain that it included all the books of the Alexandrine Bible. A new translation of the New Testament had been made by the direction of another Monophysite, Philoxenus, in the preceding century. This included in all probability translations of the disputed Catholic Epistles (2 *Peter, Jude,* 2, 3 *John*). This version was itself revised in the seventh century by Thomas of Harkel, and the Harclean New Testament contains all

The Syriac Hexaplaric Version.

the books of our New Testament except the *Apocalypse*. It is wholly uncertain at what time the version of this book which is found in the Syrian Bibles was first made.

The Canon of the Peshito was however still generally retained in the New Testament, even after the disputed books were translated. Thus JACOB OF EDESSA, in his notes on the Syriac Bible, explains words in *Baruch*, *Judith* and *Ecclesiasticus*, but not in the four controverted *Catholic Epistles* or the *Apocalypse*. At a much later time DIONYSIUS BAR SALIBI notices the doubts on the Catholic Epistles as generally current. And GREGORY (ABULPHARAGIUS) BAR HEBRÆUS, the last of the great Syrian writers, gives in the New Testament the Canon of the Peshito. In the Old Testament he comments on *Wisdom*, *Ecclesiasticus* and the *Additions to Daniel*, while he omits *Chronicles* and *Esther* as well as *Judith* and *Maccabees*. Yet in his collection of ecclesiastical laws he gives the Catalogue of the Apostolic Canons as the standard of the collection of Holy Scripture, adding to it, apparently with approbation, the notes of Athanasius on the *Apocrypha* of the Old and New Testament, of Dionysius of Alexandria on the *Apocalypse*, and of Origen on the *Epistle to the Hebrews*[1].

The general result of all that has been collected as to the Bible of the East during the

---

[1] The note ends, 'The revelation of Paul also with other revelations is received in the Church, and the letters (*sic*) of Barnabas, and Tobias, and the Shepherd, and Bar-Asira (i. e. *Ecclesiasticus*), but many do not receive the book of the Shepherd and the Revelation of John' (Mai, *Script. Vett. Coll. Nova*, x. Part 2, pp. 53, 54).

THE BIBLE OF THE MIDDLE AGES. 243

middle ages may be summed up very briefly. In CHAP. IX.
no one of the Eastern Churches was there any
fixed judgment or consistent tradition as to its
contents. The Catalogue in the Apostolic Canons, which became a part of the Ecclesiastical
law in almost every Church, gained a wide acceptance, but yet not so as to exclude or even practically to modify other opinions on the range of
Holy Scripture which were recommended by
ancient usage. In the West, the conflict on the
Canon was reduced to the comparison of the relative authority of the ecclesiastical Canon of Augustine and the critical Canon of Jerome. With
the exception of the *Epistle to the Laodicenes*
and 2 *Esdras* no single books claimed authority
or were discussed on their own merits. The
question was one of principle and not of detail.
In the East it was otherwise. The Hebrew Canon itself was not universally accepted. *Esther*,
indeed, was on the whole less supported than
Baruch. And the list of books which obtained
a partial authority was very large. Yet on the
other hand it cannot be doubted but that the
wish of the Eastern Churches, and of the Greek
Church in particular, was to confine the Old Testament to the Hebrew Canon, and to complete
the received Canon of the New Testament by the
addition of the *Apocalypse*. Popular custom Custom at
went further, and even those fathers who (like variance with
Athanasius) limited the contents of the Bible ment.
most exactly in their express judgments, commonly quoted the additional books of the Alexandrine LXX. with the same respect as those
which were universally acknowledged. But the
same sanction was not extended to the Apocrypha of the New Testament. The ecclesiastical

recognition which was accorded in the fullest terms to the Epistles of Clement, and partially to the Shepherd, never gained for those writings more than a very narrow influence. Of the former only one imperfect copy has been preserved in the Alexandrine MS. of the Bible: of the latter, besides Latin translations, only a fragment of the original Greek remains at the end of the Sinaitic MS. Yet even in the judgment of Athanasius the Shepherd was placed on the same footing as *Wisdom* or *Ecclesiasticus*.

One other fact will be noticed. The Eastern Bibles, as a general rule, became more and more corrupt as they were further removed from the direct influence of Greek literature. There was no one central power by which they could be restrained or guided; and in later times Latin influence corrupted yet more the vague traditions on Scripture which they had followed originally.

But whatever may be the errors of usage in the East, no Eastern Church is committed to error on the subject of Holy Scripture. No Council of Trent has bound any one to a decision equally untrue morally and historically. If the question of the Canon has not been absolutely settled there, it is at least capable of a right settlement. In the West, on the other hand, the steady divergence of usage and critical truth during ten centuries was fixed in a final and hopeless antagonism. How this came to pass will be traced in the next Chapter.

CHAPTER X.

THE BIBLE IN THE SIXTEENTH CENTURY.

*Think not that I came to send peace on the earth:
I came not to send peace but a sword.*—St Matt.
x. 34.

THE sixteenth century places us again face to face with the combined powers of the East and West. For a time each had gone on fulfilling its own work, but the fall of Constantinople brought them once more into contact. It was not only that 'Greece had arisen from the dead with the New Testament in her hand,' but the East had risen with a Bible which was again felt to be a record of real facts, able to quicken faith amidst the conflicts of a world struggling towards a new life. We have already seen generally the part which Palestine, and Greece and Rome had to fulfil in the history of the Canon. A work was still reserved for the German races, and when the time came for its accomplishment, men were found to do it. Whatever may be thought of some of Luther's special judgments, however hasty and self-willed and imperious they may be, it is impossible to read his comments on Holy Scripture, without feeling that he realizes its actual historic worth and consequent spiritual

The work of the German races for the Bible.

meaning in a way which was unknown before. For him the words of apostles and prophets are 'living words,' direct and immediate utterances of the Holy Spirit, penetrating to the inmost souls of men, and not mere premisses for arguments or proofs.

The elements combined in the discussion on the Bible in the 16th century.

This intense sense of the personal character of Holy Scripture, so to speak, springing out of the recognition of its primary historical origin, which found a bold and at times an exaggerated expression in Luther, was more or less characteristic of the whole period. On all sides there was a tendency in the sixteenth century, even when it was repressed, to appeal to history and reason. The mere authority of usage, which at earlier times had been denied only by scholars, was then questioned by many in all classes. The study of Greek had made criticism possible, and laid open the true approach to the investigation of the growth of the Church. But still the real force of historical evidence was as yet imperfectly understood. The materials for testing and tracing to its source a current tradition were still scattered or unknown. And even those who felt most deeply that the Books of the Bible had their origin in human life, among men of like passions with themselves, were yet far removed from a simple and absolute trust in their historical transmission and confirmation by the body to which they were delivered. On the one hand a supposed intuitive perception of the Divine authority of Scripture, immediate and final, was assumed to exist in the individual and to supersede the judgment of the Christian society. On the other an ecclesiastical usage was invested, as it were, with a creative power, by which books, which had been deliberately set aside in a second rank, were raised to a new dignity as infallible sources of doctrine.

As doctrinal controversy grew wider and keener, the question of the Canon was debated with a vehemence unknown before. To concede to the Church in every age the prerogative of extending by its own power the range of the authoritative sources and tests of doctrine, was (as it appeared) to sacrifice the historical basis of a faith once delivered to men. And at the same time the denial of the existence of an absolute living criterion of truth seemed to make it necessary to transfer to the Bible, in its collected form, every attribute of that infallibility which before had been supposed to reside in the Church or in its earthly head. The collection of Holy Scripture was first narrowed to the strict limits fixed by ancient criticism, at least in the Old Testament, and then step by step it was taken out of the field of historical inquiry. A movement which began by the assertion of the value of historical evidence ended in the suppression of all historical criticism by the later Lutheran and Genevan schools.

An antagonism of principles.

It is not part of our subject to trace the effects for good and for evil which followed from the general prevalence of this later theory of the Bible in Protestant Churches up to our own time. However repugnant it may be to the wider views of ecclesiastical history which are now opened to us, it would not, perhaps, be difficult to show that it fulfilled an important function in preserving a true sense of the Divine authority of Holy Scripture, as a whole, during a period of transition. If the tendency of the later

The debate guided by feeling more than by criticism.

schools was to reduce the Bible to a mere text book ; the Book itself was in danger of falling to pieces under the free treatment of Luther. At present it is necessary only to notice that the controversy on the Canon in the sixteenth century—the first occasion on which the subject was debated as a question of doctrine in the Catholic Church—was really conducted by feeling rather than by external evidence. The evidence on the subject was not available, even if the disputants could have made use of it. But a more summary method offered itself. In a word the Romanists followed popular usage, regarding the Bible as one only out of many original sources of truth : the Lutherans, or more strictly Luther, judged the written Word by the Gospel contained in it, now in fuller now in scantier measure, to which the Word in man bore witness : the Calvinists, accepting without hesitation the Old Testament from the Jewish Church and the New Testament from the Christian Church, set up the two records as the outward test and spring of all truth, absolutely complete in itself and isolated from all history.

It would be a fruitful inquiry to follow out the growth and antagonism of the principles involved in these general views: to trace the truth which each embodies and exaggerates : to indicate the influence which partial or faulty teaching on Scripture exercised on other parts of the Christian doctrine in which they were included; and even in the purely historical sketch to which we are now limited, a reference to these most interesting questions will give a unity and significance to what might otherwise appear a fragmentary discussion.

THE BIBLE IN THE SIXTEENTH CENTURY. 249

SECT. I. *The Roman Church.*

CHAP. X.

At the dawn of the Reformation the great Romanist scholars remained faithful to the judgment on the Canon which Jerome had followed in his translation. And Cardinal XIMENES, in the preface to his magnificent Polyglott (*Biblia Complutensia*)—the lasting monument of the University which he founded at *Complutum* or *Alcala*, and the great glory of the Spanish press—separates the *Apocrypha* from the canonical books. The books, he writes, which are without the Canon, which the Church receives rather for the edification of the people than for the establishment of ecclesiastical doctrines, are given only in Greek, but with a double translation[1].

Cardinal Ximenes
XIMENES.
A.D.
1437—1517.

Prolog. III. *b.*

Cardinal Ximenes spoke only of the disputed books of the Old Testament. His great literary rival went further. ERASMUS, in his edition of the New Testament, (the first published in the original Greek A.D. 1516,) which was dedicated to Leo X., notices the doubts which had been raised as to the controverted books, without pronouncing more than a critical judgment upon them. Thus he distinctly maintains that the *Epistle to the Hebrews* was not written by St Paul, both on the ground of its style, and also from questionable statements on points of doctrine (c. vi. 6), while he prefaces his criticism with the remark, 'I would wish you, good reader, not to consider this epistle of less value because

ERASMUS.
A.D.
1467—1536.

His opinions on *Hebrews*.

---

[1] Sixtus Senensis (see p. 258) with an obvious reference to this passage alters it most significantly: 'The books which are without the Canon *of the Hebrews*, which the Church reads for edification, are given only in Greek, &c.' (*Bibl. S.* IV. *Franciscus Xymenius.*)

many have doubted whether it is the work of Paul or some other writer. Whoever wrote it it is worthy of being read by Christians on many accounts.' So again, he supposes that the Epistles of *James* and 2, 3 *John* were written not by the Apostles, but by some other persons of the same names. On the *Apocalypse* he speaks at greater length; and his words are so characteristic that they may be quoted here as a singular illustration of the manner in which the best scholars of the sixteenth century approached the criticism of Holy Scripture. "St Jerome," he says, "bears witness that the *Apocalypse* was not received by the Greeks even in his time; and moreover that some most learned men had assailed the whole substance of the book with severe criticisms as a mere romance, on the ground that it presents no trace of Apostolic dignity, but contains only an ordinary history disguised in symbols. To say nothing at present of these opinions, I have been somewhat moved by other conjectures and also by the fact that the author while writing the Revelation is so anxious to introduce his own name: 'I John,' 'I John,' just as if he were writing a bond and not a book, and that not only against the custom of the other Apostles but much more against his own custom, since in his Gospel, though the subject is less exalted, he nowhere gives his own name, but indicates it by slight references...... Further in the Greek MSS. which I have seen the title is not 'of John the Evangelist,' but 'of John the Divine;' not to mention that the style is widely different from that of the Gospel and Epistle...These arguments, I say, would somewhat move me to decline to believe that the work belongs to John the Evangelist, unless the general consent of the world called me to another conclusion, but especially the authority of the Church, if at least the Church approves of this work with that feeling, that she wishes it to be considered the work of John the Evangelist and to be held of equal weight with the other canonical books... In fact, I observe that ancient theologians quote passages from this book rather for illustration and ornament than for the support of a serious proposition. Since even among jewels there is some difference; and some gold is purer and better than other. In sacred things also, one thing is more sacred than another. 'He who is spiritual,' as Paul says, 'judges all things, and is judged by no one.'"

With this strange conflict of criticism and authority, with this half suppressed irony, and insinuated doubt, with this assertion of a final appeal to private judgment, the great work of Erasmus closes; and it is probable that the last words best express the freedom of his real judgment. For some time his notes seem to have been unchallenged; but the spread of the reformed opinions directed attention to the statements which they contained in opposition to the current opinion of the Roman Church. An attack was made upon them before the Theological Faculty of Paris (the Sorbonne) in 1524; and in 1526 the French doctors considered and condemned a large number of propositions which were taken from his New Testament, and the defence which he had previously made. In this censure the Sorbonne declared that 'it was an error of faith to doubt as to the author of one of the books' (of the New Testament). 'Though formerly some

Du Plessis, *Collect. Jud. de nov. error.* I Jud. iv.; II. 58 ff.

252   *THE BIBLE IN THE CHURCH.*

CHAP. X. have doubted about the authors of particular books,' the decision runs, 'yet after that the Church has received them under the name of such authors by its universal usage, and has approved them by its judgment, it is not any longer right for a Christian to doubt of the fact, or to call it in question.' This general judgment is then enforced by a special affirmation of the authenticity of the *Epistle to the Hebrews* (as St Paul's), 2 *Peter* and the *Apocalypse*, with references to the Councils of Laodicea, Carthage, and the Apocryphal Council at Rome under Gelasius.

Meanwhile Erasmus had extended his criticisms to the *Apocrypha* of the Old Testament. This he was led to do in the edition of Jerome, on which he was engaged for many years. At the time when the Sorbonne was discussing his criticisms on the New Testament, he repeated what he had said in the Preface to a volume of his Jerome, but with a significant addition. 'For the rest,' he writes, 'it is not yet agreed in what spirit the Church now holds in public use books which the ancients with great consent reckoned among the Apocrypha. Whatever the authority of the Church has approved I embrace simply as a Christian man ought to do...Yet it is of great moment to know in what spirit the Church approves anything. For allowing that it assigns equal authority to the Hebrew Canon and the Four Gospels, it assuredly does not wish *Judith, Tobit* and *Wisdom* to have the same weight as the *Pentateuch*.' At a later time his judgment still wavered. In an Exposition of the Creed he gives the Hebrew Canon (without *Esther*) as containing the books of the Old Testament 'which

Tom. IV.
A.D. 1525
(quoted by Hody).

A.D. 1533.

it would be impious to doubt;' and then goes on CHAP. X.
to say 'that *Wisdom, Ecclesiasticus, Tobit, Judith, Esther*, and the *Additions to Daniel* have
been received into ecclesiastical use. Whether,
however, the Church receives them as possessing
the same authority as the others the spirit of the
Church must know.'

Erasmus was the real leader both of the literary and critical schools of the Reformation. His
influence extended both to his own Church and
to the Protestant Churches of Germany and
Switzerland; and opinions which he intimated
with hesitation and doubt found elsewhere a bold
expression. To take one example from Romanist
scholars, Cardinal CAIETAN (Jacob [Thomas] de Cardinal
Vio), the adversary of Luther at Augsburg in 1518, CAIETAN.
A.D.
gives an unhesitating adhesion to the Hebrew 1469—1534.
Canon in his *Commentary on all the Authentic
Historical Books of the Old Testament*, which
was dedicated to Clement VII. 'The whole A.D. 1532.
Latin Church,' he says, 'owes very much to Ad Clem. VII.
Pont. Max.
St Jerome...on account of his separation of the
canonical from the uncanonical books. Since by The *Apocry-*
this he freed us from the reproach of the He- *pha.*
brews, [who blamed us] for framing books or
parts of books of the ancient Canon, which they
are absolutely without.' After completing his
commentary on Esther, he adds: 'In this place *In Esth.* c. x.
we close our commentaries on the historical books
of the Old Testament, for the remaining books
(*Judith, Tobit, Maccabees* 1, 2) are reckoned by
St Jerome without the canonical books and placed
among the Apocrypha together with *Wisdom*
and *Ecclesiasticus*...Nor must you be disturbed
by the strangeness of the fact, if you shall anywhere find those books reckoned among the

Canonical books, either in the Sacred Councils or in the Sacred Doctors. For the language of Councils and Doctors must alike be revised by the judgment of Jerome; and according to his opinion those books and any others there may be like them in the Canon of the Bible are not canonical in the sense of establishing points of faith; yet they can be called canonical for the edification of the faithful, inasmuch as they are received in the Canon of the Bible for this purpose, and treated with respect. For with this distinction you will be able to understand the words of Augustine, and what was written in the Florentine Council under Eugenius IV., and what was written in the provincial Councils of Carthage and Laodicea, and by Popes Innocent and Gregory.'

The disputed books of New Testament.

The authority of Jerome had equal weight with Cardinal Caietan in dealing with the Antilegomena of the New Testament. Thus in the preface to his commentary to the *Epistle to the Hebrews* he writes, 'Since we have received the rule of Jerome let us not err in the separation of the canonical books (for those which he delivered as canonical we hold canonical, and those which he separated from the canonical books we hold without the Canon); therefore as the author of this epistle is doubtful in the opinion of Jerome, the epistle also is rendered doubtful, since unless it is Paul's it is not clear that it is canonical. Whence it comes to pass that if anything arise doubtful in faith it cannot be determined from the sole authority of this epistle. See how great mischief an anonymous book creates!' In like manner he quotes Jerome for the doubts entertained as to the authority of *St James*, 2 *Peter*, 2, 3 *John* and *St Jude*. Of the three last he expressly says that 'they are of less authority than those which are certainly Holy Scripture.' On 2 *Peter* alone he decides favourably, for the argument from style is, he maintains, very fallacious. The *Apocalypse* he dismisses in a sentence. 'I confess that I cannot interpret the *Apocalypse* according to the literal sense. Let him interpret it to whom God has given the power.'

Sub fin.
Comm. in Ep. Judæ.

These statements of Cardinal Caietan passed unchallenged during his lifetime, but shortly after his death they were assailed by CATHARINUS, a vehement controversialist whose life was spent in disputes. Yet Catharinus abandoned the argument from history, and simply took refuge in the decrees of Popes Innocent, Gelasius and Eugenius as decisive upon the extent of the Canon. This simple mode of determining the question was unhappily adopted, and probably in part through his influence, at the COUNCIL OF TRENT, in which he played an important part. The Council held its first Session on Dec. 13th, 1545. In the third session (Feb. 4th, 1546) the Nicene Creed was recited and ratified. The subject of Holy Scripture and Tradition was then brought forward for preliminary discussion on Feb. 12th. Four articles taken from the writings of Luther were proposed for consideration or rather for condemnation. Of these the first affirmed that Scripture only (without tradition) was the single and complete source of doctrine; the second that the Hebrew Canon of the Old Testament and the acknowledged books of the New Testament ought only to be admitted as authoritative. These dogmas were discussed by about thirty divines in four meetings. On the

CATHARINUS.

Annot. in Comm. Caietani, Lib. I. (1542).

The *Council of Trent.*

256 *THE BIBLE IN THE CHURCH.*

CHAP. X.

Varieties of opinion

Decree on the Canon of Scripture.

first point there was a general agreement. It was allowed that tradition was a co-ordinate source of doctrine with Scripture. On the second there was a great variety of opinion. Some proposed to follow the judgment of Cardinal Caietan and distinguish two classes of books, as, it was argued, had been the intention of Augustine. Others wished to draw the line of distinction yet more exactly, and form three classes, (1) the Acknowledged Books, (2) the Disputed Books of the New Testament, as having been afterwards generally received, (3) the Apocrypha of the Old Testament. A third party wished to give a bare list, as that of Carthage, without any further definition of the authority of the books included in it, so as to leave the subject yet open. A fourth party, influenced by a false interpretation of the earlier papal decrees, and necessarily ignorant of the grave doubts which affect their authenticity, urged the ratification of all the books of the enlarged Canon as equally of Divine authority. The first view was afterwards merged in the second, and on March 8 three minutes were drawn up embodying the three remaining opinions. These were considered privately, and on the 15th the third was carried by a majority of voices. The decree in which it was finally expressed was published on the 8th of April, and for the first time the question of the contents of the Bible was made an absolute article of faith and confirmed by an Anathema. 'The holy, œcumenical and general Council of Trent,' so the decree runs, '...following the examples of the orthodox fathers receives and venerates all the books of the Old and New Testaments...and also traditions pertaining to faith and conduct...with an equal feeling of devotion and reverence.' Then follows the list of the books of the Old and New Testaments, including *Tobit, Judith, Wisdom, Ecclesiasticus,* 1 and 2 *Maccabees,* in the same order as the decree of Eugenius IV. and the decree proceeds, 'If, however, anyone does not receive the entire books with all their parts as they are accustomed to be read in the Catholic Church and in the old Latin Vulgate edition (*i. e.* Jerome's with the additions) as sacred and canonical, and knowingly and wittingly despises the aforesaid traditions, let him be Anathema.'

This fatal decree, in which the Council, harassed by the fear of lay critics and 'grammarians,' gave a new aspect to the whole question of the Canon, was ratified by fifty-three prelates, among whom there was not one scholar distinguished for historical learning, not one who was fitted by special study to deal with a subject in which the truth could only be determined by a careful examination of the records of antiquity. How completely the decision was opposed to the spirit and letter of the original judgments of the Greek and Latin Churches, how far it was at variance in the doctrinal equalization of the disputed and acknowledged books of the Old Testament with the traditional opinion of the West, how absolutely unprecedented was the conversion of an ecclesiastical usage into an article of belief, will be seen from the evidence which has been already adduced. If historical criticism had made as much advance as grammatical criticism at the time when the decree was enacted, no anathema at least would have been directed against differences of opinion on books or parts of books; for on one point at least scholarship gained the day. It was decided after much discussion that no anathema should be added to the second part of the decree which affirmed the authority of the Latin Vulgate.

It is unnecessary to continue the history of the Canon in the Romish Church. The attempts which have been made from time to time by Romanist Scholars to claim some freedom of opinion on the subject, can find no excuse in the terms of the decree. One judgment only will be added, which has considerable interest from the circumstances under which it was pronounced.

The *Bibliotheca Sancta* of the Dominican SIXTUS SENENSIS, which was dedicated to Pius V., as 'the chief author of the Index of prohibited books and the purifier of Christian literature,' may be taken as the authorized expression of the general views which prevailed in the Council. Sixtus divides the books of the Bible into two classes. The books of the first class (Protocanonical) are those of which there has never been any doubt in the Church, or to use the term which has been already explained the 'acknowledged' books of the Old and New Testaments except *Esther*. The books of the second Class ('called Ecclesiastical in former times but now Deuterocanonical') are those which were not generally known till a late period, 'as in the Old Testament *Esther, Tobit, Judith,* and *Baruch,* the *Letter of Jeremiah,* the *Wisdom of Solomon, Ecclesiasticus,* the *Additions to Daniel, Maccabees* (2). And in the New Testament, in like manner, *Mark* xvi. 9—20; *Luke* xxii. 43, 44; *John* vii. 53—viii. 11, the *Epistle to the Hebrews, James,* 2 *Peter,* 2, 3 *John, Jude, Apocalypse,* and other books of the same kind (?), which formerly the ancient

THE BIBLE IN THE SIXTEENTH CENTURY. 259

fathers of the Church held as Apocryphal and not CHAP. X.
Canonical, and at first permitted to be read
only before catechumens (as Athanasius witnesses)...then (as Ruffinus writes) allowed to be
read before all the faithful, not for the confirmation of doctrines, but merely for the instruction of the people: and...at last willed that they
should be adopted among the Scriptures of irrefragable authority...' Apocryphal writings (in a
good sense) are those of which 'the Fathers of
the Church did not venture to decide whether
their authors were inspired by the Holy Spirit,
and therefore forbade them to be alleged for the
support of doctrines...and allowed them to be
read only privately...Such are the 3rd and 4th
Books of Esdras, the 3rd and 4th Books of Maccabees, the Appendix to Esther...'

The concessions and claims made in this passage are equally significant. The determination
of the books which come within the limits of the
Bible is taken out of the domain of historical
criticism. It is admitted that for nearly four
centuries the Hebrew Canon of the Old Testament was alone received. It is affirmed that the
Church has power not only to fix the extent of
the Canon, but also to settle questions of text.
The field of Biblical study is definitely closed
against all free research.

SECT. II. *The Saxon School of Reformers.*

Meanwhile a spirit was awakened in Ger- LUTHER.
many which for a time cast a vivid if a partial
light upon the Bible as the depository of the Divine teaching transmitted to the Church. The
discovery of a Latin Bible, we are told, turned
the thoughts of Luther into a new channel. And

17—2

Luther on his side found in the Bible something which had long been hidden from the world, not as to its doctrine only, but as to its general relation to God and men. The study of the Bible was a life-long passion with him. 'Were I but a great poet,' he said, 'I would write a magnificent poem on the utility and efficacy of the Divine word.' His judgment on the different Books is given in detail in his Prefaces. These are so full of life, and so characteristic of the man, that they can never lose their interest; and as a whole they form an important chapter of the history of the Bible. It will be sufficient to quote fragments from his remarks on the controverted books of the Old and New Testaments. 'If the truth of the history of *Judith*,' he says, 'could be established by satisfactory evidence, it would be a noble and beautiful book, which might well find a place in the Bible...As it is there are errors and doubts both as to dates and names which I cannot in any way clear up. [But if we look at it as a Divine Allegory] it is a beautiful, good, holy, profitable book, which we Christians shall do well to read. For we must so understand it, as if a spiritual, holy poet or prophet spoke by the Holy Ghost, who presents such characters [as the book describes] and through them preaches to us.'

The Book of *Wisdom* he refers to the authorship of Philo. Yet even so he affirms that 'there is very much that is good in it, and it is well worthy of being read...' It is, in fact, 'a true exposition and pattern of the first Commandment;' and from this book we can see 'how all wisdom springs and flows from this Commandment, which is the true sun whereby the wise see all they see ...And this is the chief reason why it is well to

THE BIBLE IN THE SIXTEENTH CENTURY. 261

read this book, that we may learn to fear and trust God: Thereto may He help us with grace.' CHAP. X.

'What we have said of *Judith*,' he remarks, 'we may say also of *Tobit*. If it is a history, it is a holy history. If it is a poem, it is truly a right beautiful, wholesome, profitable poem, the work of a gifted poet...*Judith* is a good, serious, brave Tragedy; *Tobit* an elegant, pleasing, godly Comedy...Therefore is the book profitable and good for us Christians also to read, as the work of an elegant Hebrew poet, who deals with no light matters, but with serious matters, and so far handles them in a Christian spirit.' *Tobit. Id.* p. 89.

Ecclesiasticus 'is a profitable book for an ordinary man; for all its purpose is to make the citizen or the head of a family God-fearing, pious and wise...We might well call it a "Book of household Discipline," or "of the virtues of a good Housholder."' *Ecclesiasticus. Id.* p. 92.

'Of very little worth is the Book of *Baruch*, whoever the worthy Baruch may be...So that I had very nearly excluded it with 3 and 4 *Ezra* (1, 2 *Esdras*) from my translation. For these two books we would not translate, because they have nothing in them which you might not find better in Æsop...However, we have admitted *Baruch*, because he writes so strongly against idolatry, and maintains the Law of Moses.' *Baruch. Id.* p. 93.

The first book of Maccabees is 'one of those which are not found in the Hebrew Bibles. Yet it presents almost the same form as other books of Holy Scripture in style and language, and would not have been unworthy to be included in the Bible, since it is a very necessary and useful book for the understanding of *Dan.* xi...For that 1 *Maccabees Id.* p. 94.

reason it is useful for us Christians to read and to be acquainted with it.'

Of the *Second Book of the Maccabees* he says, 'Rightly as the first book might have been taken into the number of the Holy Scriptures, so rightly is this book cast out, though there is some good in it.'

The *additions to Daniel and Esther* he likens to 'corn-flowers' which he had taken out of the books in which they stood in the Latin texts, but afterwards placed in a separate bed that they might not wither, because there was much good in them, especially the *Benedicite*. '*Susanna, Bel, Habacuc* and the *Dragon* appear to be pretty spiritual poems ; for their names admit of a symbolic meaning.'

The general result of these special prefaces is given in the short explanation which was prefixed to the first collected edition of the Apocrypha and preserved in the standard edition of the Bible (1545). 'The *Apocrypha*, that is books, which, while they are not placed on the same footing as the Holy Scripture, are yet profitable and good for reading[1].'

In dealing with the New Testament Luther shows equal freedom and boldness. For him there is a Gospel within the Gospel, a New Testament within the New Testament. 'From all this,' he says, 'you can rightly judge between all

---

[1] The catalogue given (I quote from the edition of 1534) is : *Judith, Wisdom, Tobias, Sirach* (*Ecclesiasticus*), *Maccabees* (1, 2), pieces in *Esther*, pieces in *Daniel*. The *Prayer of Manasses* is added at the end without note or preface, and at the conclusion of this follows 'the end of the books of the Old Testament.'

the books, and distinguish which are the best. For *St John's Gospel*, and *St Paul's Epistles*, especially that to the *Romans*, and *St Peter's First Epistle* are the true marrow and kernel of all the books; which properly also might be the first, and each Christian should be counselled to read them first and most, and make them as common by daily reading as his daily bread...Briefly *St John's Gospel* and his *first Epistle*, *St Paul's Epistles*, especially those to the *Romans, Galatians, Ephesians,* and *St Peter's first Epistle: these* (the words are emphasized in the original) *are the books which show thee Christ, and teach all which it is needful and blessed for thee to know, even if you never see or hear any other book, or any other doctrine.* Therefore is the *Epistle of St James* a right strawy Epistle compared with them, for it has no character of the Gospel in it.'

Agreeably to this general statement Luther placed the *Epistle to the Hebrews, James, Jude* and the *Apocalypse* at the end of his translation, after the other books of the New Testament, which he called 'the true and certain, Capital-books of the New Testament.' Of the Epistle to the Hebrews he says that it was certainly (ii. 3) by a disciple of the Apostles, and not by an Apostle, by one 'who did not lay the foundation of faith (vi. 1), but who yet built upon it gold, silver, precious stones. Therefore even if we find perhaps wood, straw, or hay mingled with it, that shall not prevent us from receiving such instruction with all honour; though we do not place it absolutely on the same footing with the Apostolic Epistles.'

'I admire,' he says, 'the *Epistle of St James*, though it was rejected by the ancients, and still

264   *THE BIBLE IN THE CHURCH.*

CHAP. X.
Id. p. 148.

hold it as good, for this reason that it lays down no teaching of man, and presses home the law of God. Yet to express my own opinion, without prejudice to any one, I do not hold it to be the writing of any Apostle, for these reasons: (1) It contradicts St Paul and all other Scripture in giving righteousness to works...(2) It teaches Christian people and yet does not once notice the Passion, the Resurrection, the Spirit of Christ...' Yet 'it is the duty of a true Apostle to preach

Id. p. 149.

Christ's Sufferings and Resurrection...And therein all true, holy books agree, that they preach and urge Christ. That too is the right touchstone whereby to criticise all books, whether they urge Christ or not, for all Scripture testifies of Christ (*Rom.* iii. 21)...That which does not teach Christ is still not Apostolic, even if it were the teaching of St Peter or St Paul. Again, that which preaches Christ, that were Apostolic, even if

Id. p. 150.

Judas, Annas, Pilate and Herod preached it.' 'I cannot then place it among the true Capital-books; but I will forbid no one to place and elevate it as he pleases; for there are many good sayings in it.'

Epistle of St Jude.
Id. p. 150.

The *Epistle of St Jude* is 'indisputably an extract or abstract from the Second Epistle of St Peter...Therefore, though I applaud it, it is not an Epistle which can claim to be reckoned among the Capital-books, which ought to lay the foundation of faith.'

The *Apocalypse.*

Of the *Apocalypse* he simply says (A. D. 1534)[1]

---

[1] At an earlier time (A.D. 1522) he had spoken far more disparagingly of the book. 'For several reasons I hold it to be neither apostolic nor prophetic...My spirit cannot acquiesce in the book:...I abide by the books which present Christ clear and pure to me.'

THE BIBLE IN THE SIXTEENTH CENTURY. 265

that 'no man ought to be hindered from holding it to be a work of St John or otherwise, as he will...' Reckless interpretations had brought it into dishonour. And though it was yet 'a dumb prophecy,' the true Christian, he shows, can use it for consolation and warning. 'Briefly, our Holiness is in heaven where Christ is, and not in the world before our eyes, as some paltry ware in the market. Therefore let offence, factions, heresy and wickedness be and do what they may; if only the Word of the Gospel remains pure with us, and we hold it dear and precious, we need not doubt that Christ is near and with us, even if matters go hardest; as we see in this Book that through and above all plagues, beasts, evil angels, Christ is still near and with His saints.'

CHAP. X.

Id. p. 152.

The freshness and power of Luther's judgments on the Bible, the living sense of a fellowship with the spirit which animates them, the bold independence and self-assertion which separate them from all simply critical conclusions, combined to limit their practical acceptance to individuals. Such judgments rest on no definite external evidence. They cannot be justified by the ordinary rule and measure of criticism or dogma. No Church could rest on a theory which makes private feeling the supreme authority as to doctrine and the source of doctrine. As a natural consequence the later Lutherans abandoned the teaching of their great master on the written Word. For a time the 'disputed' books of the New Testament (Antilegomena) were distinguished from the remainder; but in the early part of the seventeenth century this difference was looked upon as wholly belonging to the past, and towards its close the very letter of the printed text of

CHAP. X. Scripture was treated by great Lutheran Divines as possessing an inherent and inalienable sanctity beyond the reach of historical discussion. Yet the Lutheran Church has no recognized definition of canonicity, and no express list of the Sacred Books. The nearest approach to this is in the Lutheran Bible, in which the Apocrypha are placed by themselves and separated distinctly from 'the Holy Scripture.' But on the other hand four of the Antilegomena of the New Testament are removed equally from their places in the Latin Bible and placed as a kind of Appendix, though without any special notice. And the detailed judgments which Luther delivered are not more favourable to one class than to the other. To a certain extent therefore the question was left open; and usage alone has determined finally the subordinate position of the Apocrypha to the Old Testament, and elevated the Antilegomena of the New Testament to an equality with the remaining books.

KARLSTADT. One attempt, however, was made to investigate independently the extent of the Canon and the principles on which it was formed. Among the early friends of Luther was ANDREW BODENSTEIN of KARLSTADT (Carlstadt), who is commonly known by the name of his native town, Archdeacon of Wittenberg. As the Reformation advanced, Luther and Karlstadt were separated by theological differences, and after long sufferings Karlstadt found an honourable retreat in Switzerland. By Bullinger's recommendation he was made professor of theology at Basle and died there in 1541. While he was still working with Luther, in 1520, he published a treatise, *On the Canonical Scriptures*, which exhibits a remarkable sense of the real bearings and principles of an investigation into the constitution of the Bible. The book was in advance of the age and appears to have produced no effect at the time. It consists of five parts, (1) On the majesty of Scripture. (2) On the force and strength of Scripture. (3) On the number and order of the Sacred books. (4) On the Catalogues of Jerome and Augustine. (5) A general classification of Scripture. It is with the last division alone that we are now concerned. In this Karlstadt divides all the books of Scripture into three classes of different dignity, almost as Hugo de S. Victore had done before him. The first class contains only the *Pentateuch* and the four *Gospels*, 'the clearest luminaries of the whole Divine truth.' The second class includes the Prophets, according to the Hebrew reckoning, and the acknowledged Epistles of the New Testament (*Paul* 13, 1 *Peter*, 1 *John*). The third class contains the Hagiographa of the Hebrew Canon and the seven disputed books of the New Testament[1].

CHAP. X.

His classification of Scripture.

See p. 204 n.

Of the books of the *Apocrypha* he judges Wisdom, *Ecclesiasticus*, *Judith*, *Tobit* and 1, 2 *Maccabees* to be uncanonical and yet holy writings: '1, 2 *Esdras*, *Baruch*, the *Prayer of Manasses*, and the *Additions to Daniel* are wholly Apocryphal and to be condemned.' 'If I were asked for my opinion,' he adds, 'as to reading such books [as *Tobit*, *Wisdom* and *Ecclesiasticus*] I should thus answer: That what they contain is

On the Apocrypha.

§§ 113, 114.

§ 118.

---

[1] The *Acts* is entirely omitted. Probably the book was looked upon by Karlstadt as an Appendix to St Luke's Gospel: see *De Canonicis Scripturis*, § 136. Yet again in §§ 65 ff, he appears to pass over the book purposely.

not to be despised at once, and still that it is not right that a Christian should relieve much less slake his thirst with them. The springs which are far from all suspicion must be sought which can have no poison in them; that is, before all things the best books must be read, those which are canonical beyond all controversy; afterwards if there shall be leisure, it is allowed to peruse the controverted books, provided that you compare and collate the non-canonical books with those which are truly canonical.'

This short summary of Karlstadt's results can give no idea of the breadth and subtlety of many of his remarks. The whole evidence was not before him and consequently he erred in his conclusions; but even as it is, his treatise is not without use in the present day. It was the first clear assertion of the independent supremacy of Holy Scripture, and so far the first enunciation of the fundamental principle of the Reformation. Yet at the same time Karlstadt recognized the historic function of the Church in collecting and ratifying the sacred books. 'Why,' he asks, in reference to Luther's objections to the Epistle of St James, 'if you allow the Jews to stamp books with authority by receiving them, do you refuse to grant as much power to the Churches of Christ, since the Church is not less than the Synagogue?' And though he placed the different books of the Bible in different ranks, yet he drew a broad line between all of them and the traditions or decrees of Christian teachers. 'You see,' he writes, 'kind reader, how great is the authority of the Holy Scriptures. Whether willingly or unwillingly you will allow the extent of their authority, whose slightest sign all other arts and sciences,

THE BIBLE IN THE SIXTEENTH CENTURY. 269

as far as they affect the moulding of life, revere, CHAP. X.
regard, dread, adore. Therefore rightly the laws
of men, the canons of popes, the customs of the
people, yield to [the Bible] as their mistress, and
minister to it.' 'We judge of the opinions of all § 5.
and each from the Sacred Scriptures,' he elsewhere says, 'and therefore we pronounce [the
Bible] to be the queen and mistress of all and the
judge who judges all things while she herself is
judged by none...' 'The Divine Law, single and § 6.
alone, is placed beyond all suspicion of error, and
draws all other laws within its dominion, or utterly destroys them if they strive against it.'

SECT. III. *The Swiss School of Reformers.*

Karlstadt forms a link between the Saxon
and Swiss Reformers. While Luther was bat-
tling for the one great principle of faith, a more
comprehensive movement was begun in Switzerland. ZWINGLI, the foremost of its champions, ZWINGLI.
was only a few weeks younger than Luther, and A.D.
he had not yet heard Luther's name, as he writes, 1484—1531.
when he began to preach the Gospel. But Zwin-
gli was not contented with the compromise which
Luther was willing to make with all that was
hallowed by usage, provided it was not positively
superstitious. He aimed at forming a strictly
logical system based on Scripture only, irrespec-
tive of tradition or custom. In this respect he
carried out, in intention at least, the principles
which Karlstadt had maintained; and the method which he followed became characteristic of
the Swiss Churches. The Saxon reformation was
in essence conservative: the Swiss reformation
was in essence rationalistic.

Zwingli himself does not appear to have discussed the Canon of Scripture. In his notes on the *Epistle to the Hebrews* and *St James* he takes no account of the doubts which had been raised as to their authority. Of the *Apocalypse* alone he declares that 'it does not present the style and spirit of St John.' While Zwingli was labouring to spread his doctrines at Zurich, his friend Œcolampadius carried on the same work at Basle. In a letter to the Waldenses, Œcolampadius explains the views of his party on the Canon. 'We do not despise,' he writes, '*Judith, Tobit, Baruch,* the last two books of *Esdras,* the three books of *Maccabees,* the last two chapters of *Daniel,* but we do not allow them Divine authority, equally with those others [of the Hebrew Canon].' 'In the New Testament we receive four *Gospels,* with the *Acts of the Apostles,* and fourteen Epistles of St Paul, and seven Catholic Epistles, together with the *Apocalypse;* although we do not compare the *Apocalypse,* the Epistles of *James,* and *Jude,* and 2 *Peter* and 2, 3 *John* with the rest.'

This judgment of Œcolampadius may be taken as a fair representation of the feeling in the German Churches of Switzerland. But even before his death, which happened in the same year as that of Zwingli, Farel had begun that movement in the French cantons which under the direction of Calvin influenced more or less the theology of all Western Europe.

The famous French Bible published at Neufchâtel in 1535, under the name of Olivetan, but really by CALVIN, whatever may be its other faults, contains a clear expression of the opinion of the French Reformer upon the *Apocrypha.*

THE BIBLE IN THE SIXTEENTH CENTURY. 271

The title of the book is 'The Bible, that is all the CHAP. X.
Holy Scripture, in which are contained the Old
Testament and the New, translated in French,
the Old from the Hebrew and the New from the
Greek.' After the completion of the translation
of the books of the Hebrew Canon follows, 'The His judgment
Volume of the Apocryphal Books contained in the *crypha.*
vulgate translation which we have not found in
Hebrew or Chaldee[1].' This collection is prefaced
by an epistle on the authority of the books in
which the judgment of Jerome is given in detail[2].
These books are of doubtful authority, it is said,
but we have 'the witness of the Prophets and
Apostles more clear than the day.' The lawyer
refuses to speak without the text of human law
to support him, and how much more shall the
Christian shrink from going beyond the law of
the living God to support their faith. Rather,
'let us leave the things that are uncertain to
follow the certain, holding us and resting us on
them, and fastening our anchor there as in a sure
place.'

With regard to the *Antilegomena* of the New On the *Anti-*
Testament, Calvin expresses himself with hardly the New Tes-
less boldness than Luther, though he practically tament.
followed common usage. He gives no notes on 2 and
3 *John* or on the *Apocalypse* in his Commentary

---

[1] The books contained are 3, 4 *Esdras*, *Tobit*,
Judith, *Wisdom*, *Ecclesiasticus*, *Baruch* and the *Epistle*,
1, 2 *Maccabees*, additions to *Esther* and *Daniel*, the
Prayer of Manasses.

[2] This preface is the more interesting from the fact
that it was transferred in a translation to Matthew's
English Bible of 1537, and with one singular alteration
to Cranmer's Bible of 1540 (see p. 284). It is strange
that this curious fact should have been overlooked by
those who have written on the English Versions.

on the N. T., and writes of 1 *John* as simply 'the Epistle of John.' 'I embrace,' he says, '[the Epistle to the *Hebrews*] without doubt among the Apostolic Epistles; nor do I doubt but that it was through a device of Satan that some have questioned its authority ... Wherefore let us not allow the Church of God and ourselves to be bereft of so great a blessing; but let us vindicate for ourselves the possession of it with firmness. We need, however, feel little anxiety as to who wrote it...I cannot myself be brought to believe that Paul was the author...The method of instruction and style sufficiently show that the writer was not Paul, and he professes himself to be one of the disciples of the Apostles (ii. 3) which is wholly alien from Paul's custom...'

'The fact that Eusebius says that doubts were formerly entertained on [2 *Peter*] ought not to deter us from reading it...I am more moved by the statement of Jerome, that some, led by the difference of style, did not think Peter the author of it. For although some likeness with his style can be observed, yet I confess that there is an obvious difference which indicates a different writer. There are also other plausible conjectures from which we may gather that it was the work of some other than Peter...But if it is received as canonical, we must confess that Peter was its author, since not only is it inscribed with his name, but the writer himself witnesses that he lived with Christ...I therefore lay down that, if the Epistle be deemed worthy of credit, it proceeded from Peter, not that he wrote it himself, but that some one of his disciples at his command included in it what the necessity of the times required...Certainly, since the majesty of

the Spirit of Christ exhibits itself in every part CHAP. X.
of the Epistle, I feel a scruple at rejecting it
wholly, however much I fail to recognize in it
the genuine language of Peter.'

Of the Epistle of *St James* he speaks more *St James*.
confidently. ' It is known,' he writes, 'from the
evidence of Jerome and Eusebius, that this Epistle was not received formerly without a struggle
by many churches. There are even at the present day some who do not think it worthy of
authority. Still I willingly embrace it without
doubt, because I see no sufficiently good reason
for rejecting it...Certainly, it cannot be required
of all to treat the same topic.' And of the Epistle of *St Jude* he speaks in similar terms: ' Al- *St Jude*.
though different conflicting opinions were entertained about this Epistle also among the ancients;
still because it is useful for reading, and does
not contain anything foreign to the purity of
Apostolic doctrine, while already in former times
it gained authority with the best writers, I willingly add it to the others.'

In each case a personal and not a critical or
historical test was applied. The result could
not be long doubtful. The edition of the New
Testament which was dedicated by BEZA to BEZA.
Queen Elizabeth in the year of Calvin's death, A.D. 1564.
exhibits very clearly the influence which usage
exercised in the suppression of the early doubts
on the *Antilegomena*. In his preface to the
Epistle to the Hebrews, Beza examines and meets The *Epistle*
the arguments which had been brought against *to the Hebrews*.
the belief in its Pauline authorship, and then
concludes: ' Let us, however, allow liberty of
judgment on this point, provided only we all
agree in this, that this Epistle was truly dictated

18

274   THE BIBLE IN THE CHURCH.

CHAP. X. by the Holy Spirit...while it is written in so excellent and so exact a method, that (unless we can suppose Apollos wrote it, whose learning and eloquence combined with the greatest piety are highly praised in the Acts) scarcely any one except St Paul could have been the writer.' He afterwards notices generally the doubts entertained as to *James*, 2 *Peter*, 2, 3 *John*, *Jude* but sets them aside without discussion. His preface to the *Apocalypse* is far more elaborate. In this he discusses in some detail the objections raised by Erasmus to its Apostolic origin and pronounces them in general to be severally weak and futile. 'This being the case,' he argues, 'although I do not think that we ought to dispute too obstinately as to the name of the writer, still I should be inclined to assign the book to John the Apostle rather than to any one else...If, however, it were allowed to form a conjecture from the style, I should assign it to no one rather than Mark, who also is himself called John. The character of this book being similar to and almost identical with that of the Gospel of Mark, not only in words but also in general phraseology...Finally, we are led to believe that the Holy Spirit was pleased to gather into this most precious book those predictions of the earlier prophets which remained to be fulfilled after the coming of Christ, and also added some particulars, as far as He knew that it concerned us to be acquainted with them.'

The *Catholic Epistles*.

The *Apocalypse*.

From what has been said it will appear that the subject of the Canon was not one which excited any marked interest among the chief Swiss reformers. Custom fixed the details of their judgment, and by a gradual process the Bible

THE BIBLE IN THE SIXTEENTH CENTURY. 275

was more and more removed (as was formally CHAP. X.
the case in the Romish Church) from the region
of history. The idea of inspiration was substituted for that of canonicity. The recognition of
variety and advance in the records of revelation
was virtually forbidden. The test of authority
was placed in individual sentiment, and not in
the common witness of the congregation.

The progress of thought thus indicated is Judgments
seen yet more clearly in the public acts of the in the re-
Reformed (Calvinistic) Churches. In these also formed Con-
there is a rapid advance from a general assertion fessions.
of the claims of Holy Scripture to an exact and
rigid definition of the character and contents of
the Bible. No notice is taken of the limits of
the Canon in the confessions of faith issued by   A.D.
Zwingli. In the First Confession of Faith at   1523—1530.
Basle (1534), which is said to have been moulded
on the Confession of Œcolampadius, a general Niemeyer,
reference is made 'to Holy Biblical Scripture,' *Coll. Confess.*
to which every opinion is submitted. In the p. 104.
First Helvetic Confession (1536) Canonical Scripture, that is, 'the Word of God, given by the Holy
Spirit, and set forth by the Prophets and Apostles,' is declared to be 'the oldest and most per- *Id.* pp. 105,
fect philosophy, which alone contains completely 115.
all piety and all the rule of life.' The same general description is found in the Genevan Catechism, published by Calvin A.D. 1545, and in the p. 159.
later Helvetic Confession, 1566. The Belgian p. 467.
Confession (1561—63), which was influenced in
some degree by the English Articles, treats of
the Canon at some length. 'We embrace,' it is Art. 3—7.
said, 'Holy Scripture in those two volumes of the pp. 361—3.
Old and New Testament, which are called the
Canonical Books, about which there is no con-

18—2

troversy[1].' Then follows a list of the Hebrew Canon and of the books of the New Testament, as we receive them. 'These books alone,' the next article continues, 'we receive as sacred and Canonical, on which our faith can rest, by which it can be confirmed and established. And we believe all those things which are contained in them, and that not so much because the Church receives and approves them as Canonical, as because the Holy Spirit witnesses to our consciences that they emanated from God; and on this account also that they themselves sufficiently witness to and approve of themselves this their proper authority...' 'Moreover, we lay down a difference between these sacred books and those which men call Apocryphal, inasmuch as the Church can read the Apocryphal books, and take out proof from them so far as they agree with the Canonical books; but their authority and certainty is by no means such that any dogma of Christian faith or religion can certainly be established from their testimony...And therefore with these divine Scriptures, and this truth of God, no other human writings, however holy, no custom, nor multitude, nor antiquity, nor prescription of time, nor succession of persons, nor any councils, no decrees or statutes of men in fine, are to be compared, inasmuch as the truth of God excels all things.' Statements to the same general effect, with some verbal agreements, are found in the articles of the French reformed Church (1561); but there is this significant difference, that the *Epistle to the Hebrews* is placed in the French catalogue apart from the Epistles of St

[1] Altered afterwards to 'there never was any controversy.'

THE BIBLE IN THE SIXTEENTH CENTURY. 277

Paul. The Westminster Assembly (which first met in 1643) followed the same method in dealing with Scripture, and the words of their Confession may be taken as an exact and mature expression of the feelings of the Calvinistic churches on the subject of the Bible.

CHAP. X.

The Westminster Confession.

Art. 'i...It pleased the Lord at sundry times and in divers manners to reveal Himself and to declare His will unto His Church; and...to commit the same wholly unto writing; which maketh the Holy Scripture to be most necessary; those former ways of God's revealing His will unto His people being now ceased.

The humble advice of this Assembly of Divines... pp. 1 ff. ed 1646.

'ii. Under the name of Holy Scripture, or the Word of God written, are now contained all the books of the Old and New Testament, which are these:

'Of the Old Testament, *Genesis...Malachi.*

'Of the New Testament, *The Gospels according to Matthew...The Revelation of John.*

'All which are given by inspiration of God to be the rule of faith and life.

'iii. The Books commonly called Apocrypha, not being of Divine inspiration, are no part of the Canon of Scripture; and therefore are of no authority in the Church of God, nor to be any otherwise approved or made use of than other human writings.

'iv. The authority of the Holy Scripture, for which it ought to be believed and obeyed, dependeth not upon the testimony of any man or Church; but wholly upon God (who is truth itself) the Author thereof; and therefore it is to be received because it is the Word of God.

'v. We may be moved and induced by the testimony of the Church to an high and reverent esteem of the Holy Scripture...yet notwithstanding our full persuasion and assurance of the infallible truth and Divine authority thereof is from the inward work of the Holy Spirit bearing witness by and with the Word in our hearts.'

The controversies on the text of the Bible, which form a painful episode in the ecclesiastical annals of the seventeenth century, added yet severer precision to definitions like these, which seem sufficiently stringent. The most exact and rigid declaration of the inspiration of the Bible which is found in any public confession of faith was drawn up in the Swiss Declaration of 1675, which forms a characteristic close to this division of our history. 'Almighty God,' thus the articles commence, 'not only provided that His Word, which is a power to everyone who believes, should be committed to writing through Moses, the Prophets, and Apostles, but also has watched over it with a fatherly care up to the present time, and guarded lest it might be corrupted by the craft of Satan or any fraud of man...' Thus 'the Hebrew volume of the Old Testament, which we have received from the tradition of the Jewish Church, to which formerly the oracles of God were committed, and retain at the present day, both in its consonants, and in its vowels,—the points themselves, or at least the force of the points,— and both in its substance and in its words is divinely inspired, so that, together with the volume of the New Testament, it is the single and uncorrupted Rule of our faith and life, by whose standard, as by a touch-stone, all Versions which exist, whether Eastern or Western, must be tried, and wherever they vary be made conformable to it.'

THE BIBLE IN THE SIXTEENTH CENTURY. 279

SECT. IV. *The Arminian School.*   CHAP. X.

Yet such doctrines as these were not promulgated without opposition. Historical criticism was universally subordinate to doctrinal controversy, but still at times it made itself felt. In this respect the influence of the Arminian School upon the study of Holy Scripture was too great to be neglected in any account of the history of the Canon. The principles which were embodied in their teaching belonged to the dawn of the Reformation, though they only found adequate expression at a later time. GROTIUS (de Groot) Grotius. may be taken as their representative, and no one can have used his *Annotations* without feeling that his power of interpreting Scripture, though practically marred by many faults, was yet in several respects far superior to that of his contemporaries. His *Commentary* includes notes on the Old Testament, the Apocrypha, and the New Testament. The *Apocrypha*[1] he places together as 'the books which are without the Hebrew Canon;' and in his special prefaces he discusses their origin, showing that many of them were by Greek writers, and further arguing that they had been interpolated by Christians. Yet he does not expressly determine the limit of the respect due to them. In another place he quotes with approbation the opinion of Jerome and the practice of the English Church. 'These books *Annot. ad* were not written or approved by prophets, as *Consult. Can.* those which the Hebrews acknowledge; but the IV. p. 627 (ed. 1679).

A.D. 1583—1645.

[1] The books which he notices are: *Tobit, Judith,* Additions to *Esther* and *Daniel, Wisdom, Ecclesiasticus, Baruch* and *Letter,* 1, 2, 3 *Maccabees.* Thus he adds 3 *Maccabees* to the Apocrypha which we receive, and omits 1, 2 *Esdras* and *Prayer of Manasses.*

Christian Church, or certainly great sections of it, have believed that there is nothing in them which does not well agree with those books which all acknowledge.' On the *Antilegomena* of the New Testament he speaks in greater detail: 'It is most obvious,' he says, 'that the *Epistle to the Hebrews* was not written by St Paul, from the difference in style between this Epistle and the Epistles of St Paul;' and he then points out various reasons which lead him to attribute it to St Luke. 'Those who have rejected the *Epistle of James*...had reasons, but not good reasons, for they saw that it was opposed to their views: This I remarked that all might see how perilous it is to recede from the general agreement of the Church.' 'I believe,' he says, 'that the original title of 2 *Peter* was the Epistle of Simeon,' *i. e.* of the successor of James in the bishopric of Jerusalem; and that the present epistle was made up of two epistles by this primitive bishop, of which the second begins at the third chapter.' 'Many of the ancients,' he writes, 'believed that 2 and 3 *John* were not the works of the Apostle, with whom Eusebius and Jerome do not disagree; and there are weighty arguments in favour of that opinion.' 'I am wholly led to believe that the *Epistle of Jude* was the work of Judas, a Bishop of Jerusalem in the time of Hadrian.' On the contrary, he maintains that the *Apocalypse* is a genuine work of the Apostle. 'Those early writers believed that it was a work of the Apostle John, who justly claim our credence.' 'I believe, however, that it was kept in the care of the *presbyter* John, a disciple of the *Apostle*, and that therefore it came to pass that it was supposed by some to be his work.'

THE BIBLE IN THE SIXTEENTH CENTURY. 281

SECT. V. *The English Church.* CHAP. X.

The history of the Canon in England is clearly
reflected in the history of the English translations
of the Bible. The work which was begun by See pp. 209,
Alfric and Wycliffe was brought to a worthy com- 212.
pletion in the reign of Henry VIII. and his successors; and the various Bibles which were
issued exhibit in details of classification and order
the changes of feeling which arose with regard to
the *Apocrypha* of the Old and the *Antilegomena*
of the New Testament.

The first edition of the New Testament which TYNDALE'S
was printed in English was that of W. TYNDALE. *New Testa-*
This probably was executed at Worms in 1525; *ment.*
and in the arrangement of the books it follows
the order of Luther's Bible. The *Epistle to the
Hebrews, James, Jude,* and the *Apocalypse,* are
placed together at the end. The *Second Epistle
of St Peter* and 2, 3 *John,* on the other hand,
are placed with 1 *Peter* and 1 *John.* In his Pro- On the dis-
logues to the several books Tyndale notices the puted books.
same doubts which Luther noticed, except that See p. 263.
he passes over the *Apocalypse* in silence, though
he decides generally in favour of the authority of
the disputed books. 'Whether [the *Epistle to* Doctrinal
the Hebrews] were Paul's or no, I say not, but *Treatises, &c.*
permit it to other men's judgments; neither *Park. Soc.).*
think I it to be an article of any man's faith, but
that a man may doubt of the author.' But in
spite of these doubts 'this Epistle ought no more *Id.* p. 523.
to be refused for a holy, godly, and catholic, than
the other authentic Scriptures.' 'Though [the *Id.* p 525.
Epistle of St James] were refused in old time,
and denied of many to be the Epistle of a very
Apostle, and though also it lay not the founda-

tion of the faith of Christ...methinketh it ought of right to be taken for Holy Scripture.' 'As for the *Epistle of Judas*, though men have and yet do doubt of the author...I see not but that it ought to have the authority of Holy Scripture.' In his Prologues to 2 *Peter* and 2, 3 *John* (like Luther) he does not refer to any doubts as to the canonicity of the Epistles.

The work of Tyndale, which was most nobly conceived and executed, was interrupted by his treacherous imprisonment and martyrdom. In the meantime, however, a complete edition of the English Bible had been printed abroad in 1535. This, according to the title, was 'faithfully and truly translated out of Douche [German] and Latyn in to Englishe' by MYLES COVERDALE; and dedicated to Henry VIII.—'oure Moses' who brought us out of Egypt 'from the cruell handes of our spirituall Pharao'—in language of strange flattery. A list of the books is given, which presents some peculiarities. 'The bokes of the fyrst parte' comprise the *Pentateuch:* 'The bokes of the seconde parte,' *Joshua...Esther:* 'The bokes of the thyrde parte,' *Job...Canticles* ('Salomon's balettes'). Then follow 'the Prophetes,' including *Baruch;* and next 'the Apocrypha.' The books of the New Testament follow the same order as in Tyndale's translation[1]. The Apocrypha have a separate title-page which explains distinctly the position which they were supposed to occupy. 'Apocripha. The bokes and treatises which amonge the fathers of olde are not rekened to be of like authorite with the other bokes of the byble, nether are they foūde in the Canon of the He-

[1] The *Epistle to the Hebrews* is still called 'The Epistle of St Paul the Apostle.'

brue. The *thirde boke of Esdras*, the *fourth boke of Esdras*, The boke of *Tobias*, The boke of *Judith*, Certayne chapters of *Hester*, The boke of *Wyssdome*, *Ecclesiasticus*, The *Storye of Susanna*[1], The *Storye of Bell*, The *first boke of the Machabees*, The *seconde boke of the Machabees*. Unto these also belongeth Baruc, whom we haue set amōge the prophetes next vnto Jeremy, because he was his scrybe and in his tyme[2].' A short preface is also given, in which appeal is made to the judgment of Jerome to show that 'the Apocrypha are not judged among the doctors to be of like reputation with the other Scripture. And the chief cause thereof is this: there be many places in them, that seem to be repugnant unto the open and manifest truth in the other books of the Bible. Nevertheless I have not gathered them together (Coverdale continues) to the intent that I would have them despised or little set by, or that I should think them false, for I am not able to prove it. Yea, I doubt not verily, if they were equally conferred with the other open Scripture (time, place and circumstance in all things considered) they should neither seem contrary, nor be untruly and perversely alleged[3].'

The work of Tyndale, which was broken off by his death, was continued by his friend JOHN Ro-

[1] To this 'the Prayer of Azarias and the Song of the three Children' are added in the text.

[2] This note is specially worthy of notice. A false historical tradition was strong enough to keep *Baruch* among the Canonical Books, though on general grounds it was declared Apocryphal.

[3] In the second edition of Coverdale's Bible, printed at Zurich (London) 1550, the book of *Baruch* is placed after *Tobit*, and the *Prayer of Manasses* added after *The Story of Bel*.

CHAP. X. GERS. Tyndale had translated the Old Testament to the end of 2 *Chronicles:* Rogers completed the translation with the help of Coverdale's Version which (it is said) he revised[1]; and added Coverdale's translation of the Apocrypha. The whole work was published under the name of THOMAS MAT-THEW in 1537. The books of the Apocrypha have a separate title: 'The volume of the bookes called Apocripha contayned in the comen Transl. in Latyne, whych are not founde in the Hebrue nor in the Chalde.' Then follows a list of the books identical except in some of the titles with that in the Authorised Version; and a new Preface is added in place of Coverdale's. This Preface is a translation of that prefixed to Calvin's French Bible of Neufchâtel, and affirms in very distinct language the subordinate position of the Apocrypha, 'as they are not received nor taken as legitimate and lawful as well of the Hebrew as of the whole Church.' In the New Testament the order of Tyndale is preserved unchanged; and *the Epistle to the Hebrews*, though transposed, still bears the name of St Paul.

See p. 271.

TAVERNER'S *Bible.*

In the Bible of R. TAVERNER (London, 1539), which follows Matthew closely, there are some significant changes. The title to the Apocrypha remains unaltered, but there is no preface; and in the title of the *Epistle to the Hebrews* the name of St Paul is omitted.

CRANMER'S *Bible.*

In CRANMER's or the Great Bible of 1540, the first 'appointed to be read in Churches,' the books of the Old Testament are divided into three parts,

---

[1] It is, however, remarkable that Tyndale's translation of Jonah, which appears to have been made and published about the same time as his translation of the Pentateuch, was not inserted in it, but Coverdale's.

THE BIBLE IN THE SIXTEENTH CENTURY. 285

'the *Pentateuch*, the Historical Books, including CHAP. X.
Job, the remaining books of the Hebrew Canon
from *Psalms to Malachi*.' Then follows 'the
volume of the bokes called *Hagiographa*.' The
list is identical with that in Matthew's Bible, and
the preface of Matthew is added with one singular change. The title of *Hagiographa* is substituted for *Apocrypha* but the explanation of the
latter word is retained as if it were applicable to
the former: the books are called Hagiographa, it
is said, 'because they were wont to be read not
openly and in common, but as it were in secret
and apart.' 'The Epistle of Saynct Paul the
Apostle unto the Hebrues' is placed after that to
Philemon, and the order of the remaining books
is the same as that which is found in our Authorised Version. In the reprint of Nov. 1541,
the title of the books of the *Apocrypha* is changed.
They are no longer marked by a peculiar name,
but are described in the same terms as the books
of the former three parts: 'The iiii. parte of the
Byble contayninge these bookes' according to the
list already given. The Preface of Matthew is
also omitted, and the books as they stand appear
to form an integral and equal portion of the Old
Testament. The New Testament is unchanged.

The *Genevan* Bible, which was completed by The *Genevan*
three English exiles at Geneva in 1560, remained *Bible.*
for three quarters of a century the popular Bible
for common use in England. The books of the
Apocrypha (except the *Prayer of Manasses*) are
inserted in a new translation and with a new preface. The preface is full of interest. 'These
books that follow in order after the Prophets
unto the New Testament, are called *Apocrypha*,
that is, books which were not received by a com-

mon consent to be read and expounded publicly in the Church, neither yet served to prove any point of Christian religion, save inasmuch as they had the consent of the other Scriptures called canonical to confirm the same, or rather whereon they were grounded: but as books proceeding from godly men, were received to be read for the advancement and furtherance of the knowledge of the history and for the instruction of godly manners: which books declare that at all times God had an especial care of His Church, and left them not utterly destitute of teachers and means to confirm them in the hope of the promised Messiah, and also witness that those calamities that God sent to His Church, were according to His providence, who had both so threatened by His prophets, and so brought it to pass for the destruction of their enemies and for the trial of His children.' The order of the books in the New Testament is that of the Authorised Version. In the preface to the *Epistle to the Hebrews* notice is taken of the doubts as to whether St Paul wrote it, ('as it is not like'), but no reference is made to the doubts as to the authority of the other disputed books.

The *Bishops'* Bible.

The *Bishops'* Bible of 1568 follows Cranmer's in the arrangement of the books. In the table of contents the *Apocrypha* form 'the fourth part of the Bible called Apocryphus;' and in the general classification of 'the whole Scripture of the Bible' into 'legal, historical, sapiential and prophetical' books, the books of the *Apocrypha* (except the *Prayer of Manasses*) are ranged equally with the books of the Hebrew Canon in their respective classes. The title-page of the *Apocrypha* describes them somewhat differently. 'The volume of the bookes called Apocrypha.' No preface is added. The order of the New Testament is the same as in Cranmer's Bible, and the Epistle to the Hebrews is ascribed to 'St Paul the Apostle[1].'

In the *Authorised Version* of 1611 'the bookes called *Apocrypha*' are marked by a running title '*Apocrypha*' at the top of the page, but they have no special catalogue or preface as in earlier editions. Various renderings and references are added to them as to the other books, and in the table of lessons, which is prefixed to the Bible, they are included in the general title 'Old Testament.'

The Authorised Version.

Briefly it may be said that the English Church remained true throughout to the judgment of Jerome. The *Apocrypha* were sanctioned in every case for ecclesiastical use, but not admitted (unless perhaps in the later editions of Cranmer's Bible) to form part of the doctrinal rule. At one time the line of distinction between them and the Hebrew Canon is drawn more broadly, at another less broadly, but there can be no doubt as to the general spirit of the law by which they were included in the Bible. They were retained in the public services, as possessing a moral and historic value, but they were not allowed to have an independent dogmatic authority. Yet the English Divines, like Athanasius and Jerome, did not scruple from time to time to quote passages from the *Apocrypha* as Scripture[2]; and sentences from

Summary.

---

[1] There is no change in these respects in the edition of 1572.
[2] Thus in the *Homilies* passages from *Tobit* and *Wisdom* are quoted as Scripture, and *Baruch* is styled a prophet.

Tobit are still retained in our Communion Service.

If we turn from the indirect to the formal settlement of the English Bible-Canon, it will be seen that the subject was determined in England no less than on the Continent, without critical discussion, by the tacit consent of the leaders of the Reformation. The Articles of 1552 contain no list of the books of Holy Scripture. The 5th article, which declares that 'The doctrine of holie Scripture is sufficient to Salvation,' consists of the substance of the first paragraph only of our present 6th Article. The same general statement was repeated in the eleven (provisional) articles drawn up under the direction of Archbp. Parker, and sanctioned by the English prelates in 1559. The 6th of the *Latin* Articles of 1562 gives a list of the Scriptures of the Old Testament, and of the 'other books,' enumerating 3, 4 *Esdras*, *Wisdom*, Jesus son of Sirach (*Ecclesiasticus*), *Judith*, *Tobit*, 1, 2 *Maccabees*, which are to be read 'for example of life and instruction of manners.' The omission of *Baruch* is remarkable; and it seems likely that this book was supposed to occupy the same relation to *Jeremiah* as the apocryphal additions severally to *Esther* and *Daniel*, which are also passed over in the catalogue. In the following year an English translation of these Articles was prepared, which was afterwards presented to Parliament and ratified in 1571.

Meanwhile the list of the *Apocrypha* was completed in the *English* Articles of 1571, and took the form which it has at present. The main clauses of the Article are historically full of interest:

'In the name of Holy Scripture we do understand those canonical books of the Old and New Testament of whose authority was never any doubt in the Church.' CHAP. X.

'*The names and number of the Canonical Books.*

'*Genesis, Exodus,* &c....xii. *Prophets* the less.

'And the other books (as Jerome saith) the Church doth read for example of life and instruction of manners; but yet doth it not apply them to establish any doctrine. Such are the following:

'3 *Esdras,* 4 *Esdras*...1, 2 *Maccabees*[1].

'All the books of the New Testament as they are commonly received we do receive and account them for Canonical.'

The full list of the Apocryphal Books is given also in the Latin edition of the Articles published in 1571; and in the Irish Articles of 1615. It is likewise worthy of notice that the Irish Articles give a detailed list of the books of the New Testament in the order of the Authorized Version as well as of those of the Old Testament. 'All which,' it is added, 'we acknowledge to be given by the inspiration of God, and in that regard to be of most certain credit and highest authority. The other books, commonly called *Apocryphal,* did not proceed from such inspiration, and therefore are not of sufficient authority to establish any point of doctrine; but the Church doth read them as books containing many worthy things for

The *Irish Articles.*

Hardwick, pp. 341 f.

[1] It will be noticed that the English Church, following the usage of most Latin MSS. of the Bible, includes among the *Apocrypha* some writings which are not reckoned in the Canon by the Council of Trent: 1, 2 *Esdras,* and the *Prayer of Manasses.*

290   THE BIBLE IN THE CHURCH.

CHAP. X.   example of life and instruction of manners. Such
are these following...'

Ambiguity   One point in the language of the VIth Article
of the VIth is strangely ambiguous. The definition of Holy
Article   Scripture which is given is, 'those *canonical* books
of the Old and *New* Testament, of whose author-
See *Belgian* ity *was never any doubt in the Church.*' The
Articles, form of the definition appears to have been
p. 276   moulded chiefly with reference to the *Apocrypha*
noticed afterwards, which had confessedly gained
a partial but not a universal reception in the
Church. But at the end it is said of the 'books
of the New Testament as they are commonly
received,' that 'we receive them and *account them
Canonical.*' The last words must then either be
used loosely in the sense that, though the authority of some of the Apostolic writings had been
doubted, yet these doubts were treated as of no
moment, or be designed to express a difference
between 'Canonical books' and 'those Canonical
books of whose authority was never any doubt in
the Church.' Perhaps it may be conjectured
that some difference of opinion existed among
those who framed the Article, and that the language in which it is at present expressed was the
result of a compromise. However this may be
the fact is remarkable; and a comparison of the
Article with the corresponding articles in the
Belgian, French, Irish and Westminster Confessions makes it almost certain that the freedom
of opinion involved in the ambiguity was purposely conceded to the English clergy. But if it
were so, no one of the great English Divines in
the seventeenth or eighteenth centuries made
use of it. The differences of opinion which had
been entertained as to the disputed books of the

THE BIBLE IN THE SIXTEENTH CENTURY. 291

New Testament were forgotten or absolutely set aside. The *Apocrypha*, on the other hand, became the subject of vehement debates. The Puritans on every occasion protested against their ecclesiastical use; and among the changes which were proposed in the last conference at the Jerusalem Chamber in 1689, was the omission from the calendar of all lessons from the *Apocrypha*. The controversy was renewed in the present century; but the growing study of the Bible shews day by day more clearly the importance of the Apocrypha 'as books good and useful to be read,' which link together the Old and New Testaments, and set before the Church in vivid pictures the working of the Old Dispensation throughout the Jewish world at times when there was 'no prophet more.' They witness alike to what Judaism could do, and to what it could not do. They prove by contrast that the books of the Hebrew Canon, us a whole, are generically distinct from the ordinary religious literature of the Jews; and establish more clearly than anything else the absolute originality of the Gospel. In this respect the Church of England has followed the golden mean in adhering to the judgment of Jerome, and thereby borne witness to the true historic relations of the Bible. In this respect, as in her teaching generally, she has allowed to usage and antiquity due regard and reverence, without narrowing or enlarging the sacred limits of Faith.

CHAP. X.

CONCLUSION.

CONCLU-
SION.

IT may be well, at the end of an inquiry which has necessarily dealt in a great measure with details, to point out in a few sentences, the chief conclusions which appear to flow from it. The evidence has been already given, and any one who pleases can test their soundness. The method and the results are both purely critical; but they are not on that account to be set aside as unworthy of the notice of the spiritual student of the Bible. On the contrary, historical criticism furnishes the sure and solid basis on which the practical application of Holy Scripture rests. Its lessons claim to be welcomed as opening new harmonies in the many utterances of the One Divine Word. And even if it were not so, if they seemed to our shortsighted prudence to weaken a time-honoured tradition, they claim to be received because they are true.

1. The formation of the Christian Bible slow.

1. In the first place, then, it cannot be denied that the formation of the complete Christian Bible was slow and gradual. For at least a century after the death of our Blessed Lord, the Old Testament was the one Bible of Christians. During this period there was no wide-spread or definite idea of supplementing the records of the Old Testament by records of the New Testa-

ment. There was no sense as yet that more was needed for the guidance of the Church than the interpretation of the Law and the Prophets in the light of the Apostolic teaching. But meanwhile a written New Testament was in the very act of formation. The different types of doctrine sanctioned by the Apostles found an outward embodiment; and the original writings in which those types were preserved stood out with unchanging power amidst the shifting traditions which for a time preserved their substance. In one Church it may have been, the doctrine of St Paul prevailed at first; in another, the doctrine of St John; in another, the doctrine of St Peter or St James; but early in the second century the more frequent intercourse and wider experience of the Christian societies resulted in the definite establishment of a Catholic Church—Catholic, because it included all that was true in the partial views of heresy—and soon after, the whole Bible was received as the pledge and witness of the whole Truth.

CONCLUSION.

2. But this issue was the result of a common life, and not of any formal action. There is not the slightest evidence to show that the collection of the Sacred Books, as the depositaries of doctrine, was ever the subject of a general conference of the Churches. The Bible was formed, even as the Church itself was formed, by the action of that Holy Spirit which is the Life of both. Usage and not criticism fixed the limits of the Christian Bible; but in this case, usage is only another name for a divine instinct, a providential inspiration, a function of the Christian body. Still, however we call it, the discriminating power was seen in usage and not in law;

2. The contents of the Christian Bible ruled by usage not by formal decisions.

CONCLU-
SION.

and this is distinctly recognized by the earliest writers who treat in detail on the New Testament Canon. Thus Eusebius appeals only to the universal or general or partial approbation of churches, as fixing the authority of special books and even at a later time, Augustine accepted without the slightest misgiving, the startling conclusion, that the weight to be allowed to particular writings was to be measured by a consideration of the number and character of the churches by which they were received.

3 No absolute uniformity in the Churches as to the contents of the Bible.

3. This judgment of Augustine leads us to another remark. The usage which fixed the contents of the Bible was by no means uniform. It differed both in regard to the Old Testament and in regard to the New Testament. Of those who received the Hebrew Canon of the Old Testament only as having binding authority, some accepted and some rejected *Esther*. Indeed on the whole, if Christian evidence alone be taken, it appears that there is less evidence for the reception of this book as canonical in the fullest sense, than for the reception of *Baruch* And in the New Testament, within certain limits the greatest diversity prevailed. There was no effort, perhaps hardly a wish, to obtain absolute uniformity. Yet history teaches by the plainest examples that no one part of the Bible could be set aside without great and permanent injury to the Church which refused a portion of the apostolic heritage. We are now in a position to estimate what would have been lost if the *Epistle to the Hebrews*, or the *Epistle of St James*, or the *Apocalypse* had been excluded from the Canon. And on the other hand, we can measure the evils which flow equally from canonizing the

Apocrypha of the Old Testament, and denying to them all ecclesiastical use.

4. It follows necessarily from what has been said, that the limits of the Bible never formed an article of faith in the early Churches. Certain books, varying to some extent, were set aside for public use, but no definition of their character was imposed upon clergy or laity. Canonicity, and not inspiration, was the point to which all the chief authoritative decisions on the Bible pointed. It was not till the era of the Reformation that a question, which, in one aspect at least, is essentially a problem of history, was made the subject of a dogma; and that with the express and admitted purpose of silencing criticism. If there were any doubt on the spirit of that fatal decree of Trent—the first pattern of so many others—it would be removed by the consideration of the fact, that the same power which claimed absolute authority over the extent of the Bible, claimed equal authority over the text of it. The history of the adulterous woman (John vii. 53—viii. 11), the narrative of the Bloody Sweat (Luke xxii. 43, 44), the conclusion of St Mark's Gospel (Mark xvi. 9—20), are declared by the mere will of a Council, prior to the examination of all original evidence, to be 'scripture of irrefragable authority.' It was not thus that Origen, or Eusebius, or Athanasius, or Jerome, or Augustine spoke; and it is not thus that the Church of England speaks. With an unconscious and instinctive foresight, in which it may not be presumptuous to see the guiding power of the Divine will, the Church of England has reproduced in essence the judgments of the fourth century, by which it is our happiness to abide.

Marginalia: CONCLUSION. 4. The limits of the Bible not an article of faith in the first ages. *Bibl. Sancta* Sixti Sen. I. 1. See p. 258.

CONCLUSION.

5. The history of the Bible parallel to the history of the Church.

5. In a word, the history of the Bible is an epitome of the history of the Church. Both came to their full form slowly, silently, surely, by the combination of manifold elements. Both grew by the action of an informing power, and were not constructed from without by any foreign force. Both include treasures new and old, of which now this now that is needed for the instruction of men. Both have been overlaid by superstitious additions: both have been injured by an idolatrous reverence; but in both there is a life which makes itself felt, and refuses to be bound in one shape. The Bible, no less than the Church, is Holy, Catholic, and Apostolic: Holy, for they who wrote it were moved by the Holy Spirit: Catholic, for it embraces in essence every type of Christian truth which has gained entrance among men: Apostolic, for its limits are not extended beyond that first generation to which was committed the charge of preaching the Gospel in the fulness of its original power.

APPENDIX A.

On the History of the Canon of the Old Testament before the Christian Era.

THE history of the formation of the Canon of the Old Testament in Jewish times can be understood best by reference to the history of the formation of the Canon of the New Testament. But there is this grand difference between the two cases, that while the New Testament was formed out of writings of one age only, the Old Testament was formed out of writings which spread over many centuries. Yet the difference is one of detail and not of principle. In the case of the Old Testament the process was necessarily divided into several stages. Each great group of books had its separate history; and the national Bible, which was formed out of them, grew with the slow development of Divine revelation.

The familiar division of the Old Testament into the Law, the Prophets, and the Holy Writings (Hagiographa), probably indicates the three great forms in which the Bible was successively received by the Jews. The Law alone seems to have formed the Jewish Bible up to the Captivity. At the Return a collection of the Prophets was probably made by Ezra and added to the sacred Law. Afterwards the collection of the Hagiographa was formed, and the present Hebrew Canon completed during the period of the Persian supremacy.

i. This broad outline of the history of the Hebrew Bible is confirmed by the scanty historic notices which have been preserved. From the first 'the book of the Law' occupied a place in the sanctuary. According

APPEND. A.

A threefold Jewish Bible.

i. The *Law*.

APPEND. A. to the command of Moses it was 'put in the side of the ark' (Deut. xxxi. 25 ff.), but not *in* it (1 Kings viii. 9); and for our present purpose this testimony loses little of its value, even if it only represent the popular belief of the nation at some time after the death of Moses. This 'book of the Law' was not confined to mere precepts and enactments. It contained also general exhortations (Deut. xxviii. 61) and historical records (Ex. xvii. 14). Without assuming anything as to the origin of the Pentateuch, it is evident that the Pentateuch, as it stands at present, represents in scope and character such a book as is contemplated in these and similar passages. But there is no independent witness to its use till late in the time of the kingdom. The first clear historic reference to 'the book of the Law' is in the reign of Josiah, when Hilkiah found it 'in the house of the Lord' (2 Kings xxii. 8: comp. 2 Chron. xxxiv. 14); and there is no adequate reason to doubt that the book of Hilkiah was substantially the Pentateuch which we now have. Even at this time other records were connected with the books of Moses, which referred to the later history of the Jews in the times of Joshua (Josh. xxiv. 26) and Samuel (1 Sam. x. 25). Collections of proverbs also were made (Prov. xxv. 1); and much of the teaching of the prophets must have been preserved in the 'prophetic schools.' In this way a preparation was made for the future enlargement of the Bible in each direction[1].

ii. The *Prophets*.

ii. One proof that 'the Law' was the first Jewish Bible lies in the Bible of the Samaritans, which consists of the books of Moses only. They evidently retained a collection of sacred writings which was incomplete, and did not mutilate one which was originally of wider range. It is easy to see how this came to pass. The Samaritans were stationary at a crisis when the Jews were progressive. The chequered fortunes of the Jews were so shaped as to fit them to recognize a Divine authority in the prophetic development of the Law. When the kingdom, which had seemed at one time to offer the fulfilment of their national aspirations, was falling to pieces, the prophets rose up as spiritual

[1] In Is. xxxiv. 16 the context is supposed to shew that 'the book of the Lord' is a collection of prophetic words. To me the reference seems to be rather to the general warnings of Deuteronomy.

rulers. They claimed for themselves to be the immediate envoys of the God of Israel; and they made good their claim. Their written words were felt to have a sacred (if as yet undefined) authority. The later prophets (as Jeremiah) were evidently familiar with the writings of their predecessors. Some collections of their works must therefore have been made before the Captivity; and in the time of Zechariah the Law and the 'former prophets' were in some degree co-ordinate (Zech. vii. 12). In like manner, the title applied to the prophetic writings in the book of Daniel—'the books' (Dan. ix. 2)—shows that when that was written the collection was definitely marked out and known. Popular tradition points to Ezra and 'the great assembly'—the council by which he was assisted—as having revised and closed this collection; and the belief is supported by strong internal probability. The discipline of the Exile coming after the disasters of the kingdom had taught the Jews to welcome the wider views of God's purposes which were revealed by the prophets; and for them the new group of sacred writings must at once have assumed its true position beside the Law. But it was otherwise with those who had known nothing of this long national training. The Samaritans had hitherto learned Judaism only in its simpler form. For them the letter of the Divine ritual was more than the spirit; and when they were excluded from participation in the work of re-founding the Holy City, they naturally clung with greater pertinacity to the Law which they had first received. So from that time there were two Hebrew Bibles; of which the one led up to Christ, while the other has preserved unchanged to our own day—saddest and most venerable of all ancient rites—the typical paschal sacrifice on Mount Gerizim.

The work of EZRA.

iii. In later traditions the work of Ezra was strangely embellished. It was said that when the Scriptures had been wholly destroyed he again dictated them by the direct inspiration of God to chosen scribes (2 *Esdras* xiv. 20—48); and this wild fable was repeated in various forms by many of the earliest Christian fathers, as Irenæus, Tertullian and Clement of Alexandria; and at a later time it was borrowed from Jerome by most of the Latin writers of the West. The tradition is, in fact, as far as can be conjectured,

iii. The *Hagiographa*.

APPEND. A.

The *Great Synagogue*.

See p. 36.

the exact converse of the truth. The work which Ezra partly accomplished was continued to a much later period. The final completion of the Hebrew Bible was not the labour of one man or of one generation; and this is the truth which is contained in the story that the men of the Great Assembly 'wrote *Ezekiel*, the xii. *Minor prophets, Daniel* and *Esther*.' This *Great Assembly* or *Synagogue*, whose existence has been called in question on insufficient grounds, was the great council of the nation during the Persian period, in which the last substantive changes were made in the constitution of Judaism. The last member of it is said to have been Simon the Just (*c.* B. C. 310—290). It was organized by Ezra, and, as commonly happens, the work of the whole body was transferred to its representative member. Ezra, as we have seen, probably formed a collection of the prophetic writings; and the Assembly gathered together afterwards (as the Christian Church at a later time in corresponding circumstances) such books as were still left without the Canon, though proved to bear the stamp of the Spirit of God. The decision in the last instance (like that of Athanasius or Jerome) was, in all likelihood, the expression of a popular consent, through which (as is commonly the case in such matters) God made His will known.

The work of NEHEMIAH.

One remarkable historical statement confirms the view which has been given of the gradual formation of the later parts of the Jewish Canon during the Persian period. Nehemiah, it is said (2 *Macc.* ii. 13), 'while founding a library gathered together the [writings] concerning the kings and prophets, and the [writings] of David, and letters of kings about offerings.' In other words, if we may trust a tradition which has every mark of truth, Nehemiah completed the collection of the prophets by the addition of the later historical books, and added to them a collection of Hagiographa.

The Bible in the Maccabæan period.

The next glimpse which we have of the Jewish Bible is in the time of the Maccabæan war, when Antiochus Epiphanes sought out the 'books of the Law' and burnt them (1 Macc. i. 56), like Diocletian in his persecution of the Christians. The result of this special assault on the sacred books was, in all probability, to separate them from all the remaining literature of the nation, and Judas Maccabæus, like a second Nehemiah, 'collected again the [writings] which had been lost during the war' (2 Macc. ii. 14). After this time, as is universally acknowledged, no new book gained admission into the Hebrew Bible.

Thus the whole Palestinian, and therefore in the truest sense the whole Jewish, Bible was completed and separated from all other books; and in the Prologue to *Ecclesiasticus* (c. B.C. 131) the complex title, 'the law, the prophets, and the remainder of the books,' marks the Old Testament as distinctly as the corresponding Jewish phrase. The triple division was not indeed either arbitrary or accidental. It was a result of the discipline by which the Jews had been moulded, and an embodiment of the teaching of the successive stages through which they had passed. The *Law* was the foundation of the whole of the old dispensation, the stern power by which the chosen people was trained to fulfil its work. The *Prophetic writings* carry on the history of the struggles by which the Spirit of God led on a wilful race through triumphs and sufferings and exile to the contemplation of the spiritual antitypes of their ritual and constitution. The *Hagiographa* exhibit the working of the Divine power not in the nation, but in the individual life; and, consequently, as a whole, belong to the final period of Jewish civilization, so far as they have a popular significance.

At a later time the Greek Version of this threefold Hebrew Canon was enlarged by the addition of other, and chiefly Greek, books; but there is no indication that this took place before the Christian period; and the history of the Hebrew and Greek Bibles from the Christian era has been already traced.

APPENDIX B.

The Contents of the most ancient MSS. of the Bible.

THREE MSS. of the most venerable antiquity, known as the *Alexandrine*, the *Vatican*, and the *Sinaitic*, still remain, which severally contain a very considerable part of the Greek Bible. No one of them is absolutely complete; but enough is left of each to indicate within narrow limits its original contents. It is unnecessary to enter into the discussions which have been raised as to their relative age. They are all probably older than the first quarter of the fifth century, and certainly no one is earlier than the beginning of the fourth. Thus they are living monuments of the ecclesiastical usage of the Christian Church as to the books of Scripture at the time of its first connexion with the Empire. They seem, without doubt, to have been designed for public use; and as we look at their pages we are, as it were, transported directly into the presence of the assemblies of Christians who had known something of the terrors of the persecution of Diocletian. Their evidence consequently has an interest though not an authority greater than that which would attach to the decision of an individual. They express, in all probability, a popular and not a critical opinion. This indeed appears to follow from their contents. Each includes the books of the *Apocrypha* as well as and among the Canonical Books of the Old Testament; and the two which contain the later books of the New Testament, contain also, as part of the same collection, books which are excluded from our Canon. In both respects these earliest Christian Bibles furnish an instructive commentary on the express judgments of the Greek Fathers, and exhibit the practical tend-

APPENDIX B.

ency which exists in every age to retain as sacred every thing which has once been consecrated by custom however partial.

1. The *Alexandrine* MS. (Cod. A), which is one of the chief treasures of the British Museum, was presented to Charles I. by the reforming patriarch of Constantinople, Cyril Lucar, in 1628. The three volumes which contain the Old Testament are nearly complete. The fourth, which contains the New Testament, has several considerable lacunæ. The greater part of *St Matthew* is wanting, and besides this, about two chapters of *St John*, and eight chapters of *2 Corinthians*. After the *Apocalypse* follows in the same hand the *first Epistle of Clement*, and a fragment of the so-called *Second Epistle*. These, as appears from a table of contents prefixed to the first volume, were designed to form part of 'the New Testament.' The table itself will give a complete idea of the substance and arrangement of the MS., which is attributed with good reason to the beginning of the fifth century.

'The Creation of the World *(Genesis)*.

The departure from Egypt *(Exodus)*.

Leviticus.
Numbers.
Deuteronomy.
Joshua the son of Naue.
Judges.
Ruth.

       Together *eight* Books.

Kingdoms 1 *(Samuel* 1).
Kingdoms 2 *(Samuel* 2).
Kingdoms 3 *(Kings* 1).
Kingdoms 4 *(Kings* 2).

Paralipomena, *i.e.* Supplementary histories, 1 *(Chronicles* 1).

Paralipomena 2 *(Chronicles* 2).

       Together *Six* books.

Prophets 16.
Osee i.......
Jeremiah xiv. (*i.e.* Jeremiah, with *Baruch, Lamentations* and the *Epistle, i.e.* Baruch vi.).......
Daniel xvi. (with additions).
Esther (with additions).
Tobit.
Judith.

APPEND. B.

Ezras 1 the priest (*Esdras* 1).
Ezras 2 the priest (*Ezra* and *Nehemiah*).
History of the *Maccabees* 1.
History of the *Maccabees* 2.
History of the *Maccabees* 3.
History of the *Maccabees* 4.

The *Psalter*, with prefatory letter of Athanasius to Marcellinus, and Hymns (including the *Prayer of Manasses*).

Job.
Proverbs.
Ecclesiastes.

The Song of Songs (*The Song of Solomon*).
Wisdom, the Book of complete Virtue.
The Wisdom of Jesus the Son of Sirach (*Ecclesiasticus*).

The New Testament.

Gospels 4.
According to *Matthew*.
According to *Mark*.
According to *Luke*.
According to *John*.
Acts of Apostles.
Catholic Epistles 7 (*James*, 1, 2 *Peter*, 1, 2, 3 *John*, *Jude*).

Epistles of Paul 14 (*Romans*....2 *Thess.*, *Hebrews*, 1 *Tim....Philem.*).
Apocalypse of John.
Clement's Epistle 1.
Clement's Epistle 2.
Together......? Books.
Psalms of Solomon xviii.'

Thus briefly this Greek Bible contains in the *Old Testament*, in addition to all the books of the Hebrew Canon, the books of our *Apocrypha*, except 2 *Esdras*, and besides these, 3, 4 *Maccabees*, which we do not receive. In the New Testament it contains all the received books with the addition of 1, 2 *Clement*, which are only found in this MS. The omission of the *Shepherd*, no less than the insertion of the *Clementine Epistles*, seems to point to Syria rather than Alexandria as the real source from which this MS. was derived. The same conclusion is perhaps indicated by the order of the Old Testament. For from the arrangement of the books it appears that *Esther*—

APPENDIX B.

4 *Maccabees* formed an *Appendix* to the historical books, and *Wisdom* and *Ecclesiasticus* an *Appendix* to the Hagiographa; and that they were not treated as, in the fullest sense, canonical.

2. The history of the *Vatican* MS. (Cod. B) is unknown. It appears to have been in the Vatican Library from the close of the fifteenth century, and it has been conjectured that it was brought from the East (Constantinople) by Cardinal Bessarion. The narrative of the various attempts which have been made to collate it form one of the strangest stories in literary annals; and the edition lately published (1858) from the collation of Cardinal Mai, still leaves very much to be desired. The MS. is referred with confidence to the fourth century, and on the whole it may be pronounced to be the most correct copy of the Greek Bible, though it is not free from grave faults. It is mutilated both at the beginning and at the end, and consequently has no table of contents like that in the Alexandrine MS.; nor is there anything to show whether it originally included the *Apocalypse* or other books, as the Epistles of Clement or Hermas. The books which remain are the following:

[I. The *Octateuch.*]

Genesis (a fragment).
Exodus.
Leviticus.
Numbers.
Deuteronomy.
Joshua the son of Naue.
Judges.
Ruth.

[II. The *Historical Books.*]

Kingdoms 1 (1 *Samuel*).
Kingdoms 2 (2 *Samuel*).
Kingdoms 3 (1 *Kings*).
Kingdoms 4 (2 *Kings*).
Paralipomena 1 (1 *Chronicles*).
Paralipomena 2 (2 *Chronicles*).
Esdras 1 (*Esdras* 1).
Esdras 2 (*Ezra, Nehemiah*).

APPEND. B.

[III. The *Hagiographa*.]

Psalms (part deficient).
Proverbs.
Ecclesiastes.
Song of Solomon.
Job.
Wisdom of Solomon.
Wisdom of Sirach (*Ecclesiasticus*).
Esther (with additions).
Judith.
Tobit.

[IV. The *Prophets*.]

12 Minor Prophets (*Osee...Malachias*).
Isaiah.
Jeremiah.
Baruch.
Lamentations.
The Epistle of Jeremiah (Baruch vi.).
Ezekiel.
Daniel (with the additions).

[V. The *New Testament*.]

Gospels according to
Matthew.
Mark.
Luke.
John.
Acts of Apostles.
7 Catholic Epistles (*James*, 1, 2 *Peter*, 1, 2, 3 *John*, *Jude*).
Epistles of St Paul (*Romans*,.... 2 *Thessalonians*, *Hebrews* to ix. 14, where the MS. ends).

The book of *Daniel* is immediately followed by St *Matthew*, and from the arrangement of the quires it is certain that no books ever came between. Thus the books of *Maccabees* are wholly wanting. On the other hand, the MS. includes all the other *Apocrypha* except the *Prayer of Manasses* and 2 *Esdras*. The omission of *Maccabees* and the position of *Esther* bring the copy into very close agreement with the canon of Athanasius; and it seems probable that the Vatican

See p. 161.

MS. is the truest representation which remains of the Alexandrine Bible.

3. The *Sinaitic* MS. (Cod. ℵ) is one of the latest and most precious literary discoveries of the present century. Part of it was first detected by Tischendorf at the Monastery of St Katharine on Mount Sinai in 1844, in a basket of fragments which were destined, as he says, for the fire. What he then secured he published in 1846 under the name of *Codex Friderico-Augustanus;* and shortly afterwards he announced the discovery of another [*i.e.* other parts of the same] MS. without indicating the place where he had found it. After one fruitless journey in 1853, he succeeded in finding the treasure of which he was in quest in 1859, when he visited St Katharine's under the patronage of Alexander II., Emperor of Russia. After various negotiations, which are not very satisfactorily explained, the MS. was carried to Europe and deposited at St Petersburg, where it still remains.

The Sinaitic MS. is probably of the fourth century, and is the only one of the greatest MSS. which contains the New Testament entire. The arrangement of the books both in the Old and New Testament differs considerably from that in the Vatican and Alexandrine MSS. The accompanying table will shew what the MS. still contains.

[II. The *Historical Books.*]

1 *Chronicles* (fragments inserted in 2 Esdras from a mistake in binding in the copy from which the MS. was transcribed). [part in *Cod. Frid.-Aug.*]

2 Esdras (*Ezra* fragment, and *Nehemiah*). [*Cod. Frid.-Aug.*]

Esther. [*Cod. Frid.-Aug.*]

Tobit (nearly entire). [part in *Cod. Frid.-Aug.*]

Judith (nearly entire).

1 *Maccabees.*

4 *Maccabees.*

[III. The *Prophets.*]

Isaiah.

Jeremiah. [part in *Cod. Frid.-Aug.*]

Lamentations to ii. 20.

12 Minor Prophets (except *Hosea, Amos, Micah*).

[IV. The *Hagiographa*.]

Psalms (151).
Proverbs.
Ecclesiastes.
Song of Solomon.
Wisdom of Solomon.
Wisdom of Sirach (*Ecclesiasticus*).
Job.

[V. The *New Testament.*]

The Gospels according to
Matthew.
Mark.
Luke.
John.

14 Epistles of St Paul (*Romans....* 2 *Thessalonians, Hebrews,* 1, 2 *Timothy, Titus, Philemon*).
Acts.

7 Catholic Epistles (*James,* 1, 2 *Peter,* 1, 2, 3 *John, Jude*).
Apocalypse of John.
Epistle of Barnabas.
Shepherd (fragment).

Thus the Sinaitic MS. differs from the Alexandrine and Vatican MSS. both in the Old and in the New Testament. Of the *Apocrypha* it includes *Tobit, Judith,* 1 *Maccabees, Wisdom, Ecclesiasticus,* [*Baruch,*] among the Scriptures of the Old Testament, and adds to these 4 *Maccabees*. In the New Testament it adds to the received books the Epistle of Barnabas and the Shepherd. My attention has been called to the fact that the arrangement of the quires in the MSS. shews that 4 *Maccabees* and the *Shepherd* formed separate sections. The books are arranged in groups, and each group begins and ends a new quire. The last quire (if occasion calls for it) contains two or three instead of four sheets. From the fact that 4 *Maccabees* and the *Shepherd* thus stand by themselves, it has been conjectured that they may have formed appendices to the other generally received books.

4. The Bibles which have been hitherto examined are all of *Eastern* origin. One very remarkable list of African (that is *Western*) origin has been preserved in

APPENDIX B.

a Græco-Latin MS., which is in the Imperial Library at Paris. This MS. was found by Beza at Clermont near Beauvais, and is called from the place of its discovery the *Codex Claromontanus*. It contains St Paul's Epistles in Greek and Latin texts, and is assigned to the close of the sixth century. After the *Epistle to Philemon* and before that to the *Hebrews*, a list of '*The lines of the Holy Scriptures*' is given in the Latin text: there is nothing in the Greek text which answers to it. It is probable therefore that the scribe found the list in this place in the Latin copy, which he transcribed, and, with the usual desire of scribes to omit nothing, introduced it into his book, though it had no connexion with his immediate work. The list itself is as follows:

		Lines.
	Genesis...............................	4500
	Exodus	3700
	Leviticus.............................	2800
	Numbers	3650
	Deuteronomy.........................	3300
	Joshua................................	2000
	Judges................................	2000
	Ruth	250
1	*Kingdoms*	2500
2	*Kingdoms*	2000
3	*Kingdoms*	2600
4	*Kingdoms*	2400
	Psalms	5000
	Proverbs.............................	1600
	Ecclesiastes..........................	600
	Canticles	300
	Wisdom	1000
	Wisdom of Jesus [*Ecclesiasticus*]......	2500
12	*Prophets*	3110
	Hosea	530
	Daniel................................	1600
1	*Maccabees*	2300
2	*Maccabees*	2300
4	*Maccabees*	1000
	Judith................................	1300
	Esdras...............................	1500
	Esther	1000
	Job	1600
	Tobias	1000

APPEND. B.

	Lines.
4 Gospels.	
Matthew	2600
John	2000
Mark	1600
Luke	2900
Epistles of Paul to	
Romans	1040
1 *Corinthians*	1060
2 *Corinthians*	...70
Galatians	350
Ephesians	375
1 *Timothy*	208
2 *Timothy*	288
Titus	140
Colossians	251
Philemon	50
1 to *Peter* (thus)	200
2 to *Peter*	140
James	220
1 *John*	220
2 *John*	20
3 *John*	20
Jude	60
Epistle of Barnabas	850
Revelation of John	1200
Acts of Apostles	2600
Shepherd	4000
Acts of Paul	3560
Revelation of Peter	270

The omissions and additions of the catalogue are both worthy of notice. It omits 1, 2 *Chronicles*, and the Epistles of St Paul to the *Thessalonians* (1, 2) and *Philippians*. The omission of the last three books at any rate can only have been made through inadvertence. The *Epistle to the Hebrews*, also, is not named, but it has been acutely conjectured that this is described under the title which it bore in part, at least, of the African Church, as the *Epistle of Barnabas*. If this be correct, the list contains in the Old Testament, in addition to the Hebrew Canon, *Wisdom*, *Ecclesiasticus*, 1, 2, 4 (not 3) *Maccabees*, *Judith* and *Tobit;* and in the New Testament, in addition to the

See p. 130.

received books, the *Shepherd*, the *Acts of Paul*, and the *Revelation of Peter*. In both respects it may be taken to represent fairly the books sanctioned for ecclesiastical use in some part of the North African Church at the close of the third or the beginning of the fourth century.

5. The most important MS. of the Latin Bible, the *Codex Amiatinus*, contains four distinct enumerations of the Books of Scripture. The first is a list of the contents of the MS. itself, which exhibits several peculiarities of arrangement.

Genesis...Kings, Chronicles, Psalms (cli)...*Canticles, Wisdom, Ecclesiasticus, Isaiah...Daniel* (with additions), *Hosea...Malachi, Job, Tobit, Judith, Esther* (with additions), *Ezra and Nehemiah*, 1, 2 *Maccabees*. The *Gospels, Acts,* xiv *Epistles of St Paul (Romans... Hebrews)*. [vii] *Catholic Epistles*[1], *Apocalypse*.

According to this enumeration the whole number of Books is lxxi. *Baruch* is not found in the MS.

The table of contents is followed by a page containing a picture of Ezra with this couplet:

Codicibus sacris hostili clade perustis,
Esdra Deo fervens hoc reparavit opus.

On the next three pages are three lists of the Books of the Bible. The first is that of Jerome. This is presented in seven groups:

1. The Law: The *Pentateuch*.
2. The Prophets: *Joshua...Kings, Isaiah...Ezekiel*, xii *Prophets*.
3. The Hagiographa: *Job...Canticles, Daniel, Chronicles, Ezra, Esther*.
4. iv *Gospels*.
5. xiv *Epp. of St Paul*, 1, 2 *Peter*, 1, 2, 3 *John, James, Jude*.
6. *Acts*.
7. *Apocalypse*.

The total here is xlix Books.

The second list professes to be that of Pope Hilary and Epiphanius. It contains lxx Books.

Genesis...Chronicles.

Psalms, Proverbs, Wisdom, Ecclus, Ecclesiastes, Canticles.

---

[1] The list gives *Petri* 1, but the MS. contains both Epistles.

312   *THE BIBLE IN THE CHURCH.*

APPEND. B.

Isaiah...Daniel, Hosea...Malachi.
Job, Tobit, Esther, Judith, Ezra (2), *Macc.* (2).
iv *Gospels, Acts, Cath. Epp.* (3)[1].
xiii *Epp. of St Paul* (omitting *Helv.*).
Apocalypse.

The third list is said to be that of Augustine. The books are reckoned as lxxi in six groups. The Old Testament is divided into two parts.

1. History, xxii Books: *Genesis...Chronicles, Job Tobit, Esther, Judith, Ezra* (2), *Macc.* (2).

2. Prophecy, xxii Books: *Psalms, Books Solomon* (3), *Jesus Son of Sirach* (2), xvi *Prophets*.

3. iv *Gospels.*

4. Epistles xxi: *Romans...Hebr., Peter* (2), *John* (3), *Jude, James.*

5. *Acts.*

6. *Apocalypse*[2].

---

[1] Epist. Petri ad gentes, Jacobi, Johannis ad Parthos.

[2] For the date and history of this MS., which is of deep interest to all members of the English Church, the student is referred to a letter of the Bishop of Salisbury in the *Guardian*, Feb. 16, 1887.

[This has been supplemented by a letter of Dr Hort in the *Academy*, Feb. 26th, 1887.]

INDEX[1].

ÆTHIOPIC MSS, 238
ALEXIUS ARISTENUS, 224
ALFRIC, 208
Alogi, 138 *n*.
ALPHONSUS TOSTATUS, 201
AMPHILOCHIUS, 166
ANASTASIUS BIBLIOTHEC. 198
Antilegomena (*i.e.* Disputed Books), 133 *n*.
Antoninus of Florence, 199
Apocalypse of Peter, 115, 127, 133, 149
Apocrypha of Old Testament, alleged use of in New Testament, 45
—— Use of, 123, 130, 134, 136, 138, 146, 153, 168, 172, 173 *n*., 174, 178, 179, 182, 198, 200, 207, 214, 226, 228, 232, 237, 240.
—— in English Church, 287
Apologists, Age of, 90
Apostles, the work of, 53
APOSTOLIC CANONS, 176 *n*.
APOSTOLIC CONSTITUTIONS, 175
Apostolic Fathers, characteristics of, 72
—— their relation to the Gospels, 81
Assembly, The Great, 299, 300
ATHANASIUS, 160

[Athanasius] SYN. S. SCRIPTURÆ, 226
AUGUSTINE, 186

Balsamon, Theodorus, 224
Barnabas, Epistle of, 80, 127, 136, 149
—— i.e. *Epistle to Hebrews*, 130
Basil, 168
Bede, 208
Beza, 273.
Bible, Names of, 4
—— Historical characteristics of, 6
—— Alexandrine, Athanasian, Constantinopolitan, Syrian, 165
Biblia, 5
Bibliotheca, 5.
BODENSTEIN. See CARLSTADT.
Book of Armagh, 206

Caietan, Cardinal, 253
CALVIN, 270, 275
Canon, 110 *n*.
CARLSTADT, 266
CASSIODORUS, 197
Catharinus,
Catholic, 79
Celsus, 140
Charlemagne, 202

[1] The authorities distinguished by capitals furnish lists of the sacred books.

INDEX.

Charlemagne's Bible, 203
CHRYSOSTOM. See JOHANNES.
Clement of Alexandria, 125
Clement of Rome, 74
—— *Epistles of,* 176 *n.*, 218
Clementine Homilies, 105
Codex Alexandrinus, 303
—— *Amiatinus,* 196
—— *Claromontanus,* 308
—— *Sinaiticus,* 307
—— *Vaticanus,* 305
  See *Book of Armagh, Charlemagne's Bible.*
CONFESSION, BELGIAN, 275
—— ENGLISH, 288
—— SWISS, of 1675, 278
—— FRENCH, 276
—— WESTMINSTER, 277
Cosmas Indicopleustes, 220
COUNCIL OF CARTHAGE, 188
—— CONSTANTINOPLE (1672), 229
—— FLORENCE, 199
—— HIPPO, 185
—— JERUSALEM (1672), 229
—— LAODICEA, 169
—— QUINI-SEXTINE, 217
—— TRENT, 255
Cyril of Alexandria, 171
CYRIL OF JERUSALEM, 168
CYRIL LUCAR, 227

DAMASCENUS. See JOHANNES.
DAMASUS, 195
Didymus, 171
Diocletian, 143
Dionysius of Alexandria, 137
Dionysius of Corinth, 111 *n.*
Dispersion of the Jews, 19
Doctrine of the Apostles, 89
Donatus, 145

EBED JESU, 231
Ebionites, 69, 93
Enoch, Book of, 48
EPIPHANIUS, 172

Erasmus, 249
EUGENIUS IV., 199
EUGENIUS OF TOLEDO, 200
EUSEBIUS OF CÆSAREA (New Testament), 148
Euthalius, 171
Ezra, Legend of, 37, 299
—— Work of, 299

Firmilian, 138

GELASIUS, 195
Gnostics, 70
Gospel, Oral, 58
GRATIAN, 198
GREGORY OF NAZIANZUS, 166
Gregory of Nyssa, 168
Gregory the Great, 198
Gregory the Wonder-worker, 138
Grosseteste, R., 214
Grotius, 279

Hagiographa, 28, 37, 299
Hegesippus, 107
Heretics, earliest quotations of New Testament by, 113 *n.*
Hermas. See *Shepherd.*
Hierocles, 144
HILARY OF POITIERS (Old Testament), 180
HILDEFONSUS OF TOLEDO, 200
Homologumena (i.e. Acknowledged Books), 133, 148
Honorius, 205
HORMISDAS, 195
HORNE, ANDREW, 211
HUGO DE S. CARO, 203
HUGO DE S. VICTORE, 204

JEROME, 181
Ignatius, 76
INNOCENT I., 195
Instrumentum, 5
Johannes Balbus, 198

INDEX.

Johannes Chrysostomus, 174
Johannes Damascenus, 222
John Beleth, 205
John of Salisbury, 210
Josephus (Old Testament), 25
Irenæus, 121
Isidore of Pelusium, 171
Isidore of Seville, 200
Ivo of Chartres, 203
Junilius, 193
Justin Martyr, 97

Karlstadt. See Carlstadt.

Laodicenes, Apocryphal *Letter to*, (115) 209
Leontius, 219
Luther, 259

Macarius, 172
Marcion, 109
Marcionites, 71
Martyrdom of Ignatius, 79 n.
Melito, 112 n., 124
Memoirs of the Apostles, 100
Methodius, 138
Metrophanes Critopulus, 228
Muratorian Canon (New Testament), 112

Nazarenes, 69
Nehemiah, Work of, 300
New Testament, Historic Origin of, 57, 60, 65
Nicephorus, 225
Nicephorus Callistus, 227
Nicolaus de Lyra, 206
Notker, 207

Ockham, W., 211
Œcolampadius, 270, 275
Old Testament, History of the formation of, 297
Origen, 135

Pamphilus, 138
Papias, 95
Peter, Apocalypse of. See *Apocalypse*.
——— *Gospel according to*, 131
——— *Preaching of*, 136
Petrus Cluniacensis, 204
Petrus Comestor, 205
Petrus de Riga, 203
Philastrius, 177
Philo, 30
Photius, 223
Polycarp, 79
Porphyry, 140
Primasius, 193
Prologus galeatus, 181

Quotations from Old Testament in New Testament, summary of, 44
——— Alleged Apocryphal in New Testament, 46

Rabanus Maurus, 203
Roman Church, originally Greek, 129
Ruffinus, 178
Rupert of Deutz, 205

Samaritan Bible, 298
Septuagint, Use of, 23, 125, 130
——— Palestinian, 124
Serapion, 131
Shepherd, The, 115, 123, 127, 130, 134, 136, 148, 161, 182, 210
Sixtus Senensis, 258
'*Sixty Books, The*,' 224
Syrian MSS. of the Bible, 232

Talmud (Old Testament), 35
Tertullian, 127
Testamentum, 5
Theophilus, 131
Thomas Aquinas, 198

THOMAS OF WALDEN, 213
Tradition, Historic, recognized in New Testament, 58
Traditores, 144

VERSIONS, ÆTHIOPIC, 237
—— ARMENIAN, 239
—— EGYPTIAN, 235
—— ENGLISH :
—— —— WYCLIFFE, 211
—— —— TYNDALE, 281
—— —— COVERDALE, 282
—— —— MATTHEW, 283
—— —— CRANMER, 284
—— —— GENEVAN, 285

VERSIONS, ENGLISH:
—— —— AUTHORIZED, 287
—— GOTHIC, 155 n.
—— GREEK (Old Testament), 23, 33, 123—125
—— LATIN, OLD, 128
—— —— NEW, 181, 190
—— SYRIAC, 132, 232, 241
Ulphilas, 155 n.

Ximenes, Cardinal, 249
Xystus, 89 n.

ZONARAS, 223
Zwingli, 269, 275

www.ingramcontent.com/pod-product-compliance
Lightning Source LLC
Chambersburg PA
CBHW070230230426
43664CB00014B/2254